T0208306

"So you not only married your opposite, but someone who is downright annoying? Don't panic! You may have the makings of a terrific marriage. Chuck and Barb Snyder know. They've parlayed their remarkable differences into a tremendous relationship, and they've captured their secrets in a wonderful book that shows how you can too."

Tim Kimmel
Author of *Little House on the Freeway*

"You'll laugh, you'll cry, you'll relate…and you'll learn how to have a great marriage. This is a one-of-a-kind book, delightful and penetrating, from people who live what they teach."

Jack and Kay Arthur
Precept Ministries

"I can't think of another couple who bring more fun, commitment, faith, and *differences* to a marriage than my good friends Chuck and Barb. The Snyders have mentored pro athletes and countless couples over the years, and they've modeled a Christ-centered, loving marriage for my wife, Cindy, and me. Unless you're allergic to laughter, read this book! I recommend it to every couple who want to blend and build on their differences."

John Trent, Ph.D.
President, Encouraging Words

"Treena loves the windows open and Graham likes them closed. Treena likes *no* music, Graham likes constant classical music. But we love our differences! We also love Chuck and Barb's book—so true, so funny, and so helpful to know we are God's peculiar people. A must read for everyone!

Treena and Graham Kerr
Cocreators of the *Galloping Gourmet* television series

INCOMPATIBILITY
STILL GROUNDS FOR A GREAT
MARRIAGE

CHUCK & BARB SNYDER

Multnomah® Publishers *Sisters, Oregon*

INCOMPATIBILITY: STILL GROUNDS FOR A GREAT MARRIAGE
© 1988, 1999 by Chuck and Barb Snyder
published by Multnomah Publishers, Inc.

International Standard Book Number: 9781590528167

Cover art by Karen Cooper
© 1999 by Gemé Art, Inc. Vancouver, Washington

Unless otherwise noted, Scripture quotations in Chuck's sections are from *The Living Bible*
(TLB), © 1971 owned by assignment by KNT Charitable Trust. Published by Tyndale House
Publishers, Inc. Used by permission. Scripture quotations in Barb's sections are from the *New
America Standard Bible* (NASB) © 1960, 1977 by the Lockman Foundation. Used by permission.

Also quoted: *The Holy Bible*, New International Version (NIV) © 1973, 1984 by International
Bible Society, used by permission of Zondervan Publishing House.

Multnomah is a trademark of Multnomah Publishers, Inc., and is registered in the U.S. Patent
and Trademark Office.
The colophon is a trademark of Multnomah Publishers, Inc.

For information:
Multnomah Publishers, Inc.
Post Office Box 1720
Sisters, Oregon 97759

Library of Congress Cataloging–in–Publication Data
    Snyder, Chuck.
        Incompatibility: still grounds for a great marriage/by Chuck & Barb Snyder.   p.cm.
        ISBN (invalid) 1-57673-508-1   1. Marriage—United States—Psychological
aspects. 2. Communication in marriage—United States. 3. Interpersonal relations—United
States. 4. Difference (Psychology). I. Snyder, Barb, 1934– II. Title.
HQ734.S766   1999   99–13141   646.7'8–dc21   CIP

                              146651086

Chuck: I would like to dedicate this book to my family who have been so patient when I had to "disappear" for a while to work on it. Most of all I want to honor my precious wife Barb who is coauthoring this book with me. I am the one who has made most of the mistakes in our marriage. She has experienced most of the pain as we have worked out our marriage-friendship over the years. She has been so patient while I have been learning the lessons God has wanted to teach me. Her teaching gift has amplified God's concepts for me so I can be biblically accurate. Her sense of humor has allowed me to include some stories that she would probably tell differently. Her gifts of children and grandchildren have brought so much sunshine and laughter to my life. How do I love her? In countless ways. She is the chief reason why we can write this letter to you. She has my gratitude for eternity.

Barb: The purpose of this book is to honor our Lord Jesus Christ and show that His way works. So, I dedicate this book to Him, because He has guided us as He said He would into paths of righteousness.

And I want to honor Chuck. His obedience has been a constant source of strength to me and to our children and grandchildren. He is the picture of the Psalm 1 man:

How blessed is the man who does not walk in the counsel of the wicked,
Nor stand in the path of sinners,
Nor sit in the seat of scoffers!
But his delight is in the law of the LORD,
And in His law he meditates day and night.
And he will be like a tree firmly planted by streams of water,
Which yields its fruit in its season,
And its leaf does not wither;
And in whatever he does, he prospers.

TABLE OF CONTENTS

FOREWORD

Finally…an antibiotic for marriages.

In the eighteenth century, surgeons finally realized that post-operative infection was killing patients because they were using unsterilized instruments. The same kind of insight is available today within our "infected" marriages. The divorce epidemic is infecting our nation and world because there are specific "relationship germs" that have been isolated, and we now know what they are. Furthermore, the marriage experts know how to sterilize a couple before and after marriage to prevent divorce. Like the positive transformation in surgery, we now realize that marriages can be dramatically different. We are on the threshold of reducing the divorce rate and enhancing marriages around the world.

When it comes to applying real and effective antibiotics for couples, Chuck and Barb Snyder have come up with a book that not only can heal a couple's sicknesses, but their book is like a little bit of sugar that helps the medicine go down. In *Incompatibility: Still Grounds for a Great Marriage*, they show husbands and wives how one marriage partner's God-given differences can infect the other person over time. But these differences can actually be part of the healing balm for the other. The result is a marriage that has the stamina to endure the cuts and bruises of life, and yet also provides the softness and bandages of a fulfilling relationship.

In the face of what some couples may have thought were incompatible differences, men and women have allowed the infection to set in, but what they could have had was a great marriage strong enough to be nursing other couples back to health. Chuck and Barb show a better perspective on those differences. They remind us of an often forgotten truth that can keep your relationship going and growing for a lifetime: In diversity, there can be unity and strength.

I'm so proud to know this couple personally, and I know how their differences have blended together to produce a powerful healing prescription for couples. As you take in their humor, penetrating truth, and heart-grabbing stories, you'll give your marriage a much needed recovery.

Gary Smalley

INTRODUCTION

Chuck: Barb and I enjoy going out to eat together, and we like trying new restaurants. One time we went to a very small eating place with a fireplace in the main part of the dining room. It was crowded and Barb said to me, "You pick the table." I usually leave this choice up to her because she normally knows exactly where she would like to sit. But since she wanted my opinion this time, I picked a quiet section away from the center of the restaurant. I don't like having a lot of people so close they can notice I didn't eat all my vegetables, or sneeze in my soup. It didn't take me two nanoseconds to see that my choice of tables was wrong. Barb wanted to be near the fireplace. Why does Barb ask me where I want to sit when she knows all along where she would like to sit? Stay tuned. We'll explain.

Barb: Why can't Chuck open a cereal box, milk carton, or even a bottle of catsup without doing it upside down, tearing it, or breaking the plastic lid that is supposed to flip up? I don't understand!

Chuck: I was all ready to go to work. I had my sport coat and tie on, my briefcase in my hand, the car running, and I leaned over to kiss Barb goodbye. In the middle of my lean she asked, "Are you going to wear that tie?" Yes, as a matter of fact I was going to wear this tie because I am ready to go out the door, and I have it on along with my shirt and sport coat and pants and the car is running. Surely that should be enough of a hint to let her know I had planned to wear the tie I had on. What is she saying? Stay tuned. We'll explain.

Barb: Why is it when I put out the old butter dish with just a dab on it and a new butter dish alongside, Chuck never finishes the old one but dives right into the new one? I always have to finish up everything. I don't understand!

Chuck: I'm very goal oriented and have lots of projects going at one time. I have an audio studio in the basement of our home where I do commercials for my advertising company. I also like to make furniture in my workshop and listen to music or play my keyboard, which is also in the basement. Barb keeps telling people that I have "been in the basement" all her married life. She means I always have a hundred projects to work on at one time, and I am too restless just to sit in the evening and read or watch TV. As usual she is not entirely accurate. I haven't always been in the basement. There have been times when I was in the garage. There were also many times when I was in the bathroom. Sometimes I have been in the kitchen eating. So what's this "always-in-the-basement" routine? Stay tuned. We'll explain.

Barb: When Chuck is using the television clicker why can't he let the people finish a sentence? And why isn't he even aware that I am there? When I am clicking I'm always thinking of what HE would like. I don't understand!

Chuck: Because of our advanced age, Barb has me taking liquid minerals. She buys two styles and keeps both in the refrigerator. One style tastes bad, and the other style *really* tastes bad. One day I went to the refrigerator and took out the minerals I had been putting in my orange juice for some time. Barb said I had taken the "wrong" ones. But these were the ones I used all the time. Without telling me, she had decided to go back to the other kind and she said, "I put them in the front row." I am innocently taking the kind I usually take, and all of a sudden I'm supposed to take the ones in the front row? What happened? Stay tuned. We'll explain.

I don't know if you can relate to any of these events in your life, but these types of minor, seemingly unimportant happenings are the stuff of which marriages are made. The miscommunication seems so meaningless on the surface, but when instances add up on top of each other day-in, day-out, they begin to rub a bit and cause hard feelings.

Our book, *Incompatibility: Grounds for a Great Marriage*, was first published in 1989. We have learned so many things since then we thought we would update you on how the World's Most Opposite Couple is coming along. In many ways marriage gets easier as we get older, but we are still the same people with the same personality styles and men-women differences. Even now we occasionally have some conflicts and feel bad for a couple of days.

The advantage we have now is that over the years we have learned what's going on when we have a misunderstanding, and we try our best to be friends again quickly. One of the most important things we have discovered is the principle of just starting over. Sometimes we come to such an impasse that all we can do is put our arms around each other and say, "Let's just start over." We forget the past and go on with our lives.

At one point in our relationship all we had left was a commitment. We knew divorce was not one of God's options, and somehow, some way, we would have to learn how to live with the other person. We didn't know it then, but the key thing that happened was that we had to work *through* our problems, not try to get out of them. All of a sudden we started learning things that we "accidentally" shared with other couples going through the same thing. Pretty soon we were teaching Sunday school classes on marriage relationships. Pretty soon we were doing marriage seminars around the country. Pretty soon we were writing books—all because we worked through our problems and began living in understanding with each other, even though we truly were and will always be the World's Most Opposite Couple. We will be writing this book the way we teach—side-by-side. In this way you get a Type A's opinion and a Type B's viewpoint. You will see things through a man's eyes and also through a woman's eyes. You will hear from a high energy person and a more laid-back person. You will hear from a spender as well as a saver. You'll hear from someone who runs away from conflict and someone who pursues in conflict. Hopefully through our story you will see bits and pieces of your own relationship, and learn to laugh with us rather than cry so much. Someone has said that humor is what you have left over after all the anger, fear, and embarrassment have been squeezed out. We've been in the crying stage. Now we're able to laugh about some of the things we cried about earlier. We would like to bring you to the point where you can say, when talking about your mate, "Yep, he does that all the time." "Yep, that's just the way she is." Accepting differences rather than fighting them will bring you to the point where *you* can say with us that incompatibility is *still* grounds for a great marriage.

1

ANCIENT HISTORY

Chuck: I was born in Seattle, Washington, raised in Tacoma, Washington, and spent my summers on a farm near Coulee City, Washington. I settled my family in Seattle, and we will probably be here the rest of our lives. How's that for a quick biography?

I had an extremely happy life in my growing-up years. Our home had such a serenity about it. There was the stove, there was the davenport, there was the piano, and there was Mom. What a stability that was to me growing up, having my mom handy anytime day or night when I needed her. My dad worked hard to support the family. Some of my most delightful memories were Sunday evenings after church when my dad would build a fire in the fireplace, and the family would play games together. My brother Jim and I were four years apart. I probably made his life miserable at times being the older brother, but all I can remember was the keen competition as we played hockey in the attic and basketball and baseball in the lot next door that our folks bought for us so we would have space to play. My brother Bob was seventeen years younger than I was. I really didn't have the chance to know him as a young person because I was on my way to college a year after he was born, then went into the army, and then set up our first home in Seattle. I didn't have as much of a chance to watch him grow as I would have liked to have had.

Thinking back on those days, I can see where I was a little overprotected as most firstborns are, and I think that might have had something to do with the problems I was having with self-confidence. I remember so well walking down the streets of my hometown, sure everyone was looking and laughing at me.

When I saw a group of kids over in the corner at school, I was sure I was the target of their ridicule. In hindsight, I guess they weren't laughing at me because I was elected chairman of various school groups, president of the student body, and also president of the young people's group at church. I guess a person can appear competent on the outside but still be lacking self-confidence on the inside.

One of my physical education instructors in high school put us through some running drills, and he said I would make a terrific football player—loose hips or something like that. He thought I should turn out. So one day I brought my new jeans to school and was going to try to make the team. However, on the way to the field one of the older kids who was already on the squad said something like, "*You* are going to turn out for football?" I mumbled something, and after he left I headed home instead of to the football field—an NFL superstar nipped in the bud because of my lack of self-confidence. I was one of the stars in our intramural basketball league but never quite got up the courage to try out for the real team, and I look back with some regret that I wasn't more active in organized sports.

Our family loved music, so in junior high Mom had me take some guitar lessons. I worked hard on them, and if you can believe it, on the last day of high school I was talked into playing my guitar and singing in a talent contest during the senior assembly. I got a standing ovation, and kids came up to me afterward, amazed I could do anything like that and wondered why I had waited so long to perform. I just said, "Thanks" and looked back on what might have been if I had felt a little more sure of myself.

Although my parents insisted I go to church, God had very little to do with my life, and the Bible was a blank book to me. When I went away to college, I had a passing conversation with God once in a while when I got into trouble but nothing too meaningful. While in college, I went to church occasionally out of guilt, I suppose, then wouldn't go again for some time since church was not relevant to my everyday life. Most of the pastors and teachers in my life have given me the impression they had perfect marriages, perfect children, perfect thought lives, spent two hours reading the Bible every day, three hours in prayer, and they would be shocked to think a Christian would ever have the kind of problems I had. When I had a struggle, the *last* person in the world I would think about going to for help was the pastor or Sunday school teacher. They just wouldn't be able to understand a Christian having problems, I thought. Somehow they just didn't seem to be part of the real world.

I went to college to become a veterinarian because I loved animals. I'm forever escorting spiders outside who get trapped in the sink, or tipping beetles right side up, or fishing bumble bees out of the swimming pool.

Even though I loved animals while I was growing up, I was a loner when it came to people. College was a little threatening because I didn't know anyone, and I really didn't know how to meet or talk to strangers. We ate with the girls at the school cafeteria in college. That was interesting. I found out I liked girls a whole lot better than boys, and during my school years had a lot of girl "friends," but none of the smoochy kind. I worshiped from afar, without the courage to make any real advances.

One day I saw a note posted on the bulletin board of my dorm saying a guitar player was needed for a country music band. With the success of my last day in high school still ringing in my ears, I thought I would give it a shot. I auditioned and won a spot in the band. Soon we were playing for grange meetings and various groups on campus. Then I started doing a country disc jockey program to open the campus radio station every morning. Our band was given a live Monday night program, and we went to Spokane to be on TV. All of this was so interesting I decided to change my major from veterinary medicine, to broadcast communications, and eventually I graduated in radio and TV speech from Washington State University. I think you can see the logical tie-in there can't you—veterinary medicine to radio and TV? I thought you would. Oh, on what slender threads some of our major life decisions hang!

I had quite a few successes during my college years and enjoyed school very much. It was an exciting adventure, and I look back with such warm memories of the things I learned and the people I met.

I lived in Pine Manor, which was an independent living group organized like a fraternity. There were one hundred or so young men in the house, and we all had to do something to help earn our keep. My job was to wash breakfast dishes. My radio program started at 6:30 A.M., but I was able to make it back just in time for breakfast. Someone else swept the halls. Someone else helped serve the food. On Sundays we would have a dress-up meal. The rule was we had to look good from the table top on up, but no one cared what was below the table. Since no one cared, we would wear tennis shorts, or jeans, or pajama bottoms, or sweats on our lower half, and ties, white shirts, and sports coats on our top half. I have to laugh thinking about that. It was so typically male. Follow the letter of the law but take liberty with the spirit of it.

If I could find someplace to eat on Sundays, I would save money on my board bill, and I wouldn't have to get my "monkey suit" on, as my dad called dressing up. So once in a while I would take the band over to some of the sororities on campus to entertain. I got to play music, have a free dinner, and eat with girls. Does it get any better than that! Then after dinner we would entertain them with music. It was great fun.

One day at a sorority visit during my junior year, I sat across the table from a very attractive young lady named Barb. We had a nice conversation, but after dinner was over, a 9-foot-10-inch tall good-looking John-Wayne-type football player came in and took that little doll out for the afternoon. She didn't even have the chance to hear me do Lefty Frizzel or George Jones songs. Barb told me later her date was a 5-foot-8-inch folk singer, but he looked big and macho to me, and it was obvious my new friend was spoken for.

So, giving up easily as I usually did where girls were concerned, I made a mental note to investigate her further at some future time. I learned later, however, that Barb phoned her mother that evening and told her she had just met the man she was going to marry—*me*, not the football player (folk singer). I felt the same way, but I assumed she was taken so I just put her on the shelf with all my other unfulfilled dreams. Looking back, I think the folk singer did me a big favor. If Barb had heard me play guitar and realized how much I loved George Jones, she might not have been so quick to call her mother, and we would not now be in the position to write this book. Barb thinks George doesn't open his mouth enough when he sings, and I think her ten years of classical piano lessons (which I didn't know about until we were married) has contaminated her view of what really good music is.

It was in May that we first met, and two weeks later we both attended a YMCA-YWCA conference at a summer camp near Seattle. We were concerned with world events and formed committees to discuss what we could do about society's problems. I was cochairman of the event, so one of my jobs was to visit the various committees to see how they were doing. For some reason I spent most of my time overseeing the groups in which Barb was participating. That's probably why the world is in such a mess today. I didn't have time to work with any of the other committees.

Then tragedy struck! My shoes got wet, and I decided that I had better go to my home in Tacoma and get some dry ones. We did not have stoves that would dry shoes back in the olden days, or at least it didn't occur to me to look for one. "Barb, would you like to ride to Tacoma so I can get some dry shoes?" Where did that kind of courage come from? I wasn't sure how Mom would react to a girl in my car after midnight. The closest thing to dating I had ever done was to take some chocolate chips to a girl named Jean when we were in second grade and a couple of brief flirtations with some hired girls on the farm.

Since I was a little uneasy as to how my mom would react, I left Barb in the car while I ran in to get some more shoes. I was only going to be there a few seconds, and I would be right out. Looking back, what a comedy that must have been. It's after midnight. I burst into my home to find some shoes, and I have a girl in the car for the first time in history. And no one mentioned (at least within my hearing) how stupid it was to drive sixty miles to get new shoes after midnight. Do you suppose I was subconsciously trying to figure out a way to be with Barb some more? Naw—I just hated to slosh around in wet boots.

Barb and I returned to the conference grounds, were unofficially engaged by Friday of that week, and had our wedding planned by the time we left. Once I got the hang of it, I guess I could move fairly fast. It was kind of fun. Since things happened so fast, Barb and I decided not to tell anyone about our relationship until we returned to school the next fall for my senior year. When we got back to school, we hid the ring in her sorority mother's trunk because I couldn't find an evening to make the announcement of our engagement. In the olden days the couple had to tell everyone in their separate living groups on the same evening, and then the man was thrown into the university president's pond. It has never occurred to me until just now to wonder what the *president* thought about this, but it was probably just what kids did, and he was in the "kids" business.

The reason I couldn't find time for our joint announcement was because I was very busy going fifteen different ways at once, just as I have continued to do throughout the years. I played music with the band a couple of times a week, had drills with the ROTC unit, cut hair in the living group, did my radio programs, was on the board of the YMCA, president of my living group, and something else—oh yes, went to school. The man who played piano in my band was one of my college professors and appreciated the extra cash. He took Barb aside one day during that final year and said, "Do you really know what you're getting into?" (He meant people in the communications field tend to be very busy most of their lives.) Barb replied, "Of course," but she really didn't. Nor did I for that matter.

Because the Tacoma trip went so well, I decided to see if I could take Barb to her home in Wenatchee after the conference. I had planned to go to Coulee City to work on the farm anyway, so I would just go a few days early. "No problem! Love to go! Not out of my way at all!" (Well, actually about one hundred miles round trip, but who cared.)

We stopped at my folks' place once more to stay overnight before going across the mountains to Barb's home. This time I actually took her into the house, and Mom finally got a look at the floozy who tempted her dear son to stay out after midnight and give her a restless night or two. Barb charmed them instantly, and my folks fell in love with her as quickly as I had. I can still remember the next morning so well. I was sitting in the living room and Barb appeared in a *dress!* I had never seen her in a dress. We wore jeans at the camp. Just think! I had brought a real live girl home to meet my folks—the kind I had read and dreamed about. She was perfect! Even after forty-some years of marriage, she still looks like a teenager, and I enjoy so much being with her. We have a wonderful friendship as well as being loving marriage partners. Sure there have been some rough spots along the way. That's the reason we can write this book to help you in some of the areas in which we have struggled.

Well, I got Barb safely home to Wenatchee. I drove an old 1940 Studebaker my dad helped me fix up. I had such a wonderful Dad. He died a few years ago, and I really miss him. He worked as a mechanic and could fix anything. He had saved everything he had ever owned or found since he was four years old. He had a garage that the Smithsonian wanted when he was ready to give it up. He had all kinds of exciting things in it, such as the left rear throw-out bearing for a 1948 Jeep, the fan belt for a 1923 Model T Ford, a right rear fender for a Hupmobile in case they ever come back, a coupling for a 190-ton air compressor, one of every nut and bolt General Motors ever made, and a spare 1932 Model A motor under the workbench. You simply never knew when someone was going to stop and ask if you had handlebars for a 1937 Harley motorcycle. I loved rummaging around among the treasures in my father's garage as I was growing up, and my brothers and I have some of the treasures in *our* garages now. There's an old ancient proverb that I follow: "Wise man say never put car in garage—waste of space."

Garages are for treasures, and today I know Barb is thrilled to walk over, around, and through so many wonderful memories when she goes out to the freezer.

My mom was almost perfect. She did have one failing, however. She wanted Dad to clean up the garage. Where would he put everything? Didn't she know the stuff in the garage was worth money? The proof of Dad's wisdom came every three or four years when he would fix a faucet or a window latch or the furnace with something he had saved since high school. Mom would be so pleased to have it fixed, but I never really thought she had a true appreciation for what would have happened if Dad had not hung onto that particular bolt or screw.

And then there was Mom's car. The what's-it made noise, the muffler bearing was shot, the framas was leaking. And what did my dad do? Why, he fixed it, of course. Within just a few short months he would get right to it. He was really busy at the shop and didn't have time to be coming home every ten seconds to fix Mom's car when he had so many *other* people waiting for their cars to be fixed, and he got *paid* for those.

When he finally had time to drive Mom's car, he would exclaim in a fairly firm voice, "I don't hear any noise." It usually took another few months before her car made noise when *both* of them were in it at the same time. Once Dad discovered it was only the ringelnoffett rather than the grindandshafter, he got it fixed in no time. She was lucky it was the ringelnoffett, because otherwise it would have taken a major overhaul.

One of the things Dad couldn't fix (Mom made him throw away the part) was a glove compartment latch for the 1940 Studebaker carrying Barb and me to her home after the conference. When we would go over a bump, the glove compartment door would come unlatched and bang Barb on the knee. I had never had a passenger in my car before, but it wasn't too many miles before I would hear the click, catch the door before it hit her knee, and slam it shut again. I didn't want her to get all bruised up after I had just found her.

We arrived at her home in Wenatchee around noon, and the family had already begun to eat. Just as we drove up I heard this loud, raucous laughter coming from the little kitchen where the family was eating. I was sure they were laughing at me, of course, and how in the world could I disappear without Barb noticing I was gone! However, I got up courage and got out of the car and followed Barb into the house. It was a fairly small kitchen and had 482 people jammed into it—all Barb's relatives. Her dad was telling a joke (they told us later), and he wanted to get to the punch line before we got into the house. Anyway, after they quit laughing at me, I sat down to eat dinner with them.

Barb's mother was really strange. She fixed the oddest things to eat, like cooked broccoli, pickled beets, salad with string beans in it, corn on the cob, and other strange foreign dishes. I was a good old farm boy. I loved ham and eggs and biscuits with gravy—period! The first meal Barb's mother fixed for us included not only corn on the cob but *tea!* Tea always reminded me of water torture, the kind where the communists would drop water on a prisoner's head until he told them where the missile bases were located. I found out very early in life that if I chewed six or seven rows from the corn cob, I could turn that side up, cover part of it with the salad lettuce, and it would appear I had enjoyed my meal—until they started doing the dishes. By then it was too late. I had already left the table. I also found if I put fifteen teaspoons of sugar in the tea, I could choke it down by holding my breath and taking small sips. Anyway, I passed the test with flying colors. I often tell the exciting story of how Barb and I were officially bonded together by corn on the cob and tea.

After dinner two of Barb's small nephews began bugging me to go out and play ball with them. This would require leaving my precious Barb for a few minutes. But I knew my sacrifice would be good PR with her folks, so I got up and went outside with the boys. It also got me out of visiting.

Barb and I got married the following February and began our life together. After two days of marriage, I remarked to her as we were riding along in the car, "I wonder what all this adjustment talk we've heard about is, anyway." We had heard there might be some pressures in marriage that would require compromise and fine-tuning in the relationship. But since we hadn't had our first disagreement yet, I assumed conflict just happened in other marriages.

Barb: It's always a wonder to find out the person you thought you were marrying is not that person at all. I'm sure Chuck didn't have a clue who I was. As a matter of fact, I didn't really know who I was either. I just knew I loved Chuck very much and would do my best to make him happy for the rest of his life. However, what I thought would make him happy and what he thought would make him happy were not always the same. I'll tell you my background and what I was like and you can compare that to Chuck's background.

I was born in Wenatchee, Washington, into a family of three boys. I understand everyone was more than excited to have a girl in the family at last. I'm told my dad ran for several blocks to his folks' home yelling, "It's a girl!" I think you should know that Mom and Dad's firstborn child was a girl who died when she was four years old. This probably explains why Mom spent so much time teaching me and being with me.

They tell me I was a "smiley" child. I can remember teachers commenting that I always had a smile on my face. When I was three years old I embroidered my first dishtowels. The knots are on both the front and back side. At four years I crocheted my first doily. It was red, white, and blue and I made up my own pattern. It doesn't lay very flat but it is a real doily. In the second grade I cut out and made my first pair of pajamas. Mom was then working in the fruit business, packing cherries, apricots, or apples, and a neighbor lady took care of me. I often spent time in our house alone and during that time I found the flannel Mom kept for pajamas and a pattern. I cut them out and had the bottoms sewed before she came home. They even had a yoke on the front (which makes it more complicated for those of you who don't know about sewing).

I was in the third grade when I came down with rheumatic fever. Our home had a window seat at the end of the kitchen and the folks made a bed for me there. I could watch everything Mom did and since I am so expressive I'm sure we talked a lot. I spent most of my third grade year at home lying down. I remember I had to be carried into the living room after dinner so I could be with the family.

My Aunt Ruth called one day when I was around nine years old, and knowing my mother was working, asked me what I was having for dinner. I told her stuffed green peppers as if that was a normal thing for a child to cook. I remember inviting a friend over to play and before she got there I sprinkled some dishtowels to iron because I thought that would be great fun!

We lived on a small farm in a rural area next to a cemetery. I used to spend time by myself in the cemetery and often pretended I was a teacher while using the tombstones shaped like pulpits. We raised rabbits and chickens and had a goat and a pig. My job was to feed two hutches of rabbits. My brothers fed the rest but the folks wanted me to have an outdoor responsibility too. My brother Phil asked me if I had fed my rabbits. Of course I said yes. Then he asked if I had fed them for the past week. Again yes. He said, "You have not. We butchered them last week." Of course I have never owned up to starving my rabbits.

My mother wanted me to take piano lessons so I did until my senior year. I would get up in the morning before anyone else to practice for half an hour and then practice again after school. During apple packing season I would come home to an empty house, start the oil stove, put the breakfast dishes in to soak, and then practice. After that, I would do the dishes and prepare dinner. My brothers were always playing one sport or another so most times preparation of dinner fell to me.

By the time I was in junior high I was also doing the grocery shopping for our family. I remember being embarrassed to tell the butcher what I wanted. I thought they were laughing at me. I think they were just amazed this young girl was shopping for such big orders. (This was before prepackaged meat.)

During the eighth grade Maxine came to live with us. She was my brother Phil's girlfriend who needed a home. We divided up the housework between us and shared a room. It was a wonderful thing to have a sister. Five years later she married my brother.

Max and I made our own clothes, sometimes using print flour sacks. We packed cherries together every summer to earn money to help with our clothes budget.

In high school I chose drama for my extracurricular activity and was in several plays. I was also on the tennis team. I attended Washington State College because two of my brothers went there. At WSC (now WSU) I joined a sorority because my brothers had joined a fraternity. It was at that sorority house that I first met Chuck Snyder. Everyone raved about Chuck Snyder. He was a "big man on campus." I sat across the table from him. I was responsible for answering the phones that Sunday so spent most of the meal getting up and down. I enjoyed his sense of humor and his quiet spirit. Chuck had brought his band to our house to "play for their dinner." I was very impressed with him and wanted so badly to stay and hear his band play, but I had made a date with a folk singer. I called home that night to say I had met the man I was going to marry.

I had been asked to go to a YMCA-YWCA conference as a delegate, representing whom I don't know. I had refused. But after meeting Chuck and finding out he was chairman of the conference and was going, the next day I said I would go after all. The conference began three weeks later. At that conference I noticed every discussion committee I signed up for had Chuck's name handwritten at the end of the list of people. I think I got the clue that he was interested in me too.

We arrived on Sunday and it rained steadily. On Tuesday Chuck asked if I would like to drive with him to his home in Tacoma so he could get a dry pair of shoes. Of course I said yes. We talked easily and even discussed what kind of furniture we both liked. He wouldn't let me go into his house with him because he was afraid his mother was in her bathrobe ready for bed. She told me later she had to take two aspirin tablets to get to sleep because "Chuckie had a girl in his car!"

We became an "item" that week. By Friday Chuck said, "I've been thinking. We could get married after I graduate and spend two years in the army." Then before long he said, "I've been thinking. We could marry after graduation." I thought it was a good idea so we became engaged that Friday. Chuck took me home to meet his family and then on to Wenatchee to my home before he drove to Coulee City where he would work on his uncle's wheat ranch for the summer.

Just as we drove up to my house my dad was finishing a joke. All the doors of the house were open since it was summer and when Chuck got out of the car everyone burst out laughing. Chuck thought they were laughing at him. After dinner my nephews asked Chuck to play catch with them. When Chuck was outside my oldest brother Jim started teasing me about this guitar-playing young man I had brought home. His wife Betty said if he didn't stop she would pour a pitcher of water over him. He didn't stop, and when she started to pour, he raised up and broke the lip of the pitcher on his forehead. With blood streaming down his face, he ran screaming out the kitchen door directly toward Chuck. So that's how Chuck met my family.

When Chuck gave me my engagement ring we were sitting in his car parked in front of my home. He was just starting to put the ring on my finger when my dad suddenly stood there kicking the tires and asking Chuck about his car. Chuck jumped out, leaned back in, and while talking to my dad, put the ring on my finger. Wasn't that romantic?

During the summer Chuck continued to keep *thinking*. He'd say, "I've been *thinking*. We could get married during spring vacation in April." So we prepared our announcements with an April date on them. But before we could announce it at our separate houses on campus Chuck said, "I've been *thinking*. We could get married in between semesters." At that point my mother told him he couldn't do any more *thinking!*

When the school term started we had to stash my engagement ring in my house-mother's trunk for several weeks until Chuck could find a free date. Chuck has always been busy. Both of us had to announce it on the same evening because his house would come and serenade me at my house and then throw him into the president's pond. (It was tradition.)

We finally made the announcement and then one of Chuck's radio-speech professors asked Chuck in front of me, "Does she know what she is getting into?" I thought, "Of course I do." But I didn't. I didn't have a clue. I had no idea that for the rest of my life he would start most sentences with, "I've been *thinking*."

2

I DIDN'T KNOW
OUR MARIAGE
HAD PROBLEMS

Chuck: I am a dreamer, goal setter, and doer and have nineteen things going at once. Many of my goals involve Barb. In contrast to my do-everything-at-once style, Barb likes to do *one* thing at a time, if you can believe that. And stranger than that, she wants to *finish* a project before starting another. What fun is that? *Starting* a project is the important thing to me and is the most fun. After you've started something and all the enjoyment is out of it, just find someone to finish it while you think of ten other things you could do today that would change the world. During one of our "discussions," she finally said to me with heavy exasperation, *"I haven't had a moment's rest since I married you!"* Well that's simply not true. I remember a time in 1959 when the babies were asleep. She had a wonderful afternoon's rest. Then there was the time in 1963 when she had a couple of hours after breakfast to rest because the kids were sick in bed. In 1977 she had an hour to rest one time before our company came for dinner. And there was Christmas in 1990 when she had some time to rest because the kids and grandkids were late coming over for dinner. What does she mean never having had a moment's rest? I remember lots of moments of perfect peace for her. She tends to overstate things, but I love her anyway.

Barb: It's true, I haven't had a moment's rest since I met him. He *always* has another idea, another plan, another goal. Sometimes I'd just like to stop and rest for a while. By rest I mean mentally *and* physically. I get tired just trying to keep up with his ideas.

Chuck: Barb and I have experienced just about every marriage problem you could imagine—communications, schedules, home, finances, disciplining kids, and all the rest. There *is* one thing we didn't experience, however, and that was my midlife crisis. I know it is fashionable for a man who hits forty years of age to get tired of doing the same old things—the same old job, the same old wife, the same old car, and the same old kids. In order to feel better he buys a Mercedes and wears a gold medallion dangling around his neck in front of his hairy chest, which is exposed because his shirt is unbuttoned to his navel. He also finds some little chick to spend weekends with him in the mountains. I must have been too busy during my forty-something years because I never had time to do any of those things. And now I'm way too old to find some chick to spend weekends with me, but I *know* I would have enjoyed my Mercedes.

Barb: There was one time though. We had been invited to a family wedding. My niece had brought her boyfriend. He was a gorgeous Italian musician who looked like "Hollywood" itself. It was a warm spring day and he passed by our table. He had his shirt unbuttoned down the front with gold chains showing on his bare chest. Chuck took one look at me and started to unbutton his shirt. I said, "Honey, your undershirt is showing!"

Chuck: That was the end of my midlife crisis, but we have experienced just about everything else. So hopefully, we can help you as you go through some of the same things we went through.

There is a large group of people who think they have no marriage and relationship problems—they are called men. That's because no news is good news to a man. If his wife is not crying or throwing things, he thinks he has the best marriage going. It's when she says, "Can we talk?" that everything breaks loose for the man. If the couple is *not* talking about the relationship, the husband thinks everything is wonderful. When the couple *is* talking about the relationship, the wife thinks everything is wonderful.

I guess you could say we are walking examples of 2 Corinthians 1:3–5: "What a wonderful God we have—he is the Father of our Lord Jesus Christ, the source of every mercy, and the one who so wonderfully comforts and strengthens us in our hardships and trials. And why does he do this? So that when others are troubled, needing our sympathy and encouragement, we can pass on to them this same help and comfort God has given us."

I've already mentioned the main reason Barb and I might be able to help you with some of your marriage struggles. We have gone *through* some hard times rather than trying to get out of them, and now we can pass on to you the same comfort and encouragement God gave us as we went through the same situation. Not that we didn't *feel* like getting out of our problems from time to time, but we knew in order to please God we had to work through the tough times in our relationship.

Barb: Our purpose for this book is to tell you what the Lord has done for us, what He has taught us concerning differences, and to teach you what the Scriptures have to say about the marriage relationship as well as other relationships. We have found so many of the principles God gives us for marriage apply to our friendships too.

I think Philippians 2:3–11 holds the key to getting along with each other:

Do nothing from selfishness or empty conceit, but with humility of mind let each of you regard one another as more important than himself; do not merely look out for your own personal interests, but also for the interests of others. Have this attitude in yourselves which was also in Christ Jesus, who, although He existed in the form of God, did not regard equality with God a thing to be grasped, but emptied Himself, taking the form of a bond-servant, and being made in the likeness of men. And being found in appearance as a man, He humbled Himself by becoming obedient to the point of death, even death on a cross. Therefore also God highly exalted Him, and bestowed on Him the name which is above every name, that at the name of Jesus EVERY KNEE SHOULD BOW, of those who are in heaven, and on earth, and under the earth, and that every tongue should confess that Jesus Christ is Lord, to the glory of God the Father.

This Scripture tells us how to love each other and also how Jesus Christ loved us. Since we are told to follow His example, here is what He did and asks us to do.

First, He emptied himself. In other words He denied himself. He decided to deny Himself even while He was enjoying the benefits of His home in heaven and His position as the honored one.

Second, He became a bond-servant. A bond-servant is one who has been given his freedom, but has chosen to remain with his master and serve him for the rest of his life.

Third, He humbled Himself. He did not do what He wanted, but did what God sent Him to do, which was to become a man, to live as a man, and to go through the daily trials of living.

Fourth, He became obedient to the point of death, even death on a cross.

In all four of these, Jesus gave up His rights to benefit Himself and He put others first. This is what we must do in a marriage if it is to be all God intended it to be.

Circumstances have come your way and will continue to come where you've thought, "You've got to be kidding, Lord!" We won't know why we have to do things the Lord's way until we do them. After obedience, comes the knowledge of Christ. After obedience, you know *why* you are to:

Deny yourself

Serve

Be humble

Be obedient

All four involve putting others before yourself. It sounds simple, but it is hard to put into practice consistently.

I was asked one time what had changed my life the most. It didn't take me long to realize it was when Chuck decided to become obedient to the Lord. Things have never been the same since. I was the one who reaped most of the benefits from that decision, but Chuck disagrees because of what it says in Ephesians 5:28: "A man is really doing himself a favor and loving himself when he loves his wife" (TLB).

What we want to say over and over again is that it is okay to be different. And because of these differences, there are going to be disagreements and conflicts. That's when we have to decide to be obedient, deny ourselves, and serve each other by humbling ourselves. To give you hope, remember, the Lord said that if we would humble ourselves, He would exalt us at the proper time.

Even Chuck's and my spiritual gifts are different. Chuck has the primary gift of exhortation, and I have the primary gift of teaching. Chuck wants to emphasize living out the Lord's principles first, and I want to emphasize the Scriptures and see what they say. Then I want to see if any other Scriptures say the same thing and finally to show how to live out the principles. Chuck doesn't think I get to the living fast enough, and I think he gets there too fast without first setting a foundation. And so it goes. One of the benefits of being different, however, is when you come from different points of view and agree on an idea, you just know it has to be good.

The longer one is married, the more differences you will find. You don't raise children the same. You don't spend money the same. One person wants all the windows open when you go to bed, the other wants them closed. One wants to go to sleep with music, the other wants complete silence. Even if both want to listen to music, one will probably want classical and the other country western.

Chuck: In my opinion, the number one marriage killer is selfishness—wanting our own way. The second one is expectations—expecting our partner to react in a certain way, or remember something, or do something without being told. When we give up this way of thinking and begin focusing on our mate and what they need from us, then both our needs will be met.

Someone has said, marriage is not *finding* the right mate but *becoming* the right mate. One of the best ways to begin doing this is to start accepting rather than just enduring your partner's differences.

Now let's take a look at the World's Most Opposite Couple and learn about some of the differences we have had to work through.

3

THE WORLD'S MOST
OPPOSITE COUPLE

Chuck: I'll bet some of you thought *you* were the World's Most Opposite Couple, didn't you? There's no chance. Barb and I win hands down. We have filled two 8 1/2–by–11 sheets of paper with our differences. However, we *did* find a couple of things we had in *common* not too long ago. To our amazement, we found out we were married on the same day and have the same kids and grandkids—but that's the *end* of our compatibility.

Whether a couple's differences are hereditary, cultural, environmental, or God's design doesn't really matter much. What *does* matter is that the two marriage partners learn to *accept* the differences in order to have a harmonious marriage relationship. Each difference is really quite minor in and of itself, but as the differences accumulate they often become sources of irritation. The primary reason we talk about our differences is to give you *hope!* If we can make it, *you* can make it. Here are some of the ways in which we are different.

Barb: I hear very well.

Chuck: I have to wear hearing aids. We were in Edmonton, Canada, to speak, and we had just put down our bags in the hotel room when Barb said, "What's that whistle I hear?" She hears all kinds of strange things. A bug walks across the rug and Barb says, "What's that?" Of course I didn't hear any whistle because I had taken my hearing aids out at the airport so they didn't beep the security gate. I feel like a wimp having to wear the dumb things anyway, and I hate to have all the people standing around watching me while I'm stripped down to my shorts so the guards can find if I've hidden a gun or knife. Finally they decide the beep is caused by the batteries in my hearing things and they let me get dressed. So I took my hearing aids out, and without them I don't hear anything higher than a jet's roar without some help. For sure I am not picking up a whistle in the room. We checked the light fixtures, the elevator shaft, the refrigerator, the faucets, but the whistle persisted. Finally Barb's keener-than-most-person's hearing took her to my carry-on bag, and she discovered the whistle was coming from there. One of the batteries in my hearing aids had flopped back into place and it was ringing. Barb said, "I'm sure glad I didn't have to hear that whistle all weekend." I said, "I'm sure glad I didn't have to hear you *hearing* that whistle all weekend."

In our previous home, I liked to have three alarm clocks set to wake me up in the morning. I put one by the bed, and when it went off I knew I still had a half hour to sleep, so I peacefully dozed off again. I put the second one where I had to stretch for it a bit, and when it went off I knew I had fifteen more minutes of blissful sleep. I put the third one on the dresser so when it began dinging I actually had to get up to shut it off, and as long as I was up I might as well go to work. The problem was Barb bolted straight up at alarm number one and was awake for the rest of the day. She didn't like the three alarm system, so I had to go back to just one.

Even in those days my hearing wasn't very good, so I needed the alarm clock close to the bed. I didn't mind the ticking of a clock. It was peaceful. So after I went to bed, I would set the alarm clock on my bedside table and begin to read a book. "I can still hear it," Barb reported. So I put the alarm on the floor by my bed. "I can still hear it," she said. So I put a pillow over it. "I can still hear it." This time her voice was a little louder. So I moved the alarm out to the garage. She called out, "I can still hear it!" So I moved it out into the woods. Finally she couldn't hear it anymore and we could go to sleep. The obvious problem is that now I had to stay *awake* all night worrying about whether I would get up on time because I wouldn't be able to hear the alarm clock out in the woods. I also had to stay awake at night worrying about whether I would snore or not. That was before I moved into another bedroom. Something about Barb never getting any sleep. So in our old age at least both of us are getting our sleep now and I can hear the alarm, but I doubt whether we'll ever have any more babies.

THE WORLD'S MOST OPPOSITE COUPLE

Barb: I like to sit and read when we go on vacation.

Chuck: That's fine after you've been at the campground, motel, or hotel for a while. But soon after I arrive I'm all set to hit the road and see all the historical artifacts in the surrounding area. I like to stand where General Custer stood at the Battle of the Little Big Horn, visualize the troops, and hear the sounds of battle. I want to wander the mountains looking for the Lost Dutchman gold mine, or visit the breathtaking renovation of Ford's Theater, or explore an ancient volcano, or visit an ice cave. We can sit and read when we get home.

Barb: If I listen to music, I prefer soft strings or piano, and I want the music to be in the background.

Chuck: The problem with Barb's music is that it is so *far* in the background you can't make out whether it's on or not. She likes strange musical artists like Wag-o-neer, Show Pan, and DeBussy somebody. I enjoy more serious musicians like Ricky Skaggs, Merle Haggard, and George Jones. For me music goes to waste if it is in the background. Music is an event. I want to sit in front of my giant speakers and let the notes gently brush my hair back a little bit as Ricky sings "I See the Light," or George sings about the woman that done did him wrong. Country music is honest music and tells about life as it is. We all know a man's problems are always caused by a *woman* somewhere who has left him for another man because of a little thing like her husband not getting home from the bar until closing time. Themes like this just make us weep as we hear the truth and experience all the raw emotion that is expressed. Barb misses so much having music in the background.

Barb: I take notes in pencil with a very fine lead.

Chuck: That's hard to believe, isn't it? I think God wants us to take notes in ink. In fact, he prefers that we use a black Flair pen with a broad point where we can make a strong statement to the world and stand behind it never to change or give in. Barb's pencil says she might change her mind or give in to someone else's opinion and need to erase something. God wants us to be strong. Never erasing anything is one of the ways we can prove we are in charge.

Barb: Chuck keeps resetting my clocks ahead. I want them on "really time."

Chuck: I think we should be on time for appointments, so I set all the clocks in my life seven minutes fast so I won't be late for things. Five minutes fast would not work for me because it is too easy to compute. If my watch is seven minutes fast, then it's more complicated to figure out what "really time" is, so I just leave for the meeting when my watch says time to go. Barb is into guidelines not deadlines. She sees no reason why we have to be there on time anyway since they always start the meeting late. She swears she is always on time, but she isn't. I try to ease her kitchen clock ahead to a more comfortable time, but she has just installed a new microwave and regular oven in our kitchen, and they both have digital clocks. So at a glance she can compare the three clocks and see if I've been messing with them.

Barb: I like to balance my checkbook to the penny.

Chuck: I don't want to spend my sunset years trying to balance my checkbook, so I have what I call my "E" factor. When I get my statement from the bank, I check to see if the bank and I agree on how much I have in the account. If the bank says I have a little more than I thought, I just put E (for error) in my bankbook and add the difference. If they say I have a little less than I thought, I just put E in my bankbook and subtract the difference. I come out to the *penny* every time and know exactly how much I have in the account. I figure if I am within twenty bucks of agreeing, I'm not going to spend my terminal years trying to figure out who was wrong. It was either me or the bank, so I just use the E factor and get on with my life.

Barb: I came from a loud family that sometimes was boisterous and joked around a lot. We were free to express angry feelings to each other and then be friends again quickly.

Chuck: I came from a very quiet family. No one ever raised their voices and we surely never expressed a difference of opinion. As I look back now I can remember a few times when my dad seemed to get quiet or tensed up a bit, but I never took that as anger. I thought people had to SHOUT and throw things if they were angry. Mom was very dominant so I'm sure there were times when Dad went into his garage and kicked the Model A Ford—but I never knew it. Therefore, when Barb and I got together and had a "discussion," I thought we had failed miserably. She thought we had succeeded wonderfully.

Barb: I'm laid back and take life pretty much as it comes.

Chuck: I'm a driven person and try to *make* life happen. I'm always looking for shortcuts around red lights. Barb looks at red lights as an instrument in God's hands to bring order into our lives. I, of course, look at red lights as very much a tool of Satan to disrupt my schedule. I have books filled with single spaced pages listing hundreds of projects I want to get done. I love to cross off the items as I finally get them accomplished. It's very hard for me to sit for more than half an hour or so before my back goes into spasms and my legs get restless. Barb can sit all evening with her hand work and enjoy winding down with some TV programs.

I also tend to look at the big picture and sometimes don't pay enough attention to the details of life. Gary Smalley has been a friend of ours from way back before he became famous. One time we brought him to Seattle to speak for our Sunday school retreat. He's a dreamer like I am. He was up front talking about his dream to reach one hundred thousand men for Christ. As I remember, it involved a newsletter mailing. His wife Norma was in the back with Barb and I, and she leaned over and said, "I wonder who is going to lick the stamps."

I am like the guy at the circus with one hundred plates spinning on sticks. When one plate starts to wobble, I run over and spin it again. Then I run to another plate and spin it just before it falls. If Barb was performing at the circus, she would have just one plate and one stick and be content to keep the one plate spinning the rest of her life.

Barb: I love cooked vegetables.

Chuck: I *hate* cooked vegetables. If God had wanted us to eat cooked vegetables, He would have *grown* them cooked. I don't believe the Bible supports eating cooked vegetables. To see what I mean, check out the third chapter, second verse of First Samson. I'll read it in the King James. "Cursed is the cook who boileth the weed in its own juice and crammeth it down the throats of the brethren."

Barb: I like brown, nutritious bread—especially the kind I make myself with wheat germ, bran, brewer's yeast, soy flour and all sorts of extra things to make it good. It's really delicious!

Chuck: Like rocks, asphalt, sand, and zinc pellets, Barb's bread is very heavy. When you come to visit us for breakfast don't have a second slice. You won't be able to get up from the table. I think Wonder Bread is the bread God eats. It's white and fluffy and builds bodies twelve ways. You can roll it up into little balls and throw them at each other. And it lasts a long time too because of all the preservatives.

Barb: I like jam with fruit lumps.

Chuck: I don't like food with lumps in it. I never know what the lumps are, and I always like to know what I am eating. Barb grew up on a little farm where her mom often made jam with lumps in it. When I would visit, I noticed the beetle and tomato worm population went down whenever her mom made jam with lumps. I was always suspicious, especially when I saw the lumps move a couple of times. I think God would prefer we eat jelly. You can see right through it and make sure it is pure and contains no foreign substances.

Barb: I like a great variety of food.

Chuck: I like the same old thing. If you find something you like, solder it! Why would you want to keep trying new things all the time? If you ever come to Seattle be sure to visit the Wedgewood Broiler at North Ninetieth & Thirty-fifth Northeast. Ask for Phyllis or Krissy when you go in, and they will tell you what I have every time I stop by to eat. When they see me coming through the door, they start my salad. They have warned me to call ahead if I ever want to change my order. Why in the world would I want to change what I eat when it's something I like?

The problem is, Barb *enjoys* cooking new things like "Oh La La De Phooey De Dwaaa." I have no idea what it is, and besides that, it has lumps in it. If I don't run around the table twirling my napkin in the air and have a second bowl, Barb feels bad. If I *do* have a second bowl, I feel bad. I'm afraid we'll never see eye-to-eye on food.

Barb: When we go over the mountains to visit my family, I like to take Stevens Pass. The scenery is beautiful and it looks like the Swiss Alps.

Chuck: The problem with Stevens Pass is it only has two lanes, and you get behind 576 logging trucks, 384 Greyhound buses, 275 campers, and six people over one hundred years old who want to drive fifteen miles an hour and look at the scenery—and all of them are in front of me. There are some cut-outs once in a while, and I finally succeed getting past a few trucks, buses, RVs and a couple of the people over one hundred years old just as Barb says, "Let's eat." So there I am in the booth at the restaurant watching all of the trucks, campers, buses, and old people go by. The ones I had worked *so hard* to get in front of.

Folks, if you ever come to Seattle and want to cross the mountains, I suggest you take Snoqualmie Pass. It has four beautiful lanes to help you get around all those people and get on with your life. It took us two weeks to make the 140-mile trip the last time we went Barb's way. How can I ever be a success if I'm spending that much time sitting still?

Barb: When I get lost, I ask directions quickly.

Chuck: And of course I feel asking directions is a sign of weakness. We should just keep the car moving until we see the little halo over the right address or a glow in the distance showing us the way. Barb wants to stop and disrupt some guy's life at the 7-Eleven store asking, "Where are we?" I think we should know where we are at all times. Besides, the guy at the 7-Eleven doesn't know where the address is any better than I do, so we would have saved time just keeping the car moving and asking God to guide us.

Barb: I'm left-handed.

Chuck: I'm right-handed. There is a positive note in this, however. It is a real advantage in hotel bathrooms. The towel, drinking glass, and toothbrush on the right side of the sink are mine. Those on the left side are Barb's. It works great! The way this all started was one time early on in our marriage when I used Barb's toothbrush. She kept getting tested for beriberi all the next week. It cuts down on trips to the doctor if I just use the one on the right side.

Barb: I want my toilet paper to come off the *top* of the roll.

Chuck: This has never been a very high priority for me, but I'm learning. We travel quite a bit, so when I am in the men's room at the Atlanta or Dallas airport, I change all the rolls just in case Barb ever goes in there and is offended.

Chuck: We're going to list some more of our other differences, but some of you have read the list in our first book, or have heard us talk about them on *Focus on the Family.* So if you want to skip to the next chapter, be our guest.

Barb: I like butter.

Chuck: I much prefer margarine.

Barb: I have lower energy.

Chuck: I have high energy.

Barb: I like my applesauce hot.

Chuck: I like *ice* crystals in my applesauce.

Barb: I like my honey thin.

Chuck: I like my honey sugary thick.

Barb: I'm relationship oriented.

Chuck: I'm goal oriented.

Barb: I'm practical.

Chuck: I'm a dreamer.

Barb: It's harder for me to make decisions.

Chuck: It's easy for me to make decisions.

Barb: I like to be very accurate with details.

Chuck: I tend to exaggerate at times.

Barb: When I'm angry, I want to talk.

Chuck: The *last* thing I want to do is talk when I'm angry or when we are having a conflict. In fact, since you've finished your dinner, I can tell you that for me talking during a conflict is like vomiting! I hate to get to it, but I *do* feel better after it's over.

Barb: I'm not in the least threatened by teary TV programs or books.

Chuck: There are enough tears in the world. I like to laugh with *F-Troop*, *McHale's Navy*, or *Laurel and Hardy*. Who would want to cry on purpose?

Barb: I sometimes run my hair dryer on low.

Chuck: I couldn't believe it. We were at one of our pro athlete conferences in Phoenix, and when I went to dry my hair I found the switch on low. How can our ship come in if we use our dryer on low? The thing to do is to put the switch on "blowtorch" and get on with life.

Barb: I want to resolve conflict immediately.

Chuck: I want to *avoid* conflict immediately.

Barb: I plan for things to go right.

Chuck: I'm in business. I know that plan A will never work out quite right. So I always have a Plan B that I can slip right into when everything goes wrong.

Barb: At least I don't worry about it.

Chuck: I don't worry about it either. Worry is a sin. I'm *concerned*, however.

Barb: I take main roads when I drive the car.

Chuck: I take shortcuts. My goal is to keep the car moving at all times.

Barb: I'm a perfectionist.

Chuck: I'm disorderly.

Barb: I love clothes and have pretty good taste.

Chuck: I could care less about clothes. The only taste I have is in my mouth, and Barb wonders about that sometimes.

Barb: I like a clean desk.

Chuck: I have a roll top.

Barb: I like my coffee black.

Chuck: I must have sugar and cream.

Barb: I'd rather talk on the phone than write notes.

Chuck: I much prefer writing notes. I don't like talking on the phone.

Barb: I like small intimate groups where we can share deeply.

Chuck: I like *large* intimate groups where we *don't* have to share.

Barb: I prefer just one or two pets and at this stage of our life none.

Chuck: I think Noah had a wonderful deal with two animals of every kind. What a treat.

Barb: I like sour-tart things.

Chuck: I have the world's biggest sweet tooth.

Barb: I'm a saver.

Chuck: I'm a spender.

Barb: I'm a planner.

Chuck: I'm impulsive

Barb: I can take things back to a store easily.

Chuck: I have a garage full of things I should have taken back to the store easily.

Barb: I love healthy nutritious food. The Good Earth is one of my favorite restaurants.

Chuck: I much prefer McDonald's, Wendy's, Burger King, and Skipper's. They kicked us out of the Good Earth the last time we went there. I ordered bacon, and we haven't been invited back since.

Barb: I take my time.

Chuck: I'm always in a hurry trying to get something done.

Barb: I do one thing at a time to conclusion.

Chuck: I like to do many things at once, and someday I hope to conclude something.

Barb: I hate paperwork.

Chuck: I handle paperwork easily.

Barb: I'm pretty good at small talk and keeping a conversation going.

Chuck: I hate small talk and don't consider myself a good conversationalist unless, of course, the person is contemplating a suicide or divorce. In that case, I can talk all night.

Barb: I prefer red clam chowder.

Chuck: I prefer white clam chowder.

Barb: I am known to endure to the end.

Chuck: I'm changeable. Why would you want to do the same thing for more than fifteen minutes?

Barb: I'm a good navigator in the car.

Chuck: I lose my way easily.

Barb: I prefer creamy peanut butter.

Chuck: I prefer chunky peanut butter.

Barb: I like my toast almost burned.

Chuck: I ask the cook just to breathe on it.

Barb: I prefer mayonnaise.

Chuck: I prefer salad dressing.

Barb: I have been known to smash bugs in the house and kill spiders that have fallen into the bathtub.

Chuck: I carefully lift them out to safety on the back of an old envelope or something.

Barb: We don't have time to go boating, but if we did I would want to get a small quiet sailboat.

Chuck: I'm suspicious of people in sailboats sitting out there on the lake waiting for a breeze. How can you be a success in life that way? What I would have is a ninety-horse Johnson so we could get to where we were going quickly and get on with our life. People in sailboats obviously have no goals in life. They wouldn't have a goal to *rest,* would they?

Now doesn't that give you hope? I thought it would. We could probably stop this book right here and you will have gotten your money's worth. Accepting our partner's differences is one of the keys to a better marriage. Many people seem to feel that differences in marriage are simply to be endured. In fact, isn't "incompatibility" one of our culture's most frequent excuses for divorce? We've found that Barb's strengths tend to be my weaknesses, and my strengths tend to be her weaknesses. Each of us completes the other. On the other hand, it is not wrong or strange to be the same, so don't panic if this is the case with you. We're just talking about the tendencies we've noticed in talking to other people and in our own relationship too.

What we'd like you to do is sit down with your wife or husband and list all the differences you have between you. Then have a meeting with the Lord when you present your lists to Him. Thank Him for making your mate so different, so he or she can be a completer to you by adding strengths you don't have. When you *celebrate* the differences, your marriage will take on a whole new meaning, and conflicts over differences will begin to fade away as you accept each other right where you are.

Just because Barb and I have gone through some communication struggles in our relationship and have passed through the crying stage into the laughing stage does not mean we no longer have conflicts. The big difference for us when we have a conflict now is we have a name for it, and we have more knowledge of what the other person needs in the area of our differences. Our reward comes not only with a better marriage, but we have the chance to help other people going through the same things we have experienced—only sometimes they are still in the crying stage.

Now let's find out how most of us happened to end up marrying someone who is our opposite. We surely didn't mean to. What happened?

4

I DATED ONE MAN
BUT MARRIED ANOTHER

Chuck: We have made our living in the advertising business over the years, and almost by accident we became involved in the lives of pro athletes. I have mentioned that I have an audio studio in our home. That way I can do commercials for my clients at way below the market rate and also do projects for the Lord and other worthy causes free. I had been asked to do some public service radio spots about cystic fibrosis. The Seahawks had just come to town, and they asked Jim Zorn to do the commercial. He was trying out for the starting quarterback job. He came to the house to do his spots on the very day he was chosen to start for Seattle's new expansion football team. He was so excited and so were we. It took us about five minutes to discover he was a Christian, and a wonderful friendship began. Over the course of the next few months we met Steve Largent and some of the other players and began friendships with them. The couples had been listening to tapes for their Bible study and asked if Barb and I would teach them. We said, "Sure."

Within a year or so after meeting Jim, we got acquainted with a number of the Seattle Mariners baseball players and wives, and they asked us to do a wives' tea at our home. We said, "Sure." The Lord had given us a big home near downtown Seattle so we had the room to do this easily. Then some months went by and the Mariners wives asked Barb to teach their women's Bible study. She said, "Sure." Then the Mariners couples asked us to do their couples' Bible study. We said, "Sure."

Then Norm Evans asked if we would be on his associate staff and do personal and marriage counseling for a ministry called Pro Athlete's Outreach. We said, "Sure." Then the national director of Baseball Chapel asked if I would be the chapel coordinator for the Mariners at the Kingdome. I said, "Sure."

Then Don James, the University of Washington Husky football coach, now a member of the coaches' Hall of Fame, asked us if Barb and I would be cochaplains for the football team. We said, "Sure." Our chief qualification for doing all these things was that we were old enough to be parents for the players, and since I worked for myself, we were able to carve out the time needed to do the travel involved in these activities.

Most of the pros were married, so we had a chance to do some teaching on parenting and marriage relationships. But when we began serving as chaplains for the University of Washington Husky football team, we started having single athletes come into our life too. Now, in addition to helping people with marriages, we were doing premarital counseling for the singles. All of a sudden we discovered something we knew instinctively but hadn't put into words. Most of the singles in a dating situation don't think they will ever have problems. They are looking for someone who has everything in common with them. And they usually have found them. Their present dating partner seems to like the same kind of music and food. They like the same entertainment, enjoy the same sports, and both of them are so much alike. And for sure they are not sharing negatives. If they ever were to have a disagreement, they don't say to each other, "That's dumb." They say, "My, what an interesting viewpoint. I don't think I have ever looked at the situation like that. Tell me more about how you feel."

The woman's knight in shining armor is so considerate and caring. He is always bringing her little presents and calling to see how she is if they have been away from each other for more than a day or two. He enjoys looking into her eyes and visiting with her for hours on end, if not in person, at least on the telephone. He visits with her mom about family matters and discusses the world situation or baseball standings with her dad. He makes time to play ball with her little brother after having dinner at her home. If the couple has a disagreement, her boyfriend is so quick to talk about it and get it solved. His whole world seems to center around her. When Barb and I were in school, I would go clear across campus just to walk Barb a couple of doors to her next class. I wanted to be with her every time I could.

The woman in a dating situation knows that her husband-to-be loves to tinker with old cars. So on Saturday she packs a little lunch for the two of them, comes to his garage, sits on the fender of his latest project, and asks him to explain how carburetors work, what alternators do, and how radiators cool the water. In dating situations women have even been known to watch *football* games willingly. She loves to hear him discuss the advantages of using the 4–3 defense rather than the 3–4 in a particular game situation. She saw the wisdom of the 3–4 where you could put more pressure on the quarterback. But at times the 4–3 made more sense to her when the other team was completing short passes underneath.

As I mentioned earlier, I had a country band in college, and Barb would bring her hand work to where we were playing. She would sit there with a big smile. She *loved* to hear me sing George Jones and Hank Williams songs. It was only after we got married that I discovered she liked Mozart better.

Let's say instead of cars the young man loves boats. He spends every waking moment out sailing. When he tells his girlfriend about his interest in boats, she's excited! She wants to share this part of his life too. He likes it, so she assumes she will too. She can visualize the wind blowing through her hair and the fresh salt spray caressing her face.

The girl tells him about how her family always goes to the county fair each year. She especially likes the produce barn where they arrange various types of fruit in patterns. She loves the cross-stitch exhibit and never misses the new paintings by her favorite impressionist artists that are displayed in the art barn. He says, "Be still my heart. That sounds like so much fun." He marks down the date in his daytimer so he can't possibly forget the dates for the fair. Where she goes, he wants to go, too.

Then the couple gets married, and all of a sudden they have *nothing* in common. She likes vegetables. He likes grease. She likes Chopin. He likes Joe Rash and the Pimples Rock Band. They begin to disagree all the time, and he *never* wants to talk about the conflicts they are having. He just retreats. He tries to "fix" her when she has a problem. He seldom visits with her anymore, and if he does, he is looking out the window rather than into her eyes. She finds out he hates ice skating, and yet they watched the skating finals a number of times while they were dating. He even asked about the scoring. He never brings her presents anymore. He doesn't call when he will be late coming home from work. He hates going over to her folks because he has to "visit" all the time. He can't imagine anything more boring than seeing apples arranged in patterns or some artist and his weird paintings that could have been done better by his two-year-old brother. Besides, he saw the fair once. Why would he want to see it again? And her dad doesn't know what he is talking about as far as the Bosnia situation is concerned, and her little brother is a *pain*.

On the other hand, she is not impressed with having four or five old cars in the backyard for all the neighbors to see. She wants him to take them to the dump. Besides, he spends way too much time tinkering with them. She couldn't care less what the carburetor does, or how the radiator cools. Her eyes glaze over when he wants to discuss the merits of the 4–3 vs. the 3–4. She gets sick on the boat, and all of a sudden it dawns on them. They are *different!* How in the world did *that* happen? They had so much in common when they were dating.

The main reason this happens is something women aren't aware of. After the wedding ceremony, the woman goes to change her dress, and her new husband goes in for brain surgery. The church usually sets up a little clinic in the nursery or Christian education room. The doctor on duty removes the communication lobe, the shopping lobe, the visiting lobe, the listening lobe, the mother lobe, and the ice skating lobe. He replaces them with a Monday Night Football lobe, career lobe, golf handicap lobe, Indy 500 lobe, and a workshop/golf/tennis/TV/Internet lobe, depending on what the husband put on the list he gave to the doctor. The woman finishes getting dressed, says a thousand good-byes, exchanges tears with Mom (Dad is anxious to "get on with the rest of his life"), and is so excited to see her husband again. She is anxious to watch him begin to work on his life-long goal of caring for her, showing compassion to her, giving to her, serving her needs, and visiting with her.

What a shock. The man she meets after she changes her dress is completely *different* from the man that she married just a few minutes ago. She expected her shining knight to continue talking with her as he snuggled with her on the blanket under the stars. She expected him to be excited (or at least *go*) to the county fair. She expected him to enjoy shopping with her as much as he did while they were dating. She expected him to take the old cars to the dump when he realized how uncomfortable they made her in front of the neighbors. When these things don't happen, she is devastated. Now he's off to his career, Monday Night Football, tennis, or hobby, and she wonders where he went. She looks into his eyes and there is no one home. They glaze over when she talks to him about her world. During the dating process they were wide open to each other, sharing dreams, desires, interests, judgments, values, and preferences.

When they were dating, he even went *shopping* with her, which by the way, is the highest honor a man can give to a woman. Now he *hates* to shop and quickly makes plans to meet her in forty minutes as he takes off for the hardware store or bookshop. What happened to his love of shoe and blouse shopping? The two of them spent lots of time visiting and sharing their lives when they dated. During this time they both focused on positives rather than on negatives. They both went along with each other's wishes just to honor the other person and value the relationship. Then not too long after the honeymoon is over, both of them start noticing all the times the other person does things "wrong." Pretty soon they begin looking more at the negatives than on the positives, and the relationship slowly deteriorates. I feel like apologizing to all the women in the world because we men simply do not know what is needed to keep a relationship going. A woman knows instinctively by God's design what it takes to have a good marriage, and she is so offended and hurt when her husband doesn't do his "part." I don't blame women for feeling that way, but we men don't mean to be beasts. We just don't know *how* to have a meaningful relationship with our wife until someone comes into our life to teach us.

We didn't have books on marriage way back in the olden days when we were in the early years of our relationship. All we had were the Dead Sea Scrolls. It was hot down there in the desert, but I wanted to be everything Barb needed, so I would climb up to the cave once in a while to study. One time as I was reading the Genesis scroll, I stumbled across Genesis 2:18 that said: "And the LORD God said, It is not good that the man should be alone; I will make him an help meet for him" (KJV).

I asked around and no one seemed to know what a "help meet" was. Even my pastors didn't sound like they knew what it meant. It appeared to me Barb was to be my helper, follow me around, pick up my shorts and socks, and come to bed early whenever I felt in the mood. That sounded terrific. After all God had said the husband and wife were *one* flesh.

Barb: And Chuck thought he was the *one!*

Chuck: Well, that's the way it sounded to me, and I was all for it. However, as we began having some struggles in our marriage, we decided we had to find out more about this "one flesh" business. Barb has a marvelous teaching gift and she looked up the Hebrew word for "help meet" and found out that it meant "completer." That startled me because it meant that differences between men and women in a marriage were *designed* by God. Evidently it wasn't an accident that Barb and I were so different. This was the first time I realized God thought I was not complete without Barb. And this meant she would bring wisdom and gifts to our relationship that I didn't have, and I would contribute a few she didn't have. Together we would be stronger than either one of us individually. In order for a man and woman to *complete* each other, they had to be different. And we were *very* different!

But here's the good news. The longer you're married the less you sweat the little things like shopping together. During the first few years of marriage you want to do everything together, and that's great. But as the years go by and you relax a little bit more, all you have to do is synchronize your watches at the mall and each go your own separate ways. I don't get much joy looking at women's shoes, and Barb doesn't appreciate the finer things about a bandsaw blade. We are different and it is okay.

Barb: It takes work to have a harmonious relationship. It isn't 50–50 as we so often hear. It is 100–100. Both partners must give all of themselves to the other and become servants and ministers to each other. We come into marriage wanting our own way and think our mates will fulfill all our needs. It takes an effort to focus on the other person's needs. Our tendency in marriage is to drift apart. It's easy to go our own way.

A good marriage is forged, rather than simply formed. It is forged in the furnace of trials we go through together and in the heat of tensions and conflicts that we have and work through.

The thing we as couples love most about each other in a dating situation soon becomes our greatest irritation after marriage. Chuck saw this friendly, outgoing person in me, and I saw his quiet, gentle spirit. But after we were married, he would think, *Good grief, does she have to talk to everyone?* And I had to learn that when Chuck got angry he didn't talk for three days. When I got angry I wanted to get it over with and be friends, so I pursued.

Chuck: Attacked!

Barb: I just wanted to deal with it right then, but Chuck thought I was attacking him. I had a hard time with that. Chuck's way of handling conflict is a little more dignified than my way. He prides himself on being "submissive" on a temperament test we took. What he overlooks, however, is when he answered the same questions on me, he graded me more submissive than himself. The truth is neither of us feel submissive inside ourselves. We may act it out but we are being submissive because the Bible tells us to. Chuck seems submissive when it comes to conflict though because he often remains silent and it looks like he's agreeing. We have since taken another test where he scored *really* dominant!

Chuck: Lovingly dominant.

Barb: *Dominant!* And I turned out compliant.

Chuck: Compliant to your own way of doing things.

Barb: You're right. I want things done a certain way, and he wants things done a certain way. When you have two people in a relationship who feel they are "right," then you are bound to have sparks. In fact, one marriage counselor told us we had the hardest type of match: two dominant people in the same marriage.

Chuck: I happen to be more "right" than Barb because I'm president of the world. This means I get irritated when someone else uses *my* freeways, *my* bank lines, *my* restaurants, or is doing construction on *my* street when I am in a hurry. Let's face it, *you* get in my way sometimes, and this irritates me a great deal.

Some of the differences we talk about in this book are cultural; some involve personalities, temperaments, and heredity. The type of parenting we received also plays a part. However, there *are* some God-designed differences between men and women we'll talk about later that also make us come at things differently.

I know this bothers some of our feminist friends, but we hope they will have an open mind as they hear us out. Actually, the women's movement has been responsible for some good things in our society. More equal pay in the marketplace for women, more management opportunities, better working conditions, and more respect. A woman corporation president should have the same pay, privileges, and perks that a man would have in the same position. Where I think some people get off the track, however, is trying to make men and women the *same*. We can be equal, but we'll *never* be the same.

And by the way, if men had been doing what they should have been doing in the marriage relationship down through the years, there would not have been a need for a women's movement.

Barb: Once we were invited to a local radio station to be interviewed about the first edition of our *Incompatibility* book. The nationally known host was in Seattle broadcasting his program back to California.

He came out to the lobby and greeted us both enthusiastically, but when we got to the studio he said, "Mrs. Snyder, you sit in the corner."

I said, "Oh, you aren't going to interview both of us?"

He looked at the book and said, "Oh, you did help write this book. Well, sit here but point the microphone toward Chuck."

Soon, however, the engineer came in with another mike for me. Then the host introduced us to the radio audience as "Chuck and *Jean* Snyder."

We talked about servant-headship on the program and a man called in and with an angry voice said this topic had only been taught this way since women's lib. I wish I could have thought faster and answered him on the spot. But later after thinking about it I said, "We would never have *had* women's lib if this topic had been taught correctly."

On the way home I said to Chuck, "Could you do your best work if you were told to sit in the corner, and had then been told, 'Okay, sit there because you did help write the book, but point the microphone toward Barb,' and had then been introduced as *George* and Barb Snyder?"

Chuck replied, "I'd think that would make you try even harder to show them how good you are."

I exclaimed, *"That's exactly why we have the women's movement!"*

Chuck: It's a man's world, no doubt about that, and women have just barely begun to get the respect they deserve. But we're different in so many ways. Whether these differences are hereditary, cultural, environmental, or God's design doesn't really matter much. What does matter is that the two partners learn to *accept* the differences in order to have a harmonious marriage relationship.

I like to look at a marriage like a car battery. If you put a jumper cable on the battery and touch the positive and negative wires together you get much flashing, snapping, popping, and fireworks. But if the battery is hooked up to a car, there is strength, motion, and power. Sure there will be some sparks and fireworks at some time in a marriage as two opposites try to have contact. But when the marriage partners act as a team—each adding the gifts that God gave them—there is strength, motion, and power in the relationship.

One of our nation's founding fathers said the tree of freedom had to be watered from time to time by the blood of martyrs. I think something similar could be said about marriage. The flower of marriage has to be watered by conflicts from time to time to help it grow into a beautiful plant.

The first time God said something in his creation was not good was when man was alone. I'm reminded of this every time Barb goes home to visit her family or when she goes to teach somewhere like the Ukraine or Israel. I have all these great plans and lists of things I am going to get done while she is gone. I can work twenty-four hours a day if I want to. I don't have to eat, or I can eat nineteen meals a day. I am independent and can come and go as I like. Then she leaves. Suddenly all my plans and goals don't seem so exciting anymore, and I tend to mope around, watch too much TV, and go to bed too early. I can hardly wait for Barb to return, and that's after forty-plus years of marriage!

Now let's take a look at some different personality styles. These are not right or wrong—just different.

5

TALK ABOUT PERSONALITY!

"If I do not want what you want, please try not to tell me that my want is wrong."

"Or if I believe other than you, at least pause before you correct my view."

"Or if my emotion is less than yours, or more, given the same circumstances, try not to ask me to feel more strongly or weakly."

"I do not, for the moment at least, ask you to understand me. That will come only when you are willing to give up *changing* me into a copy of you."

"To put up with me is the first step to understanding me. Not that you embrace my ways as right for you, but that you are no longer irritated or disappointed with me for my seeming waywardness. And in understanding me you might come to *prize* my differences from you, and, far from seeking to change me, preserve and even nurture those differences."

Chuck: What profound wisdom from the book *Please Understand Me* by David Keirsey and Marilyn Bates. They have caught the essence of marriage harmony. The book is about personality styles. The authors include a wonderful self-grading test to let you find out what your basic personality is. It's one of those books that you can read over and over and still gain something each time you read it.

One of the temperament styles they talk about is the SJ. This is the rule maker. Keirsey and Bates write: "School is made for SJs and largely run by SJs and kept mainly to transform these frolicking puppies [students] into serious, duty-oriented little parents who seek only to know what they are 'supposed to do.'" (p. # 40)

The problem is, not everyone is made that way. My son Tim, our firstborn granddaughter Kjersten, my secondborn grandson Connor, my dog Molly, and myself have what the book calls an NF personality style. We have what they call the "Apollonian" temperament. Here's my summary of what the authors say about people with this temperament.

The goal of the Apollonian is extraordinary! Their goal in life is to have a goal. Their purpose in life is to have a purpose in life. To be a grain of sand on a beach is to be nothing. To have the same meaning as others is not to be at all. No matter how they structure their relationships or time it *must* make sense and have meaning. The NF is apt to be passionate in the pursuit of a creative effort; an intellectual butterfly, flitting from idea to idea. He or she is future-oriented and focused on what *might* be. In Greek mythology, Apollo stood as a direct link between gods and men. The NF is often a self-appointed bearer of truth, a spokesperson for the gods.

I laughed when I read that description because that was *exactly* Barb's perception of me early on in our marriage, and I'm sure it still is. One of her favorite phrases was, "When the King speaks, no one speaks after the King." I didn't mean to come off kingly. I just happened to be right in most situations. That's not my fault. That's the way God made me—His design, His plan, His goal, His desire, and His passion. He wants me to be His representative to you mere mortals here on earth. It is a high calling but I'm more than happy to do it. (Are you convinced yet? I didn't think so.)

Because only 12 percent of the population are NFs, that means 88 percent of the people walking around don't understand us. What happens when the SJ teacher and the NF student meet in the classroom? Chaos might be one of the first words that comes to mind. Let's say there is a class of thirty-two splendidly different boys and girls; twelve SJs like the teacher; twelve SPs who are outgoing people-person types; four NTs who are scientists; and four NFs like me. The teacher arranges everyone in rows and columns. The role of the SJ teacher, quoting from Keirsey & Bates, is to see to it that:

All of the children do their work neatly, diligently, and on time, so that they will "develop good study habits" and eventually become "dependable, helpful, honest, and responsible citizens ready willing and able to do their part,"…she will set out to GET THE CHILDREN TO WANT those things coveted by SJs. The children are regarded as all the same in this… Any messages to the contrary from the twenty children who don't get their jollies from the SJ corner are instantly (albeit unconsciously) disqualified, i.e., are met with attribution, or imperviousness, or disconfirmation, or even intrusion. That's if she doesn't realize that many of the children are incredibly different from her and from each other. (p. #99)

There have been a number of good books written on the subject of personalities. Three of my favorites are Dr. James Dobson's *Strong-Willed Child,* Dr. Grant Martin's *The Hyperactive Child,* and personality expert Cynthia Ulrick Tobias's book called *The Way They Learn.*

Tobias bases her approach on the work of Anthony Gregorc and Kathleen Butler. She has become an expert in all the various learning styles, but the Concrete Random, called the CR, is her specialty, because she is one. The CR sounds a lot like the NF we talked about, so that means I'm a CR too. So is Tim. So is Kjersten, so is Connor, so is Molly our dog.

Tobias lists some of the characteristics of the CR. She says we are investigative, intuitive, curious, realistic, creative, innovative, divergent, and adventurous. We see many opinions and solutions. We contribute unusual and diverse ideas. We are out of the main stream. We live in the future. We redesign and restructure. We are tolerant of all types of people. We hate restrictions, limitations, formal reports, and routine. We don't like redoing anything once it's done, keeping detailed records, showing someone how we got a particular answer, having to choose just one answer, or having to have no opinion on something. We may do anything just to be different, lose patience with those who can't keep up, jump to conclusions without sufficient information, refuse to deal with problems at the time they are brought up, and may abandon a project before it is completed. We learn best through practical, hands-on experiences, by inspiration, through problem solving, experiments, open-ended activities, games and simulations, independent study, and by creating products. And we are often heard to say things like "Why?" "I've got a really great idea," "Well, yeah that's what I meant." And here's the kicker. We *hate* authority and being told what to do.

Barb and I were traveling to do our marriage seminar in a town on Highway 2 going from Seattle to eastern Washington. For years there has been a sign on that road that says: "Turn On Your Headlights. Test Area." While we were driving by it, I said to Barb, "I hate that sign!"

She asked why I felt that way. "Because it is *yelling* at me."

Barb: I told him the sign was *not* yelling. It was simply asking him to turn on his lights.

Chuck: I plainly heard the sign yelling, "Turn on your headlights (fathead)! This is a test area (stupo)!" The words in the parentheses are not on the sign, but that's the way I feel every time I read the sign. I *never* turn on my lights. Why should I do that? I don't know who is giving the test. I don't know why it is taking so long to finish the test. No one has ever asked me to take the test. I don't know what the test is testing, so why would I turn on my lights? Only robots would do that. And besides, I *hate* being told what to do!

When we got to the retreat, I used this little story in the seminar as I explained my learning style, and a guy stood up and said, "The reason for the sign is that we have lots of head-on accidents on that stretch of highway." That makes sense, but for my learning style here is what the sign should read: Please turn on your headlights to prevent head-on accidents. I'd snap those lights on instantly.

Barb: What he fails to tell you is I had told him exactly the same thing in the car, but he didn't believe me.

Chuck: I think I am missing something here. Barb did not mention the part about head-on accidents. She assumes I can read her mind, but she really doesn't give me enough information to go on. Oh well, so it goes with the World's Most Opposite Couple.

I also hate it when I call the telephone directory service, because after the computer operator gives me the number she says, "Make a note of it (Lame brain)!" Lady, I wouldn't have *called* if I hadn't planned to make a note of it so I could remember it. You don't have to tell me every time to make a note of it.

I'm not stupid. Maybe I would like to *memorize* the number instead of making a note of it. You can't run my life. This is a free country! You can't tell me what to do with a phone number!

Excuse me, I got a little carried away there, but the lady does irritate me a great deal. It also bothers me to get bills where the amount I owe is typed in by the computer, but there is a little box below it that says "indicate amount paid." First of all, with light bills, insurance bills, gas bills, water bills, and mortgage bills, you either pay the entire amount or are strung up by your thumbs. The only bills I can think of where you might make a partial payment would be department stores or credit cards. But they *want* you to make partial payments. They love the 25 percent or whatever they are charging you as interest. Since I have to pay most bills in full, it is *dumb* to ask me how much I paid! It is right there in front of their eyes written by the computer and on my check. So I just circle the amount with an arrow to the box. I shouldn't even take the time to do that for such a dumb request. Maybe I'll stop doing this and see if they foreclose on my home.

One of the tragedies of our culture is that almost all of the characteristics of the CR person are the same traits for children we say have Attention Deficit Hyperactive Disorder (ADHD). Our society often drugs these ADHD kids with Prozac and Ritalin assuming they have some kind of chemical deficiency. I think most of these ADHD kids are being drugged because their learning style is not compatible with our school system. Obviously some children need and are helped by drugs so they can concentrate and learn. But my guess is the majority of these ADHD kids are simply CRs (or NFs) who are not understood by SJ people.

Dr. Grant Martin, author of *The Hyperactive Child*, is a good friend of mine. I read in his book that people were doing research to see if the childhood ADHD tendencies continued into adulthood. I called Grant and told him not to let the researchers spend one more dime in research. The tendencies *do* go into adulthood, and I am a prime example. I don't know if he ever got credit for finding me, but hopefully the research people saved some money. I did an analysis on this in my book for women called *Men: Some Assembly Required*. I found out I fit every one of the characteristics of the ADHD child. I'll mention a few and maybe you'll see what I mean.

One of my similarities to an ADHD person is having trouble maintaining a sustained interest in reading. I guess my question is, what Bible verse says you have to finish every book you start? I have probably two thousand books staring down at me from the shelves in the study where I am writing these words. I have another couple hundred on shelves in other rooms of the house. At this time I probably have fifty by and under my bed. Okay, there is one negative with this. Our insurance policy does not cover Barb when she is making the bed. If she trips over one of the fifty books, we have to pay the hospital bills. The insurance company is simply not going to take that sort of risk. She solved that by having *me* make the bed.

I sometimes change books two or three times a night. I will start with a Calvin & Hobbes cartoon book for a good laugh. Then I'll switch to a relationship book where I can learn something and I underline the main points. That keeps me interested and awake. When I want to go to sleep I switch to a political, geological, or history book, and I'm snoring before I've turned a couple of pages. I have finished quite a few books, but I have started *hundreds* more that I probably will never finish. No, I'm not good at sustained reading. I've heard some structured SJ people say you have to finish everything you start, but I can't seem to find it in the Bible. I haven't found one person who can give me a good reason why I need to do something more than ten or fifteen minutes at a time, with the exception of the things Barb needs. I'll talk about that in the chapter on the home. But for everyone else, it doesn't matter. The fun part is *starting* projects, not finishing them. Who says we have to finish them anyway?

Barb: I don't believe there is a verse that says, "Cleanliness is next to godliness." But the Bible does say that "God is not the author of confusion" and most people feel confused when things are not in order. When things are "finished" and "in order" I have a sense of peace. Even Chuck sometimes says he feels confused when there is too much disorder, but I want to clear up the messes right now and Chuck can live with them a little longer.

Chuck: ADHD (CR/NF) folks also have problems reading instructions. For one thing, I hate being told what to do. Second, I simply want to get going on the assembly process. It's hard for me to read about putting tab C into tab D before you connect tabs A and B. I read instructions only when I get stuck.

I've tried to learn Spanish because I would love to be able to talk to the

Hispanic workers in some of the hotels we stay in for the pro athlete conferences. I have four or five sets of tapes that were supposed to teach me conversational Spanish in just twenty minutes. I would sound like Santa Ana himself. The tapes didn't work for me. I signed up for a community college Spanish class one time, but my first evening was spent hearing the teacher speak in Spanish. I never did figure out what she was saying so I never went back. I took two years of Spanish in high school but it never stuck. So you can see I have given it a good shot. I did learn one phrase, however. *"Su tiene piedras in su cabeza."* It means "You have rocks in your head." You'd be amazed how seldom that comes up in general conversation.

Here's another example of my impulsiveness. I put together a metal building at our cabin one time. What's so hard about putting a metal building together? You have four walls, a roof, a couple of doors, no big deal. Why in the world would you bother with instructions? So I assembled it. When I stepped back to admire my work, I stumbled over a bag of white things. So I checked the instructions under "white things" and found out they were the five hundred grommets I should have put under the roof screws to keep the roof from leaking. This might not be a problem where you live, but here in Seattle it is a major problem. But being a true creative ADHD (CR/NF), I just took my caulking gun and zapped all the screws. Not one drop of rain has ever seeped through the roof. It doesn't *look* as professional as if Barb had put the shed up, but we don't take our visitors out there anyway, so who cares. And I haven't spent my last years of life reading instructions.

ADHD people are also criticized for having trouble maintaining an organized living/work place. I can't seem to find a Bible verse on this either or even think of a good reason (other than a mate's needs) why we would even *want* an organized work or living place. I have piles of things all over the house—that is until you come to visit. Then I'll cram the stuff under the bed, in the closet, in my rolltop desk, and you'll think I'm a neat-nik. I do that for Barb and Barb alone. She's the only one who cares. I sit here shaking my head in amazement that there are people who would think being unorganized is something "bad" or undesired.

The SJs also think we should have a consistent work performance. I'm not sure what this means, but for us ADHD folks some days we feel like working ten hours, and some days we want to take a nap in the afternoon. Some of us work best from 8:00 P.M. to 3:00 A.M. Other people are like me. My brain goes to jelly around 6:00 P.M., but I'm bright, alert, and creative at 5:30 A.M.—if I can convince myself it is important to get up.

My purpose here is not to criticize my precious SJ friends like Barb or the experts who are so freely doling out Prozac and Ritalin. I just wanted to make sure you knew that my CR/NF personality/learning style fits the characteristics of the ADHD person *exactly,* and I hope parents and teachers will take that into consideration before they start drugging kids who seem to be a little out of step with everyone else.

It's so much fun to watch various personalities in action. We have meetings with our tax accountant and attorney once in a while. Our attorney, Skeeter Ellis, who has since gone to be with the Lord, was very spontaneous, and Don Kurth, our tax advisor is quite orderly just like we want our tax people to be. I remember so well at our breakfast meetings when they would both order oatmeal with raisins and brown sugar. Don picked up each raisin and placed them individually on the oatmeal in precise order, one at a time. Skeeter would just take his bowl of raisins and dump them on top of the oatmeal, and begin to eat. Neither man was wrong—just different.

Another common way of looking at personality types divides people into Type A or Type B personalities. Type A people are driven by the clock. They set unrealistic deadlines for themselves. They are restless. They always need to be doing something. They hate red lights, stop signs, and bank lines, and are very goal oriented. Type B people, on the other hand, take life more as it comes. They are more laid back, are more content, treat deadlines more as guidelines, and are able just to sit and read. They are not clock-driven. They don't mind red lights, stop signs, or bank lines because they enjoy the process more than the Type A personality.

Barb: It isn't easy living with a Type A, impulsive, driven-type person, but at least it keeps life interesting. Frustrating at times, but interesting. Chuck used to give me a list of goals to accomplish. I'd get one or two done and want to enjoy the accomplishment, but he'd say, "When are you going to get this done?" Or "How's that project coming?" He wasn't even enjoying the ones I had gotten done!

Chuck: What is the logical thing to do when you have accomplished a goal? Set another goal of course. Barb wants to rest if you can believe that.

Barb: That's right. I do want to rest. I enjoy the process of getting something done more than Chuck does. He just wants to get it done and then get on with something else.

Another word for impulsive is changeable. When Chuck comes up with an idea and tells me about it, he makes me feel that it is the most important thing in the world to him. I think about it, decide to go along with the idea, and make my adjustment to his way of thinking. He has sold me on the idea with all the conviction in the world. He would even sign a contract in blood if I asked him to. So I begin following along. But before I know it he is going in a different direction, or has decided that's not a good idea after all and he says, "Let's do this instead!"

Impulsive people feel they have the best idea around and have to do it *right now!* Not only that, it often involves money. That's okay if you can afford it, but so often you can't. For nine years I waited to buy new carpet for the first home we owned. It was the time when Chuck was starting his production company for radio and TV commercials. I was keeping the financial books for the company, and I would see where we were going to have enough money to buy the carpet—just as he had another idea for a piece of business equipment.

One time it was an electric organ for musical jingles. As he often did, he said, "It's for you, it's for the business." Somehow it never seemed like it was for me. Of course he thought it was for me because he was my provider, but I really thought he could provide best for me by letting me buy new carpet. I finally agreed that he should buy the organ, but then I noticed that he only used it for one or two commercials. It wasn't long before he had another idea "for the business."

A friend of ours, Larry Burkett, is involved in financial counseling and has what he calls his thirty-day plan. He loves tools, but when he sees a tool he just *has* to have, he makes himself wait for thirty days. By the time thirty days are up, there is usually something else he just *has* to have. This is how he controls his impulsiveness.

We have another friend, Gary Smalley, who is almost a carbon copy of Chuck in the area of dreaming and impulsiveness. Chuck and Gary always have what they call their "noncompleters" lunch when Gary and his family come for a visit. This means they don't take Norma and me along. They can dream and plan and solve the world's problems without anyone saying, "Have you thought about this?" "What are you going to do about that?" "How will you pay for it?" "Where are you going to park it?" And other practical things that come to a woman's mind.

One time Gary asked Chuck if he and I could come to a conference and give a temperament test to a group of business leaders. Chuck was very excited and decided that would be a great thing to do. Then I called Norma and asked a few questions. "How long is the conference?" (Two-and-a-half days.) "How many people will be there?" (Three hundred.) "Norma, we can't grade, chart, and analyze the test for that many people in two-and-a-half days." As Norma reported these facts to Gary I could hear him in the background saying, "Oh yeah, I guess we won't have time." The two men were all set to do this impossible task and have us travel miles and miles because they had their eyes on the goal. Norma and I were thinking through the process of how we were going to accomplish their goal.

It's vital that you know what personality style your mate has. There are a variety of tests that will determine this. The Taylor-Johnson test is one of the best. When you know the strengths and weaknesses of the various personality styles, you can be more tolerant and understanding and say, "That's just the way they are."

Chuck bought a universal gym and after buying it found it was too tall to put in our basement. So he had to have an exercise house built which cost many more thousands of dollars than either of us had imagined—something about a hillside sliding or something. We ended up with a fabulous exercise house that was seldom (very seldom) used, and it eventually became his office at home.

Chuck: It's not true that I seldom used the exercise room. I clearly remember going in there quite often—to get some birdseed I kept there.

I guess one of my biggest problems is wanting instant results. Every year on January second (I don't want to ruin New Year's dinner on the first), I resolve to get in better shape. So I make out a plan to do forty push-ups each morning and forty before I go to bed at night, too. I plan to go to Greenlake and run six miles. I plan to go out to my exercise house every morning after doing the push-ups and pump iron for an hour. I did this for a couple of weeks religiously, but when I looked in the mirror to see my rippling muscles, the rippling I saw wasn't muscles. So I rewarded myself for the good effort with some pizza and ice cream. Who wants to go through all that abuse if it isn't going to work?

Barb: You said you would use your exercise house faithfully.

Chuck: I never said that. You might have assumed that, but those words have never come out of my mouth. Just because I bought the stuff and brought it home was no guarantee I would use it for the rest of my life. After my two weeks of hard work and noticing no change in my figure, I just put it aside until some other day when I have more time. If I can't look like a football player in two weeks then let's get on to something else that will produce faster results.

Actually I'm more structured than it appears from Barb's comments. For instance, I have a stamp collection with all the plate blocks and individual stamps I've saved since high school. I'm sure collecting stamps sounds like too exacting a hobby for an impulsive person, but I also have all the stamp albums I need to put them in, too. And someday I'll put the stamps in the books. Right now they are in a box, but I know I'll enjoy doing that when the time is right.

I also collect coins, but they are still in cans even though I have the coin books. I'll get to them one of these days. My impulsiveness makes it hard for me to put the little plastic tab back on the bread wrapper to keep it fresh. Or take the fringes off postage stamps before I lick them and affix them to the envelope. How in the world is my ship ever going to come in if I keep taking fringes off stamps and putting tabs on bread wrappers? I need to keep moving.

Then there are those times when Barb goes to visit her family and leaves me to tend to the house myself. When I get up in the morning, why would I make the bed? I'm just going to get back in it tonight. Why bother? And the dishes? We have dishes in the cupboard we haven't used since our wedding over forty years ago. We keep washing the ones in the front row, so we never get to the back of the cupboard. We take a few out, use them, wash them, put them back—over and over. We have some of Edison's first dishes that have never seen the light of day. When Barb's gone, however, I just use new dishes from the cupboard each day and put them into the sink after I eat. They stack nicely. The plates fit nicely with other plates, the saucers with other saucers, and the cups with other cups. It looks very orderly. Then just before Barb comes home, I make the bed and wash the dishes once. Everyone's happy, and I don't spend my declining years making beds and washing dishes when no one cares.

I've had a new understanding of Barb since my grandson Cameron came along. His two younger brothers and my granddaughters are more like I am. They are dreamers and can handle fantasy. I will say to the girls and Cameron's brothers: "Remember when we went to the moon and I got our spaceship too close to the sun? Remember how hot it got? How many tentacles did those monsters on the moon have?" And they can remember and tell me how many tentacles the moon monsters had.

I tried to do the same type of thing with Cameron. When he was smaller he would hide in the living room, and I would come in and say, "Where's Cameron?" He would be standing in plain sight with the blanket over his head. It wasn't long before he would take the blanket off and say, "BaPa, I'm right here!"

His two brothers, however, thought it was fun that I couldn't see them and were so tickled when I finally "found" them underneath the blanket, or behind the couch, or under the coffee table.

I was telling Cam some stories at the table and said, "Remember, Cam, when Engineer Bob was sleepy and you drove the train yourself?" My tone of voice implied that of course he would remember this, but his face would show confusion and concern. From time to time he would stamp his little foot in frustration with something I was saying. Poor little precious doll. I was driving him crazy. Cam needs stability of the truth standing firm—no fantasy, no dreams, no stretching the truth.

Barb: As I watched Cam react to Chuck I realized it's because that's the way I am. I am so literal that when I was little I hated to pretend. I just kept thinking *this is not real.* Remember, I'm the one who thought ironing dish towels was fun. I told Chuck, "When you watch Cam, you're watching me." So after forty plus years Chuck understands me better.

Chuck: Even though I try to honor Cam's personality style, I still try to stretch his brain a little bit once in a while, and he's a pretty good sport. I took the three boys to the "mysterious" beach the other day. This is a strip of sand hidden behind a marina, and I tell them that no one else in the world knows that our mysterious beach is there. Since we go during the day, there are times when no one is there, and we have it all to ourselves. The last time we went to the mysterious beach, I wanted them to help me find pirate things. We found a piece of metal from a pirate boat right there on that beach. No wonder it's so mysterious. Then we found some chains that were used on the legs of prisoners and some dragon's teeth in one of the dirt banks by the beach. We also found some petrified eyes from monsters. Connor and Caleb of course were amazed at all these exciting things. Even though Cameron was a little skeptical, he did put a couple of pirate artifacts in the plastic sack we had brought along to carry all the treasures we were going to find. As he was putting a couple of things in the bag, I said once again how wonderful it was to find pirate things. He just couldn't take it anymore. He said, "BaPa, these are just rocks and sand!"

On another trip to the beach I picked up a handful of mud and was telling the kids about how the aliens used mud as gasoline for their spaceships. Connor and Caleb were amazed. Cameron reached down, picked up a handful of mud, stared at it for a few minutes intently, and then said, "Well, I would call it mud!" Barb said, "That's *me*," and I had a new understanding of how she was designed. I'm sorry it took me so long.

By now you are probably thinking, poor Barb. Look what she has to live with. Well she's not so perfect. Take her potato drawer for instance. You have to be very careful when you go out to the garage, because the potatoes have long sprouts on them that reach out and trip you deliberately when you go by. Once in a while I will go to the refrigerator and a fuzzy green feeler will lash out at me from one of the Tupperware dishes holding leftovers in the refrigerator. It's the macaroni and cheese from Christmas. We had some environmental protesters come by the house last week. They chained themselves to the refrigerator and held up signs saying: "Protect the fungus among us" and "Mold should have a chance to live, too."

I have this dream to build a CHUCKLAND near Seattle somewhere. I've asked Barb whether she wanted to make jam in the morning like Mrs. Knotts did at the berry farm or take tickets in the afternoon. Or take tickets in the morning and make jam in the afternoon. She can't make up her mind, so I'm stuck. She has not picked out the color of the backpack she wants for our fifty-mile hike into the mountains. She has not decided between a Harley or Honda for our five-hundred-mile motorcycle togetherness ride I want to take in the Baja desert. How can we accomplish the wonderful goals I have in mind when she can't make up her mind on important issues like these?

Another major decision that Barb has been putting off since the sixth grade is whether she would rather freeze to death or burn to death. I remember the great debates we would have in school on this heavy subject. Barb keeps wavering back and forth on this decision depending on whether it is winter or summer. She's got to make up her mind before she dies.

I remember the time when we were bumped up to first class on one of our airline trips. We had never thought the extra money was worth the prestige, but we were excited when we found ourselves up in the linen napkin compartment. A tragedy happened, however. Barb dropped her dinner roll and it rolled all the way back to the tail of the airplane. This embarrassed the SJ stewardesses who like things orderly. We've never been asked to sit in first class since.

Barb's folks had fruit trees at their home, and they used to load up our car trunk when we visited. When we got home I would take the fruit from the trunk to the garage. We really appreciated their thoughtfulness, but Barb never quite got around to using all the fruit before it got rotten. Then I would take the fruit from the garage to the garbage can. I suggested one time to Barb that it would be lots more efficient if I just took the boxes directly from the trunk to the garbage. It would save all that storage. She didn't quite see it that way.

Barb: This sounds worse than it was. The folks really did send a lot of fruit home with us. I would use most of it and some would get rotten. Chuck has teased me so much about letting the fruit rot that once I packed each apple individually in paper so if one went bad it would not touch another and cause it to go bad too. When I went to get some apples Chuck had thrown *that* box out. So I can't win.

Chuck: It gets worse. Barb still has nine thank-you cards to write that she has never sent out for our wedding gifts back in 1955. I have kept after her over the years, but she has been busy. Now after waiting all these years she says it's no use to send them because the people are probably dead by now anyway. I of course suggested her insensitivity hastened their demise. On their death beds they were probably saying, "Good grief, what kind of a girl did Chuck marry anyway?"

And here's the most serious flaw in Barb's character. It's the reason I could never run for president of the United States. The reporters are sure to dig *this* skeleton out of our closet. Barb is addicted to Haagen-Dazs Rum Raisin Ice Cream. She has even been known to—hang onto your bonnets—eat a whole pint at one sitting. I can see the headlines now: Presidential candidate Snyder withdraws from race due to wife's addiction! See? She's not so perfect.

Barb: I love that ice cream. I don't mean to eat the whole thing but it's like this. I eat around the edges because it melts a little there and is *so* good. Then I decide I should flatten out the middle and then I'll put it back in the freezer. But don't you know, it's melted a little around the edges again, and I think that maybe I'll just eat a little around the edge again and so it goes. First thing I know it's close to the bottom. "Well, there's just a little left so I may as well eat it!" Before I know it the whole pint is gone.

Once I was outside working in the garden. When I came in, a pint of rum raisin ice cream with a spoon stuck in it stood in the middle of the open door-way. Chuck tells me he was just testing my willpower. I didn't have any!

Chuck: Well, actually she *is* perfect, or at least almost. As I mentioned in the introduction, she is the main reason I have anything to share with you in regard to making a marriage work. If anyone can relate to some of the things we say, I defer all the credit to her and God. They were the team that changed my life.

We've talked about personality differences. Now let's see if God made men and women different.

6

MEN AND WOMEN
ARE DIFFERENT—
SURPRISE, SURPRISE!

Several years ago, *USA TODAY* ran an article on the findings by some scientists who suggested that men all descended from a common male ancestor about 270,000 years ago. Yale University biologist Robert Dorit said, "The new study doesn't indicate the origin of 'Adam,' but when taken with the Eve studies, it bolsters the idea that all humans came from the same family or gene pool."

Chuck: The scientists seemed to be amazed that they can trace men and women back to common ancestors. The Bible has said all along that God created one woman and one man to start the human race. I know the idea about God is a stretch for some of you who don't believe there is such a person, but I'm impressed that even our secular scientists are agreeing with the Bible without really meaning to.

Another *USA TODAY* article talks about how scientists in the past thought the moon was a chip off the earth. Now they have had to admit that the moon is completely different from the earth and have had to rewrite their textbooks.

Another *USA TODAY* article from a couple of years ago talked about the findings from a group of scientists studying the moon's composition. Paul Lucey, a University of Hawaii scientist said, "We've concluded that the moon did not form from the same source material as the Earth. This means that two of the four major theories about lunar origin are wrong, and that only one theory—the 'giant impact hypothesis'—is most likely correct." Graham Ryder, a staff scientist at the Lunar and Planetary Institute in Houston said, "The

[Lucey] study is really excellent, but it doesn't prove the theory. But giant impact is the only model we have that fits these data."

I love the final statement in the article saying giant impact is the only model they have that fits the data. It isn't much of a stretch for me to believe the Bible when it says God created the moon, sun, stars, and earth *differently*. The Bible also says the flesh of birds, animals, fish, and humans is different. Each type of flesh has unique characteristics. I know this will *really* stretch you, but do you suppose God made men and women different too?

In her wonderful book called *He and She,* Cris Evatt quotes Tim Clutton-Brock, an ecologist from Cambridge University who says: "Only by regarding males and females as if they were two different species are we likely to understand why it is that the sexes differ so widely in anatomy, physiology and behavior."

In the introduction of her book Evatt asks the question, "Why are men and women different? No one knows for sure." With deep respect for Evatt, I have to differ. We *do* know for sure why this happened. The Bible tells us in Genesis 2:18 that the woman was made by God to *complete* the man. This implies to me that if my wife Barb is to complete me, she must be *different!*

I'm going to recommend you read Evatt's book as well as John Gray's *Men Are from Mars, Women Are from Venus* for most of the details on the differences between men and women. But I did want to add a few things I have observed from a Christian viewpoint that seem to confirm that men and women really are different from each other by God's design. My feminist friends get all nervous when God is referred to as a "he" in the Bible. What they don't realize is that God has *both* male and female characteristics. He divided himself, so to speak, when He made Adam and Eve, and we've been trying frantically to get back together ever since.

The feminist movement has also tried hard to explain away most of the differences they see between men and women. They say these are caused by environment, personality, learning styles, parenting, and cultural stereotypes among other things. This totally overlooks the fact that men's and women's brains are wired differently at birth, women's hips are hooked up differently to make childbirth possible, women's red blood cell count is 20 percent less than men's. Women have smaller bones and less muscle mass. They have an extra layer of fat on their bodies that men do not have. Men feel pain less than women. More men are left-handed. Men have thicker skins. Men's metabolic rate is higher. Men lose weight easier than women. Men have longer vocal chords, and they change their minds more often than women.

Barb: Even magazines recognize a difference between men and women. Women's magazines deal mostly with relationships and the home. Things like marriage, motherhood, children, sex, food, fashions, furnishings, medicine, and psychology. Women want to understand themselves, their mates, and their children.

Men's magazines, on the other hand, are more performance oriented. There are many articles on setting records of some kind. There is less emphasis on relationships. Men's interests center around cars and sports like boxing and football, rather than ice skating. They enjoy stories about war, fighting, spy action, adventure, business, and of course sex, but mostly in a visual orientation rather than in the context of a relationship.

Chuck: Men tend to shop differently than women do. A man sees what he wants, picks it up, takes it to the checkout counter, and he's gone. He is not into doing much comparing or checking other stores or brands. He just wants to get on with his life. Most women, on the other hand, enjoy the process of shopping more than a man does. Comparing, checking, and evaluating are important parts of her trip to the mall or supermarket.

Barb: I long ago gave up the idea of shopping with Chuck. When he goes with me, I feel this great pressure to hurry up and get done, and I can't really shop the way I want to. I like to look at things and then look some more. When I find something I think I might like, I want to try it on. I'll take two sizes into the dressing room just in case one doesn't fit, maybe the other will. I don't even like to shop with other women because I can't think when I'm with someone else. Chuck is patient, but I always feel like he's looking at me! It's like when our kids were small and sitting in the backseat of the car. Tim would often exclaim, "She's staring at me!" or vice versa. So I'm thankful when Chuck goes off to look for a bookstore.

Chuck: Vinod Chabra of the Hearst Feature Service wrote an article based on some studies by Cornell University and *Better Homes and Gardens* which talked about men shoppers. Here are some of the things they found:

1. Men are 70.9 percent less likely than women to clip coupons.

2. Men are impulsive. If something strikes them as interesting or challenging, consider it sold.

3. Men know only two types of meat; hamburger and sirloin steak. Their seafood choice is usually lobster.

4. Men don't read food ads very often, or bother with shopping lists.

5. Men buy a lot of snacks, especially pretzels and chips.

6. Men don't bother with nutritional labels. They are quick to substitute and aren't fussy over expiration dates.

7. Men don't squirrel away sale items. Even toothpaste and toilet paper are purchased on an "as-and-when-needed basis."

8. Men are far more brand-loyal. They avoid comparison shopping and reach for the best, even when it comes to pet food.

Even though I don't do much of the family shopping, I see where I would fit the pattern mentioned above almost exactly. There's been a lot of talk about more men shopping these days. With more women in the marketplace, I would agree that it's only natural that the couple would take turns shopping. I'd like to suggest, however, that if the wife does not make a list for her husband, she is playing with financial fire. If a man goes on his own to the supermarket without a list, he will get little smokies, stuffed olives, chips, hamburger, cheese, pop, teriyaki chicken breasts, ice cream, frozen jam, and fresh strawberries. He checks out and goes home carrying all his packages. The problem is when his wife starts putting the things away (he can't remember where they go), she asks, "Where's the flour and milk?" "Flour and milk? I *knew* I was forgetting something." But it's not his fault, ladies. The conniving supermarket people put the smokies, chips, jam, pop, and stuffed olives right at eye level when he goes down the aisle. But they put the flour, sugar, salt, milk, and bread *way* in the back hidden behind the kumquats or broccoli. You have to want or at least *remember* milk and flour because there's no chance you would accidentally go by it. Here's a practical tip, ladies. Make him a list. It will cut down on the extra items he brings home, and there is a better than average chance he will bring home boring things like flour and milk.

I don't ever recall hearing anyone talk about the subject, but I wonder if music taste is one of the differences between a man and woman. To this day I can never remember having a car pull up beside me at a stop sign with a woman behind the wheel and the doors bulging out in time with Empty Head and the Four Hairs rock band. There might be a few women around who do this, but I'll bet they are rare. A woman is by nature softer, and it seems like her music might be, too. For sure there are women in the front row at the arena when Hot News and the Four Papers come to town to peel the paint off the coliseum with their music. I think, however, the women are there to share the evening with their boyfriends, not because of the music. I could be completely wrong, but that's my impression. I really think music is more of an event to a man than a woman. He cranks up his six-foot speakers and listens to his music at 1100-scorch decibels! My guess is women use music more as a background to set a mood, especially as they get a little older.

I think road rage is a male thing. Once in a while I will have a woman tailgate me closer than I would like, but it's hard for me to remember ever noticing a woman darting in and out of traffic, running up to the car in front of them, jamming on their brakes, flashing their lights, or waving greetings to people with their fingers. On the other hand, I see twenty men do this on every trip I take down the freeway.

I even think anger is more of a man thing than a woman's trait. Have you ever heard of two women at a bar saying to each other, "Let's step outside and settle this woman-to-woman?" If they did step outside to settle the dispute woman-to-woman, they would probably find a table, sit down, talk out the problem, and go shopping together. You seldom see women tossed through the Saddle Saloon's front window. It's laughable even thinking about that scene in your mind.

War is also a man thing. I feel so sorry for the women recruits who have been deceived by our culture to join the military and have their heads shaved and put up with some jerk yelling in their face all the time. It insults every part of their feminine being. Women are not designed for abuse. I'm so sorry they have to go through that just to prove they are equal, when everyone knows women are *superior*. For the life of me I can't see why women want to come from superior down to just being equal. It beats me.

I am absolutely opposed to cobasic training in the military. We do need women in some of the more sensitive areas of our defense. They have more patience as a rule. They can do two or three things at once. They bring wonderful gifts to the military, but please don't bunk them together with men or have a man and woman in a foxhole on guard duty together at night. I don't know if my feminist friends have ever taken biology in college, but that's where I learned about hormones that flare up when we're single and alone with a member of the opposite sex. That even happens with *married* people once in a while, and it is an open invitation to infidelity big time. Sure you find women in motorcycle and street gangs, but in my opinion they are just reflecting what they see their men friends do. The hard drinking, sleeping around, smoking, foul language, and anger are men things, and I hate to have women contaminated by them. Hard broads are created by hard men. It is not a woman's nature to fight unless her primary relationship is doing it.

Male and female differences are very much in evidence at birth. One avid feminist in our area got married and had a daughter. She was very sure conditioning, culture, and parenting had everything to do with how the child was maturing. Then she had a son, and she said, "I was wrong!" He is *completely* different.

You can see this at school carnivals where the one- and two-year-olds have a roped off section of their own so the older kids can participate in the games without worrying about tripping over them. The two-year-old girls are very active jumping and skipping and throwing balls to each other well under control. On the other hand, the little two-year-old boys are *trashing* the place, bouncing off the walls, knocking down the chairs, running over people with little or no respect for anyone else's space.

We named Caleb, our little two-year-old grandson, "El Destructo" because he runs rough-shod all over what his two-year-old girl cousin Allysen is playing with. Allysen is very considerate and wants to mother Ubby, as we call him. He doesn't need a woman in his life right now and resists her with all his might. Allysen is kind and sweet and considerate. Ubby is gruff and selfish and pouts when Allysen is around. Let's lighten up and not feel so guilty about buying our baby boy a racing helmet and our baby girl a doll.

Sometimes a woman's words are not what they seem. For instance, there have been times when Barb and I would have a conflict and she would go to the bedroom to cry. I would cautiously make my way up there after steeling my courage and would be greeted with, "Go away." Since I have a logical brain and am used to dealing with facts and doing what people say, I would go away. But that was not what she really wanted. What she was really saying was, "Come here, hold me in your arms. Cut through my raised voice and tears and prove to me I'm important to you." My computer readout was saying, "Go away." Barb was saying, "Stay here." Now that's tough to explain to a man, but it's true, and it is up to the husband to live with his wife in understanding so he can do the right thing, which is not always (to him) the logical thing.

Barb: It's true. I may still be upset with Chuck when he comes to talk. If he doesn't understand what I'm saying after I've tried to explain it to him, I'll get frustrated and say, "Oh, just go away!" *But* I would rather have him hang in there with me and not give up. I don't want him silent either. I want him to be strong *for* me and not *against* me. I want him to show me that this relationship is worth fighting for, even if he doesn't always understand me. The first time Chuck did that I *knew* he cared.

Chuck: Women's humor is much softer than a man's. A woman wouldn't think of putting someone down. They are into connection. On the other hand, much of a man's humor is teasing, even cutting at times. I have a young pastor in my men's Bible study, and he adds a great deal to the group. He recently started a new church. He was telling the men of his vision for the new church. He said he wanted a strong music program and a stirring message from God's Word. I asked him where he was going to get someone to do the stirring message—yuk, yuk. Men's humor.

Barb and I were in a hotel coffee shop one time. A man came into the coffee shop, spotted someone he had not seen in a long time, and they hit each other on the shoulders. This was followed by mock punches to the stomach, pushes and light shoves in a mini wrestling match, and exchanges of insults. "You old such and such, how'd you get so fat?" "You don't look a day over eighty-five." "What, are you pregnant or something?" I whispered to Barb, "They love each other." They weren't showing love in the way *she* would show love, but she trusted my statement. Much of the content of male stand-up comic routines is ridicule, put-downs, and downright insults to other people.

It's a cutting, harsh humor that is a little bit funny but in an uncomfortable way for most of us.

Men tend to talk more in a social situation, and women tend to talk more in a home or relationship setting. When we're out for dinner with another couple or in a small group setting, I love to tell jokes about what we have learned concerning marriage relationships. So what if I get a few of the details mixed up between last week and last year, and I might exaggerate a tiny bit to make the situation a little more funny than it was? I call it artist's liberty, and I take advantage of that every time I can. The problem comes on the way home from the event. Barb is hurt and feels put down and says we went to Mount Vernon in *February* of 1986, not May. I sometimes get carried away and mis- state her feelings about something I talked about. I don't mean to. One of the elements of humor is slight exaggeration, but I had to learn that if I am going to bring Barb up as one of the subjects for my jokes, it had better be true. Truth is not always that funny, but I try to be more careful for her.

When someone has a problem, a woman wants to grieve with them, feel their pain, bring them dinner, give them hugs, weep with them, connect by sharing common experiences, and say things like, "I know how you feel." It wouldn't even occur to them to try to help the person get over the problem, or tell them what to do. They just want to give comfort.

Men, on the other hand, are notorious for trying to fix problems. John Gray in his book *Men Are from Mars; Women Are from Venus*, gives a wonderful word picture of the man when he has a problem. He goes into his cave to figure out what he is going to do about it. When he comes out, he knows what the prob- lem is and what the solution is. The mistake the woman makes is trying to talk with the man when he is in his cave. If she goes in, she gets burned by his dragon of anger. So she sits by the entrance saying, "Are you through yet?" "Are you ready to come out of your cave yet?" This just causes him to go deeper into the cavern. What the woman needs to do is go shopping. Eventually, he'll come out and be ready to talk, but you can't short-circuit the process.

Most women don't even know what the problem *is* until they start talking about it. During the process of talking, they discover what the problem is, and after talking some more, find some possible solutions. It would be laughable if it wasn't so tragic for the woman, but when the man and woman get together to talk, and she gives him an emotional message about a problem, he immediately takes out his verbal tool-box and starts fixing her problem. She doesn't even know what the problem *is* yet, let alone want a solution as to how to fix it. So she keeps talking searching for the problem. He keeps fixing wondering why she isn't taking his advice, and both are hurt and don't understand the other. Not much communication is accomplished.

I learned that understanding just meant reflecting Barb's feelings back to her in my own words, even if I didn't necessarily agree. For instance, we used the envelope system for our finances when we were first married. We would divide our take-home pay and put so much into the food envelope, so much into the clothing envelope, so much into the entertainment envelope, and so much into the miscellaneous envelope. Near the end of the month she would say, "I'm just about out of food money."

My usual response was, "You'll make it." What I should have said was, "I'll bet that makes you uneasy, doesn't it? You worry about the kids having enough milk, don't you? Thanks for taking our finances seriously." As I became the mirror to her feelings, she knew I understood. All she wanted was for me to be sensitive to how she felt.

It really *does* sound like you women want our advice when you have a problem. Let's say the wife says, "I feel so unappreciated at my job. Everyone is making more money than I am, and I do all the work."

The typical husband, wanting to help, would say, "Just march into your boss's office and demand a raise, and take along a list of all the things you are doing that she probably doesn't know you are doing."

What the typical woman would rather hear is, "I know that frustrates you. You deserve more, that's for sure. I'm your biggest fan!"

Or the wife will say, "The kids are driving me batty. We need a bigger house!" The typical husband will point out the impossibilities of buying a home right now with all their debts and pick her up a couple of books on child raising.

What she would rather have him do is take her in his arms and say, "I don't know how you survive. You are such a good Mom. Thanks for being so wonderful. Let me take care of the kids tonight and you have a girl's night out with someone if you'd like to."

Sometimes we men need to give up a little pride or control when serving wives. Barb and I hated to answer the phone in our previous home. It was quite large, and it was hard to find the other person. Barb might be in her sewing room. I might be in the shop with the saw going, or doing radio commercials in the basement. I never have the phone on in the studio. For some reason my clients don't appreciate phones ringing in their commercials. I realize that's nit-picky, but that's the way they are.

One time I was in doing some commercials and had the phone off as usual. I finished and went back to my desk just as Barb came huffing (my word) down the stairs and demanded, "Did you hear the intercom?"

"No, I didn't hear the intercom," I said. And further, using my best Christ-like attitude, I said, "And if I *had* heard it I would have *answered* it!" I was being falsely accused. Here I was trying to make a living for this woman. I don't have phones on in the studio. I just got back. I'm justified, completely innocent, and pure. I resent being accused of not hearing the intercom.

Barb: This is the way I remember the incident! Many times in the past I tried to reach Chuck on the intercom and he would not answer me. I would ask him if he had heard it and he would insist that he had answered it. We found out later he was holding the button down that he should have released. So I really didn't know if he had heard me or not. This time I thought I "innocently" asked him if he had heard the intercom and suddenly he was angry. I think it was like that sign yelling at him. He just thought I was "huffing" down the stairs.

Chuck: She *huffed* down the stairs. Trust me. We felt bad, but I could have prevented the whole thing by realizing she was leaving the house and wanted to let me know she was leaving. She was frustrated because she couldn't find me on the intercom. What I could have said when she asked if I heard the intercom was, "No, and I'm sorry." What would I have lost? A little pride I guess. Putting up with being falsely accused I suppose. But I would have met her needs a whole lot more with that simple answer.

I don't seem to be able to keep communication going when I'm confronted with something. I tend to defend myself, which only makes things worse. Much of it has to do with my temperament and the way I am emotionally designed. I can choose to grit my teeth and try to communicate at the height of emotion, but I fail far more than I succeed. What Barb desperately needs is for me to understand her feelings, accept her for *having* feelings, and not show disapproval for her getting emotional. This is such a hard area for me, but I'm working on it.

Just this year I made up a special list for my men's Bible study to use when their wives give them an emotional message, or start talking to them about a problem.

Ways to respond when your wife or girlfriend gives an emotional message:

That really ties you up in knots, doesn't it?
Tell me more about that.
That was really frustrating, wasn't it?
My, my.
And then what happened?
And what else do you feel?
That was real difficult, wasn't it?
Isn't that something?
For goodness sake!
I'll bet you couldn't believe it, could you?
I'll bet you felt helpless, didn't you?
That made you so sad, didn't it?
What else did she say?
How did that make you feel?
How about that? Can you believe it?
Did you expect that?
What did your heart feel?
That must have hurt.

Men, just make a copy of this page and put it in your wallet. Then just before you come home from work, or go out to dinner, or go for a car ride, or go to the park for a walk, glance at the items and try to memorize the first couple so you don't have to refer to your list when you are trying to listen to her heart. After you have used the first two, then excuse yourself to go to the bathroom, and memorize the next three items. Then resume your insightful sympathy. The first thing your wife or girlfriend will do is smell your breath to see if you're on something. After a while, however, she will know you are for real and think you really care—and you do, but it usually wouldn't dawn on you to listen to her rather than fix her. That's why I've given you the list. By the way, guys, don't give the whole list for just one feeling. Stretch it out so it will last a while.

John Kasay was the place-kicker for the Seahawks for a while, and like many of the pro athletes he and his wife Laura became our "kids" because we're old enough to be their parents. We love them because they *breathe,* not because they play football, baseball, or ride broncos. John was picking up a couple of additional credits for his advertising major by working for my agency in the off-season. John is very linear, just like we want our kickers to be. We want him to be exactly 3.2 feet to the side of the ball, take 2.8 steps to meet it squarely, swing the leg through in an arc direct to the goal post, and put the ball through the uprights. John fit this mold very well.

One day he was upset because he didn't seem to be meeting Laura's needs when she had a problem. He was amazed that all his insightful advice and well-thought-out solutions were met with frustration. He asked my advice, so I had him get his legal pad and I gave him the list of responses I have given you. He laughed and didn't think they would work, but I said, "Trust me." So he did. That afternoon it was sunny in Seattle. (We only have sun on July 5th and August 16th. The rest of the year it rains and rains and rains and rains. Spread the word. Tell all your friends.) So John and Laura decided to walk around the lake we have in the middle of town. (It has seaweed in it. You wouldn't like it.) Pretty soon Laura gave John an emotional message about a problem she was having. He had memorized the first couple of responses, so he said, "That...really...ties...you...up...in...knots,...doesn't...it?" (This is so foreign to a man's nature it's hard to get the words out.) John said she stopped, reached over and took off *his* sunglasses and asked, "What did you say?"

John blinked a little bit and repeated a bit more fluently, "That really ties you up in knots, doesn't it?"

She started laughing. "You've been talking to *Chuck,* haven't you?" He admitted he had, and half of the time during the rest of their walk she was laughing about him talking to me, but the rest of the time she thought he *really cared*. And he did, and he does. It's just not our nature as men to listen, and I'm so sorry.

Barb: When a woman gets into a conflict, she desperately wants to share what she is feeling and to have some understanding from her husband. Instead of giving her understanding, the man will usually tell the woman to *do* something to get rid of her problem. The impression they give us is, "Here are five easy steps to solve your crisis. What other little problems do you have?" We don't want solutions. We want understanding. When the man gives us solutions too quickly, it makes us feel like our problems aren't very important, and we feel devalued and dishonored.

We have a *Cathy* cartoon on our refrigerator. She and her boyfriend have just watched a football game. Cathy tells her boyfriend about seeing the pre-game warm-up, the coach's preview, the predictions show, starting lineups, the game with a hundred replays, the post-game show, the coach's wrap, the locker-room show, and the after-game-call-in program, and now she wants to talk about their relationship. Her boyfriend says, "Isn't that just like a woman—always wants to *rehash* everything."

Sometimes a husband will say to his wife, "You're just too sensitive." It's true we are sensitive compared to them. We see and feel lots of things men do not. We know when all is not going well between us. I was aware that one couple in our life was having problems, and the young wife was aware of it also. In fact, she had spoken to her husband about it many times over a period of months. But it wasn't until she created a crisis that the young husband said, "I thought for a couple of days there might be something wrong."

Women have a need for their relationships to be right with everyone. We're sensitive to the needs of others and show it by being the driving force to get our men to go to weddings, funerals, anniversary celebrations, and the like. We know when others need to be honored. I think, however, our husbands would much rather watch golf or the NFL football game on TV, or go fishing.

Chuck: Another difference between men and women is that women are usually glad to accept help, but accepting help makes men feel weak, so we resist anyone trying to help us. We men want to do things by ourselves, like tie our shoes when we are three years old, take *all* the garbage out at one time, fix the car out on the freeway, or find the address without asking for directions.

I was picking up some things at Home Depot. As I went back to my car, I passed a guy wrestling a filing cabinet into his pickup. He was red in the face and his veins were ready to burst as he inched this heavy monster bit by bit onto the truck bed. I stopped and asked, "Can I help?"

And of course he said in a raspy, choked voice, "No thanks. I'm doing fine." I continued to my car. I understood perfectly what was going on. The hospital bill will be covered by insurance anyway, and his wife will think he is just working too hard.

When Barb and I are traveling in the car and have clear, written directions on how to find our destination, we're still different. Barb looks ahead to the final destination and has clearly in mind all of the details on how to get there. I can only handle one thing at a time as far as directions are concerned, so I ask Barb only to tell me whether I am in the correct lane to turn the right way when we get to the light. She still forgets that and will say something like, "We turn right on Jefferson, go 4.2 miles to a Texaco, turn left, but keep to the right, and watch for a Y in the road where we veer to the left, and go 2.3 miles to a fire station, turn right, and it is the fourth street on the right. They live in the white house with the green shutters and have an old car out front." My brain goes blank and I say, "What way did you say to turn on Jefferson?" Just tell me the rest of the journey step by step.

Sometimes when we're going to a place that's familiar to both of us Barb will say, "Go any way you want." I'm pretty pumped about that statement, so I start going any way I want. It isn't very long before she says, "Why did you turn there?" Or "It's easier if you stay on the left." Or "I think it would be shorter to go by the Kingdome." Now this is in no way a put-down of Barb. She is the navigator in the car. She is the expert in the big picture. She can see the path from where we are to the final destination. The only problem is I thought I heard her say, "Go any way you want." That's the thing that is confusing.

Women use sports as exercise or a reason to be with someone. Men's main goal for sports is to win the game no matter what it takes. They have no compassion for people on the other team.

When women visit they usually talk about people and relationships. When men visit they usually talk about *things* like golf scores, last night's ball game, cars, assignments they bring home from work, shop projects, schedules, and so on. Very few *people* make it into men's conversation except in a negative way.

I mentioned in the intro that I would explain why Barb asked, as I was ready to go out the door to work one time, "Are you going to wear that tie?" Yes, I was going to wear this tie. I had it on along with my coat. I had my briefcase and the car was running. Yes, this is the tie I have chosen to wear today. I had no idea the way I looked affected Barb. I thought people would hold *me* responsible for choosing my tie, wearing clean pants, and not wearing two left shoes.

Barb: I believe women are more indirect than men. We have been accused of being "bossy" or "aggressive" so often we try to soften our approach. I used to tell the secretaries in the office I would always come at them softly like, "If you have time, will you type this up for me?" But I told them I really meant I would like this done. The problem was it never got done.

Chuck, on the other hand, would tell them to type up this and do that and he needed it by five o'clock and thank you. He would have it by five o'clock. A woman just doesn't speak that way, and if she did she would be criticized.

It's the same with Chuck. He tells me he wants me to be direct and I am many times. But I feel (know) he couldn't handle it if I came at him directly all the time. I know he *says* he could, but I wonder!

Chuck: A man might say to an employee on the loading dock, "Jim, I need those cases moved immediately please." A woman will be more apt to say, "Jim, when you have a minute or can work it into your schedule, would you mind moving those cases? I would really appreciate your help." The problem comes when Jim (a man) takes the woman's words literally. "When you have a minute" means to do it when he can fit moving the cases in with the other things he has on his list this week. The woman is upset when she visits the dock the next morning and the cases are still there. She will feel she had asked to have them moved and Jim ignored her. Jim knows she is in no hurry because she said, "When you have a minute," and he has not had a minute yet. So Barb doesn't say, "That tie looks terrible! The polka dots don't go with your blue striped shirt. Please find another one." Instead, she asks, "Are you going to wear that tie?" Yes, I had planned to wear this tie and so on.

I've had a number of women complain their husband did not love them anymore. I asked how they knew that. Among the things they tell me is the fact her husband never looks at her when they talk. He keeps looking out the window or at the wall. And more than that, he never *says* anything while she's talking to acknowledge he is even hearing her. I tried to explain that normally men don't look into people's eyes when they talk, especially if it is in a conflict situation. They just wait until the other person is through before they offer anything. I tested this on one of the guys in my Bible study. I kept looking into his eyes as I talked to him, and pretty soon he said, "Stop looking at me, will you. That gives me the *willies.*"

If possible, when a woman talks with another woman, they would like to be face to face as they look into each other's eyes and talk. Women also make noises when they talk with each other. The one listening will say things like, "Is that so? Can you believe that? My goodness, isn't that something! Oh my word! Well, I never would have thought," as the other one is talking. Two men are usually side by side watching the game on TV or reading the paper together. Once in a while one of them will quickly glance over to see if the other guy is still there, but they surely are not looking into each other's eyes or making noise.

There are many more differences between men and women, but I'll ask Cris Evatt and John Gray to give you the rest of the instances when you read their wonderful books. Our culture is slowly but surely turning around to admit there are differences between the sexes, and that it's okay. In fact, the differences make us laugh as the TV program *Home Improvement* reminds us every night. Remember, being different was God's idea in the first place. He likes it when we bring our individual gifts to a marriage to make it stronger. Don't try to change each other. Delight in the other person's gifts. Encourage and support them, and this will turn some of your tears from sadness to laughter.

Now here's a question about the differences between men and women you may not have thought about. Does estrogen fog a woman's brain? The next chapter might make you think so.

7

ESTROGEN
FOGS THE BRAIN

Chuck: The reason I think Barb has a hormone problem is that she assumes I will understand what she means even though sometimes she doesn't give me all the information I need to keep up with her. I have no other explanation for the following miscommunication examples in our marriage except to say Barb's brain has been fogged by estrogen.

For instance, on the third floor living area of our former home I had a shower in my bathroom, and Barb had a bathtub in hers. Once in a while she would come over to use the shower in the morning while I was shaving. One time she was showering away and she called out, "Is the hot water on?"

"No," I said.

She said, "Put it on." So I turned the hot water on in the sink. I thought maybe it was affecting the water temperature of her shower. So I kept on shaving. She was confused that I didn't leave. What I didn't know was she had asked would I put the hot water on *under the teakettle* down in the kitchen. She forgot three essential words: *under the teakettle*. She thought I should just *know* what she meant.

Barb: You need to know that for *years* every morning Chuck would get up, get the paper, go to the kitchen, fill the teakettle and put it on the stove to heat because we used a Melitta drip coffeepot and the water needed to be hot in order to make coffee. So when I asked him, "Is the water on?" it was in context with our morning routine. He just gets slower in our old age to put two and two together.

Chuck: I still think the words *under the teakettle* would have been helpful. Barb often gives me instructions that are very clear in her mind, but never arrive in my mind. One time we were in an airplane during a layover. We usually have aisle seats across from each other. At our age we get up and down a lot and this makes it easier. Barb had a seat-mate so she took all her carry-on material up to a vacant seat so she could have a little more room to work. She often does her Bible study when we travel on airplanes. After the plane had cleared out, she called back and wanted to know, "Is my seat-mate gone?"

"Yes, he's gone," I said. I had seen him leave. So she gathered up all her books and papers and came back but found his stuff still under the seat. She was amazed that I said he was gone when obviously he wasn't gone. I was supposed to catch the difference between "Was he gone?" (forever) and "Was he gone?" (until the plane left again). I think that's asking a lot.

We were on our way in the car to speak at a conference. We were driving along and Barb said, "You'll enjoy meeting her." Well I'm sure I would, but I didn't know who "her" was, nor where I would meet her. Was she a member of our Sunday school class, Barb's Bible study group, or some extended family member coming to the conference? I really didn't have much to go on. She thought I should know who she meant.

I was reading the paper at the breakfast table. Barb was too. All of a sudden she put down her paper and said, "Will you have what's-his-name fix that thing?" Now I ask you, can you get many clues from that statement as to who should fix what? Barb just thought I should know.

We just got back from a cabin where I was trying to finish a book. On vacation I feel free to eat what God eats: Wonder Bread, baloney, eggs and bacon, a nice steak, baked potatoes with more things on top than most people think I should have, and all the pop I want to drink. Usually I conform more to Barb's nutritional standards at home, but on vacation I want to eat like I would if I were in heaven. So I did all that and was enjoying myself immensely at the dinner table when Barb said, "Who do you want to give money gifts to when you die?" I thought she agreed not to give me a bad time about my vacation eating. What she had forgotten to tell me was she was thinking about the owner of the cabin who had lost her husband in his forties. What I needed was some sort of introductory paragraph like, "I was thinking of all the grief Annie has gone through, but because of her husband's death she has been able to give cash gifts to some of the organizations that she wanted to support." Then the question about my dying would have been a little less abrupt.

Or there are those times when Barb *swears* she told me something and I am equally as sure those words have never come out of her mouth. She was talking to her mom, her girlfriend, the butcher, the neighbor, but she had never brought up the subject within my hearing range. I'm sure she had said to the neighbor, "I think I will ask Chuck to take out the garbage," but she never asks *me*. She'll tell her friends, "I think I'll have Chuck clean the gutters this weekend," but I never get the information.

Worse than Barb telling someone else what she is going to ask me, she sometimes just *thinks* about something and then is sure she has mentioned it to me out loud. My feeling is I am *sure* I would have remembered something *that* important if she had told me. We saw a cartoon once where the wife was in the kitchen preparing dinner, the husband was reading his paper, and there was a baby crawling across the floor. The husband says, "I *know* I would have remembered if you had told me you were pregnant!"

Barb: There have been times when Chuck and I have had long conversations on a subject. We come to agreement—like going to a wedding. Then when the time comes to go he says, "We've *never* talked about that!" I then proceed to tell him where we were, what we were eating, what we were wearing, and how we looked at each other when we talked about the wedding. He *insists*, "We never talked about it."

Yesterday the tables were turned. I went to Sears to get a replacement part for a carpet cleaner. I came home with one, and after Chuck put it on I proceeded to break that one, too. He said, "Did you get two."

"No."

"I told you to get two." I did not hear him say that.

Now what we experienced yesterday is different than when *he* says I never told him. I immediately told him he was probably right and I just missed it. But Chuck is *still* defending himself when he hasn't heard me for forty some years.

Chuck: This just proves what a wonderful person Barb is, but I think the difference between the two episodes is very clear. I *knew* I had told Barb to get two parts. She *thinks* she told me about the wedding. It is plain to see who is "fogged" in this part of our lives.

Wives don't give proper transitions either. We will be driving along in the car talking about Aunt Suzie's haircut and all of a sudden Barb will be giving some details that have nothing to do with the subject at hand. I'll listen to a little bit of it and ask what that has to do with Aunt Suzie's haircut. I find out Barb is now talking about Uncle Ted's violin but has failed to give a proper transition. Or she will be talking about how wonderful George is so I'm going along with her in my mind that George Toles is a great person. All of a sudden she will mention his home in Twisp. George doesn't live in Twisp so I challenge her. I find out she is talking about George Parker. He's also a great guy, but then I have to go back over the whole conversation and bring my brain up to date with the new name. She thinks it should be obvious who she is talking about.

When we decide to go out to a restaurant, I would like to go where Barb would like to eat, so I will ask her, "Where do you want to eat?"

She will say, "I don't care, where do *you* want to eat."

I say, "I don't care, where do *you* want to eat."

She says, "I don't care, where do *you* want to eat."

Okay, it sounds like she wants to know where I would like to eat so I say, "Let's go get fish and chips."

She will say, "Yuck! How about some pizza?"

I could have sworn she said, "Where do *you* want to eat?"

Barb: First off, I don't mean "Yuck." I'm negotiating. We're discussing this. Chuck thinks since I have spoken it is a final decision. It's not! I still want to keep talking until we can come to an agreement. Maybe he doesn't understand rhetorical questions.

Chuck: I wouldn't know a rhetorical question if I heard it, so I guess I'll let her comment pass. All I know is that fish and chips is the wrong answer.

Sometimes we'll go to a stadium or theater where our seats are not assigned, and I will ask, "Where do you want to sit?"

She says, "I don't care, where do you want to sit?"

I say, "I don't care, where do *you* want to sit?"

She says, "I don't care, where do *you* want to sit?"

It sounds like she is saying, "Where do you want to sit?" so I say, "How about here." She says, "No, let's go down front." Why *ask* if she doesn't want my opinion.

Barb: It's true, I do that all the time. I guess I just want to involve him in a conversation. Who knows? We laugh at other couples all the time when we watch them go through the same scenario. Must be just the way we are.

Chuck: I'm easy. I'll eat and go and sit anywhere she wants. Barb says she thinks we are still discussing it. It surely doesn't sound like a discussion when *she* decides where we will eat or sit.

I also believe God wants us to be on time for things like airport schedules. Scripture says we are to be at the airport one hour before our flight takes off. When we are in the planning stage, Barb will ask me when I think we should leave for the airport. I hate to give an opinion because I know it will be wrong, but eventually I will say, "10:30 A.M."

She will think a minute and then say, "How about 11:00 A.M.?" If she didn't want to take my decision, why does she ask? I will never understand why she wants me to make a decision if she is going to change it.

Barb: Chuck used to try and trick me into going at exactly the time he wanted to go. He would tell me 9:00 A.M. when he really wanted to leave at 10:00 A.M. So naturally I would say 10:00 A.M. and he would be happy, but he never let me forget that I had changed the time. Finally I caught on, and *now* when I ask him when he wants to leave, he only starts a half hour earlier. I do change the time he wants to leave, but it's this little game we play. I know exactly what he's doing.

Chuck: I go to another old ancient proverb that says: "Wise woman never asks honorable husband questions she already knows answers to."

Barb is not as impressed with ancient wisdom as I am, except for the two-thousand-year-old book she calls the Bible.

One time we attended an event at the Convention Center in downtown Seattle. I let Barb off at the door as I usually do and went to park. After the event was over I started for the door near where our car was parked, but for some reason Barb thought we should go another way. I had parked the car. She had no idea where it was, but I am so tuned in to going along with what Barb wants that we walked completely around the center, through dark alleys and mugging parks, and finally got to the car. We laughed, but she wanted to know why I didn't stand up for my convictions. I just didn't want to get into a debate, so I just went along with her wishes, even though I knew where the car was parked. Dumb? Not really. It was good practice honoring Barb and trying to please her.

Barb: That has to be the most ridiculous thing we've ever done. Chuck told me where the car was parked, I *knew* where it was parked but I thought if we went out this door it would be a shortcut. It turned out to be very long, and through all the dark places Chuck described. We laughed a lot but he keeps changing the story to make it sound better.

Chuck: Barb also thinks restaurant menus are guidelines. The leaders of the restaurant industry spend millions of dollars every year planning, printing, and distributing menus. The way to order from a menu is simply to say, "I will have number one, eggs over easy." Barb, however, wants to *change* number one on the menu God wrote. She says, "May I have two salads please, one with blue cheese and one with French, and I want my dressing on the side. I would like my toast almost burned, but dry, and don't let the cook put any butter on the eggs, and I'd like some lemon wedges for my water, and do you have any orange marmalade?" It used to embarrass me that Barb would have the courage to upset our nation's economy so badly by making the poor restaurant person go through all those hoops.

Barb: Restaurants don't have the right combinations on their menus, so since we are paying for the meal I figure it's all right to have what I like. I don't think it bothers Chuck much anymore, but when we were first married it was a real trial for him. And it was even worse for our son when he was a teenager. I really embarrassed him by changing the menu around.

Chuck: I have learned so much from Dr. Norman Wright's books over the years, especially the one called *Communication: Key to Your Marriage*. Of course good communication is the key to all of our relationships: business, ministry, church, neighborhood, kids, parents, in-laws, investment partners, and just about every other area of life you can think about. But in my mind, communication in marriage is the cornerstone of our society and the world, for that matter. As the family goes, so goes just about everything else. Communication is the key to marriage, and we need to have a stronger commitment to finding out how our mate is designed, what they need from us, and how they communicate. Then we must alter our style to fit theirs as much as possible. When both the husband and wife do that, they understand each other better, and everyone benefits.

Now let's talk about another common misunderstanding in marriage—the tug-of-war between women who value relationships and men who value goals.

8

DO I HAVE TO GO?

Chuck: I was asked to speak to a Northwest Writers' conference on how to write humor. Well in the first place I don't write humor, I just report on the things that are happening in my life. Second, I didn't think I could teach anyone to do it who didn't have a funny life like I did, but I agreed to speak anyway, and I think they had a good time.

Marriage differences always enter into my remarks no matter what the subject is, because I see such a need for couples to begin accepting and understanding the other person in spite of what they are doing or not doing. I often tease about how weddings are one example of the differences between men and women. The reason I resist going to weddings is they are not very efficient.

If I was asked how to do weddings right, I would get things like lighting the candles and seating the mothers out of the way before the people arrived so everything would be ready for the main event. At least the men are ready. They usually come out of a side door at the front of the church in a glump: the pastor, the groom, and the best man. They are ready for the wedding to begin. What do the women do? Traipse one by one to the front of the church to some funeral music on the arm of another man who has also been waiting patiently for everything to get going. The traipsing takes about forty-five minutes, and finally everyone is ready. Then we have to find out if anyone in the audience doesn't want this event to happen. I've never heard anyone object yet, so we could just eliminate that part from the service. Then after the audience sits down, the two mothers come up front slowly to light two of three candles on the altar. (The other people should have done that while they were up there.) By this time my back is going into spasms because I have been sitting for two hours waiting for the ceremony to start.

Then the pastor has to preach a long sermon because he knows he won't get another shot at most of the audience until Easter. Then there is communion, which is fine, but they could have done that in the dressing room since only the bride and groom are involved in this. Finally after six or seven hours, depending on how many songs people sing, the bride and groom rush out the middle aisle, and the ordinary people are then ushered out of the church. I think someone should just say, "Dismissed." Maybe the church wants to impute some more of Adam's original sin to the men sitting there while they release the prisoners row by row.

Finally we are on the front steps. I am ready to start changing the world and getting on with my life. "Thank God Almighty, I'm free at last." I'm jingling the car keys in my pocket in anticipation to hitting the road, and then Barb says, "The reception is in the basement." *Reception?* I thought we signed a book! Couldn't they just look at the book next week in their new little nest and exclaim when they read our names, "Isn't that nice, Chuck and Barb were at our wedding."

Some people have even been callused enough to schedule weddings at 1:00 P.M. on Saturday afternoon during college basketball's Final Four, or the NFL playoffs, or some other spiritual event. And it even gets more barbaric sometimes. I've been to weddings where the bride and groom have to *hug* everyone one at a time as they get up to file out of the church. I'm getting weak just thinking about all this, so I think I will continue my story about the writer's conference.

I gave them some yuk yuk stories about weddings. When I tell my wedding jokes during our marriage seminars, there are people rolling in the aisles during my monologue. But at the writers' conference, it was strangely silent. The faces were still smiling and accepting, but I heard no indignant "amens" and "right-ons" like I usually did when I talked about weddings at our seminars. They just smiled. Later they told me how much fun they had and asked me to come again. However, on the way home I was feeling a little bit uneasy about why my jokes on weddings bombed. Then almost like a bolt from the blue I realized that about 90 percent of the audience were *women*. No wonder they didn't think my wedding monologue was so funny. *They* were the ones who *did* the traipsing and candle lighting and wished it would have lasted longer. The women at the writers' conference were very kind and affirming, but they didn't have a clue what was so funny. I'm going to have to do a better job of analyzing the groups I speak to. I guess it was the *men* who were rolling in the aisles during our marriage seminars.

I've done some costly research on how this relationship-goal difference alters our everyday life. Using a huge sample and the latest computers, I have discovered the average man spends 22.8 years of his life waiting for weddings to get over. I found out that even going to the *bathroom* is a relationship thing. The average man spends 19.7 years of his life waiting for his girlfriend, and later his wife, to get out of the restroom. The problem, of course, is that they always take someone in with them. You've seen women, like I have, get up from a table and say, "Anyone want to go to the ladies' room with me?" Six women get up like they didn't know they even had to go until then. I've never been in a ladies' room, but I assume they talk about all of their relationships and catch up on what's happening in each other's lives. If a man got up from the table and said, "Anyone want to go into the bathroom with me?" there would be some eyebrows raised that's for sure.

My survey also proved that 11.9 years of the average man's life is spent waiting at the mall for his wife to finish her shopping. Now this is lower than you would expect because I had to factor in the time during his dating days when he *wanted* to go shopping at the mall with his girlfriend. This messes up the figures a bit, but this is as close as I could come. Even though the shopping lobe was taken out of a man's brain after the wedding ceremony, sometimes he still has a faint recollection that he has been at a mall once. After he is married and goes once, he immediately sees the reasons why he would never have the need to go again. Therefore, the number of years of total waiting is lower than it would be on a strictly gender basis. I'm sure you appreciate my scientific approach.

I love the Gaither Southern Gospel videos. It's probably the closest I come to a true worship experience. I'm always in tears watching them. In fact, I have some in my eyes now as I think about how much they minister to my life.

Even though I am very touched, I do notice they have very few women piano players, at least on any of the tapes I have. Anthony Berger and Bill Gaither are pretty low-key, but most of the other piano players (all men) are show biz; sparkly rings, hands coming up high, standing up while they play, wearing funny hats. It's almost like they are *attacking* the piano, and they make spectacular music. They are the center of attention—in charge on stage—doing God's will, and it feels good to them and the audience.

If they ever have any women piano players on the program, I'll bet they will be less noticeable and more in the background. The TV director won't take many tight shots of them because they won't be standing on their heads playing the piano with their nose. The women on the tapes glow with the glory of the Lord, but they don't seem to have the need to be noticed or the center of attention. They are just enjoying the relationships they have with the other singers.

Now this is not a put-down to the men in any way. I just wish I could do the breathtaking things those men do with a piano, too. I'm just pointing out—again—the God-designed differences between most men and most women. Men are more into goals (being on stage), while women are more into relationships and content to be part of the group. There are exceptions to all this of course, but it's fun to watch the tendencies.

Barb: Men are usually into *things* and *doing,* and women are into *persons* and *being.* Men like to count, weigh, combine, and amass things. According to Paul Tournier in his book *The Gift of Feeling,* a man does this to increase his power. He talks about how men judge the value of a sports person to one one-hundredth of a second, feeling there is no more irrefutable proof than figures. Women, on the other hand, will make up their minds on the attractiveness of his or her style. Descartes said, "I think, therefore I am." Tournier suggests a woman would say, "I relate, therefore I am." A woman has no real consciousness of existing except through relationships.

Tournier goes on to say that women express feelings more easily than men. A man finds it much harder than a woman to let his heart speak. Someone has said when a man speaks, he gives you a piece of his mind. When a woman speaks, she gives you a piece of her heart. The man is much more at ease in the world of objects than the world of persons. Therefore, it follows that most men are into "quantity," and most women are into "quality." Or "how many" versus "how good." A man may have many friends but not really know any of them very well. A woman may not have as many friends, but it doesn't matter because she is concerned about the depth of the relationship and how well she knows the person.

Another thing Paul Tournier talks about is women in the marketplace. When some women start working, they try to become "men" by being more concerned about getting ahead than about the people involved in their work. This makes women appear hard and aggressive. If women could only understand they could be a force in the marketplace and still express their softness and concern for others, they would be so far ahead of men in general. Actually there has to be a balance for both sexes—not just a desire for things and getting ahead in a career, and not just personal relationships. It takes a combination of both.

I have a sister-in-law who went into the fresh and silk flower business with a friend. In one month after buying the shop, they doubled the business. The reason they could do this is because they are concerned about and take care of their customers. They know what colors they like. They know the customer's names, how many are in the families, and their likes and dislikes. They are not just pushing for the sale. They are caring for the people involved too.

Chuck has already mentioned the phone as an example of our different approach. Some men love to talk on the phone, but most men's business conversations go something like this: "Hi, Jim. How's the old golf game? Missed the birdie on three did you? Say, I need fourteen more cases of oil by Friday. Can you get it here? Great. Say hello to Margaret. Good-bye."

On the other hand, a woman would probably say: "Hello, Sally, how was your weekend? Oh really, was he sick the whole time? Are the other kids okay? Sure hope your mom doesn't come down with it for being there. (A few more minutes of relationship talk.) Well, I better go. Oh, by the way, I need fourteen more cases of oil by Friday. Any problem? Good. Sure hope the kids get better. Let's have lunch soon. We never seem to have enough time to talk. Good-bye."

Even though their business conversations are not long, many times women will be the best of friends without ever having met each other in person. They will know how many children each other has, what their husbands do, where they are from, what area of the city they live in, and so on. Two men might talk on the phone weekly for years and know very little about each other.

My guess is that a man could exist much longer on a deserted island than a woman could. He would be into getting things organized. She would probably die quickly for lack of meaningful relationships. Chuck says, "Maybe that's why we've never heard of Roberta Crusoe—just Robinson."

Chuck: You say men don't visit? Well, you're wrong. We visit a lot when we are together. For instance, when we play golf we talk all the time. We say things like, "Nice putt!" "Hooking a little bit today, aren't you?" "Watch the rough on the next hole." "Find your ball?" "Way to go." "Do you want a Coke or Pepsi at the break?" Now if that isn't visiting, I don't know what is.

Barb: I guess that's proof that when we share our lives, men and women don't share the same things. When women are eating out, the waitress comes forty-five minutes after they have been seated, and they haven't even looked at the menu yet. The first thing a group of men do is take the menu and decide what they are going to order, and *then* they begin talking.

Another way men and women are different is the way they introduce themselves. Chuck says, "Hi, I'm Chuck Snyder and I'm in advertising," while I say, "Hi, I'm Barb Snyder and I'm married to Chuck. We have three children: Tim who is married to Tammie and they have three daughters. Then we have Bev who is married to David and they have three sons. Next we have Deb whom we adopted when she was thirty-four years old. Deb's Mom died when she was twenty years old and she did not have a continuing relationship with her stepfather. So one day I thought, every young person needs to belong— really belong. I talked to Chuck about adopting her and he was excited. Before we could ask Tim and Bev how they felt about it, Tim looked at Deb one day and said, 'Deb, why don't you let us adopt you?' That was a confirmation to me. At Deb's birthday dinner the whole family asked her if we could adopt her. We all went to court on August 3, 1988, signed the papers and, since then, have lived happily ever after."

When I'm at church alone, I look for a person I know to sit with because I want to share the experience with someone. When a man goes to church alone, he just goes in and sits down. His goal is to attend church, and that is what he does.

Each Sunday when the church service ends, Chuck's goal is to go home and get on with his life while mine is to stay around and talk. So we've compromised. Chuck goes out to the car and listens to Chuck Swindoll tapes or reads a book, while I catch up on my relationships. It's not that he doesn't like people. It's just that his comfort zone is in the car. On the other hand, when we go to a retreat to speak, it just amazes me to see Chuck going around from table to table, or person to person to welcome them and make them feel comfortable. He has a goal to touch people's lives, and he is in control of the situation. When he is at a party, wedding, anniversary celebration, or other social event where he is *not* in charge, he is uncomfortable just making small talk.

Chuck: One time Barb mentioned a youth program at church she wanted to go to. I said, "Have a good time." Slight problem. She wanted *me* to go too. I was trying to change the world and didn't have time to go. Besides, I had seen a youth program one time, and why would I want to see another. I love youth, but their programs are always the same—some guitars and songs I don't know, some testimonies about how cool the Malibu camp was, and what they learned, and how cute the boys were and on and on. This is all good stuff, but I personally would not have anything to add to the evening, so why should I go?

"So people will see you and know you care," Barb said.

"I do care, and I'll write a check to prove it, and you can take it to them."

"I think *you* should go," sounded like the final word. Barb had a need to do this, and God has asked me to meet Barb's needs, so I really had no choice. The problem was after it was settled that I would be going, my back went into spasms, my neck was so stiff I couldn't turn my head, every muscle in my body hurt, and I was dizzy. I was afraid to take my blood pressure for fear that the extra pressure would do me in.

The evening came and all the way to the church my back, neck, muscles, mind, and lymph nodes were all churning in opposition to doing such a thing. Fortunately there was room on the back pew where I could be in misery without anyone seeing me. The program was way worse than I could have thought—and longer than it should have been. All in all, I had a miserable evening. On the way back home my misery increased when Barb said, "You never... You always... Why couldn't you... When will you... I couldn't believe you wouldn't… Someday maybe you'll…" I didn't mean to make her miserable.

Barb: I was unhappy with Chuck that evening because I seldom ask him to go anywhere he doesn't want to go. But this particular evening looked to be so inviting and interesting that I asked if he would go with me. Not only did he act out his misery in church with many, many whispered comments, but he also kept it up all afternoon before we left for church. I planned to enjoy the evening so much but instead had to listen to Chuck's remarks. On the way home I simply asked him, "Why is it that I can go to any and everything you want me to, with a happy face, without making life miserable for you before, during, and after the event? And furthermore…!" Well, you see how it went.

Chuck: So I went out to breakfast with myself the next morning to see if I could figure out why I made her feel bad. I love Barb. I want to meet her needs, but I failed miserably. After thinking about what happened, I hit on the answer. If I went with a happy face, Barb would probably want to *go again* sometime. Unconsciously, I thought if I could make her miserable enough, she might leave me home the next time. Well, I apologized and asked for a compromise. I promised her that the next time we went to a social event I would go with a happy face. But when she looked over and saw my smiling face visiting with someone at the reception, she was to assume I was *miserable* and get me out of there as soon as she could—maybe stay five hours instead of six hours visiting. She agreed she could do that. The next event came and I went with a happy face. But Barb forgot our deal because later she said when she looked over and saw me having such a good time visiting, she decided to stay longer.

I've come up with a principle, ladies. It's called the principle of grieving. Do not expect instant approval or acceptance from your husband when you tell him about the wedding, or graduation party, or church reception that will take place during the critical playoff game on TV. When you break this heartbreaking news, he'll start going through a grieving process. His whole world will have just come to an end. His back, neck, feet, bones, muscles, and sinuses will go into spasms. His eyes will roll back in his head. He might even vomit a little bit. He will get dizzy and feel faint. Rather than do what you normally do and say, "You never and you always," just go shopping for a little while. When you come home, he probably will have recovered enough from this horrible event in his life to commit to going with you and doing the right thing. He loves you and would do anything for you, but don't expect him to recover quickly when he has this sort of loss come into his life. Don't expect him to change—ever! Just praise him for loving you enough to go, and tell him how much you appreciate his sacrifice. He will never be as much into relationships as you are.

I love it when Barb goes to minister to all the ladies in her Precept Bible class on Tuesdays. Barb teaches her part, and then they watch a tape by Kay Arthur from 11:00 A.M. to noon. Then they have a short lunch from noon to 5:00 P.M. and everyone goes home. I ask her what they talk about for so long, and she tries to think about what they covered but can't come up with much besides husbands. I feel so good when she can go to a women's event. I will never meet all her relationship needs, so this is her outlet. What a gift that is to me and to Barb. She can fellowship with people who understand her completely. She can talk heart-to-heart and knee-to-knee. She can cry and no one gets uncomfortable. She can trouble talk and no one thinks any less of me or anyone else coming up in the conversation. Barb must have an opportunity to do this sort of thing without me along. As much as I try to be supportive, I am threatened by tears. I can only have a meaningful conversation with someone for five to ten minutes unless they are going to commit suicide or get a divorce. I hate just standing around trying to think of things to talk about. When Barb goes to her women things alone, she doesn't have this giant pressure standing next to her wanting to know when they can go home.

Barb: There can also be a big difference in the way a man and woman come home from work. The woman can come in from the marketplace very tired, but within half an hour or so she's ready to visit about her day. The man comes home tired, too, but he just grabs his newspaper or flips on the TV and *never* feels like visiting or at least says he needs some space to recover from his day. Or maybe the woman is a homemaker and wants some adult talk after a day of potty training, reading stories, making meals, and settling arguments between her little ones.

They do spend time together. Hopefully the results of his evening of talking will make him want to do it again sometime. It's really lots of fun and vital to keeping a relationship fresh. If we don't make sure we talk to each other, this is what often happens. The wife has been trying for years to get her husband to talk to her, to pay attention to her, to see her as a worthwhile, interesting individual. When this doesn't happen—say after twenty to twenty-five years of noncommunication by the husband—she decides to get a job so she can get some approval somewhere. If she can't get approval at home, then maybe she can get it from a job.

At the same time the husband has come to realize he will never be president of the company and decides home and wife look pretty good after all. Just as he comes home for a relationship, she goes out the door to find a job. All she needed was a relationship that was not so one sided. She needed some approval at home.

When the kids were small, Chuck and I always did our best communicating after dinner. There were usually children's shows on TV between six and seven in the evening. So after dinner, the kids would leave the table to watch TV, the dogs would hop up on Chuck's lap, and we would visit and talk about the events of the day. This fulfilled my need to talk with an adult and touch base with the most important person in my life. Then after we had visited, Chuck was free to go to his workshop or do anything else he wanted to do that evening. I would read a book or do whatever I wanted to do. After we were through visiting, the kids would come back in the kitchen and wash the dishes. Wasn't that good planning? Now that our family is raised, we still find dinner the best time to visit, but now it is often at a restaurant.

In the book *Passive Men and Wild Women*, Pierre Mornell explains that when a man comes home at the end of the day, the most important part of his day is over; he has provided for his family. His wife, on the other hand, is just *beginning* the most important part of her day, and that is making contact with her husband. She wants to talk. He wants to be left alone because he has talked all day. She doesn't understand and gives him disapproval. He doesn't understand and resists her disapproval. She presses him to talk. He resists her more. Finally she goes to the telephone and calls a friend. Days later when she once more tries to get her husband to talk, he says, "How can I talk to you when you're always on the phone?" That's when she becomes wild and hysterical, and he wonders what's wrong with her.

Dr. Mornell suggests that when a woman says, "Can we talk?" the man thinks he will have to talk with her the whole evening. He feels like he is being thrown into a swimming pool, and he can't swim or see the edge of the pool. He thinks he will drown. The couple could even set a time limit on talking at first, maybe committing as little as ten minutes or so and it would probably fulfill the woman's need to visit and his need for some time by himself. The limit on time means they both have hope.

We women do not expect our husbands to fulfill all our needs for visiting. That's why we have lunch with friends, coffee with neighbors, and Bible studies together.

Some of the best times of my life were when the children were small and my friends and I would get together to iron clothes, sew, can fruit, or knit. We enjoyed one another, accomplished things that needed to be done and made close friendships that have lasted through the years. This is something young women could enjoy even today.

Because we are more relationship oriented than men, we are also more emotionally responsive. We easily get caught up in the relationships of a good book or movie. Women are often more open. Men are usually more closed. There are emotional men, too, but you don't often find a man crying over a good book, movie, or TV program where emotion is involved in the dialogue. Women *do* cry easier, and some of this has to do with a woman having more prolactin in her system than a man does. A man is usually more in control of his feelings and will often stuff them and walk away in silence also. A man might not hear a woman until she creates a crisis of some kind. Tears get the man's attention even though the tears might not be intentional.

Women are more able or willing to share problems with each other. It's called "trouble talk." We women counsel each other all the time. We understand each other very well, and never think it's a negative if someone is having a problem. A man seldom shares his problems. He wants to pretend he doesn't have any, and if he does, it's the woman's fault. You almost always find a woman in a counseling office before her husband.

I remember early in our marriage Chuck saying, "I would never share my problems with anyone." I laugh now because he is sharing what he has learned with almost everyone with whom he comes in contact. In fact, he even wrote a book about his failures, and everyone thinks he's wonderful because he is so real.

In our former home we had a tennis court. Right after we moved in, Chuck wanted to put a cover over it. It rains a lot in the winter in Seattle, and he thought we could use it more if it was covered. Since he wanted me to let him dream without asking him about all the details, I just let him talk and dream and talk and dream. I knew there was no way we could afford the cover, and more than that, I just didn't want to ruin the feel of the woods and the peacefulness of the setting. One day one of our clients placed a big order, and all of a sudden Chuck thought we could afford the cover. He was so excited. Then I had to say, "There is something I haven't told you. I don't *want* a cover on the tennis court because it will look like a warehouse and won't fit in the woods." He was amazed I had not said anything earlier. In fact, he thought it was funny!

Chuck: I did?

Barb: Yes, you did. You laughed a lot.

Chuck: That's not the way I remember it, but since I'm not into details I'll give you the benefit of the doubt. We never did get a cover over our tennis court. Think of all the extra exercise I would have gotten. I wanted to make sure if I had a heart attack, Barb would not have to sell the house to pay taxes and move to skid row. In fact, I feel a little weak right now, but maybe it will pass.

One of my biggest failures, past and present, is stretching Barb too much. For instance, when we moved into our big home, I really had some big plans to match it. I figured with this large house we could easily handle groups of at least a hundred. In fact, 150 would be better. All Barb had to do was rig up a dessert of some kind—no big deal. I found out later she had different expectations. She had dreamed about entertaining couples or singles—people who came through town and needed a place to stay. And here I was, suddenly inviting the entire town of Tacoma over for lunch! The first clue I had that I was pressing her too hard in our new home was the time I teased my sister-in-law about our plan to have the University of Washington marching band over for some tea that weekend, and she believed me!

One evening Barb and I started out to go to a basketball game and stopped at a restaurant on the way. Barb began to cry and couldn't quit. She wanted to quit but couldn't. She was too stretched and tired. Evidently I had been sharing "tons" of goals (Barb's word) with her and was all excited about changing the world. It seems like I shared only a few goals, but if Barb says "tons" I'll have to believe her because I don't keep track of things like that.

I can just hear all you wives saying, "You beast!" And you're right. I guess I was, but I didn't mean to be so insensitive. I was just ignorant of what Barb was feeling as she did her best to support me in the things I was planning. I really failed her. Even now I'm not as sensitive to her needs and energy level and goals as I should be. I need to learn what Barb needs to help her grow and provide it for her.

I think this goal-relationship difference between men and women starts in the womb but really manifests itself as the small child begins to make friends. The boys are "doing" and the girls are "being." You can see the difference in sports. Our granddaughter Brooke is the family athlete. She runs track, plays basketball, soccer, and T-ball. Her school has this peculiar idea that men and women can compete in sports straight up, but God didn't make a woman's hips for speed in the same way he made a man's hips. Sure there are some fast women. Let me rephrase that. Sure there are women who run fast, some faster than men, but remember we're talking about tendencies and not the exceptions.

One time we went to a track meet that included girls and boys from Brooke's kindergarten class. Everyone was at the starting line ready to go. The gun sounded and everyone was off. Coming out of the first turn it was obvious to the little girls they were not going to compete, so they paired off. Ladies, this is a *race!* Every person for him- or herself! Focus! Races are not run together! But the girls think it is okay, and when they go by the grandstand they are waving to their friends in the stands. Ladies, this is a *race!* Focus on the finish line, please! The boys of course win and bump chests and preen around for a while. The girls are not worried. They had a nice run with a companion and some of their friends saw them compete. It was a wonderful day.

We go to Brooke's soccer games, too. There is a marked-off area in front of each of the goals on the field. That is the goalie's territory where the goalie can touch the ball with their hands. No one else can touch the ball with their hands in that area. It was fun to see the girls battle for the ball and take it toward the goal. But when they got to the goalie's area the girls would stop and stand there. It would hurt a relationship with the goalie if they were to go after the ball in that marked-off area. Sure women learn how to be more competitive as they grow older, but my point is this ability is more acquired than it is natural like it is with a man. I think a woman has to work harder at sports than a man does.

We enjoy watching Brooke play basketball too. I noticed that every time she or a teammate scored they jumped up with their arms in the air, looked to the stands and sometimes waved. When the boys scored on the court next door, they might touch hands, but they were much more into themselves. They really were not aware as much that there were people there to see them play. They were into a goal—to win the game. The girls wanted to win also, but relationships played an important part, too.

I recently went to a time management seminar. I go every time one comes to town. I have more things on my to do list than I will ever get done before the Lord comes, so I am constantly trying to find ways to improve my time priorities. One of the subjects during the seminar was how much a telephone interrupts our life. The instructor was giving all sorts of great ideas about how to handle this. One thing you could do was right in the middle of a conversation *you* could hit the receiver button so it sounded like you were cut off. He told how important it was to let your answering machine screen your calls. He suggested buying a buzzer, and when you have talked a few minutes punch the button and say, "Oops, there's my other line. Got to go. Talk to you another time." Or you could take the receiver away from your mouth and say, "I'll be right with you, hang in there." Of course there is no one there, and as Christians we couldn't lie like this, but it was a secular seminar, so there were no rules other than how we could cut phone conversations short. I always sit in the back so I can sneak out if it isn't worthwhile by 10:00 A.M. I was getting the biggest bang out of watching the women in the audience softly shake their heads no without even knowing they were doing it. What he was saying violated *all* relationship rules, and they were incredulous anyone would be rude enough to do those things. On the other hand the men were taking notes furiously because of the teacher's great insights into how we could save time on the phone. You'll notice I remembered them all. Men look at the phone as a horrible interruption most of the time. Most of the women looked at the phone as a relationship.

The problem Barb has with the phone is she doesn't know how to keep a phone conversation short. After a few minutes on the phone there is usually a pause which is a wonderful time to get out of the conversation by saying, "Well, I hope we will be able to see you sometime."

Instead of doing that, she says, "How's your mom?" Oh, *now* you're in for it. Stuck for at least twenty minutes. Then instead of saying, "It's sure been nice talking with you," she says, "What else did your husband say?" Or, "Did you catch the Nordstrom sale? It's on for another week, and you won't believe what I found…" And the conversation goes on for another hour. I have a headache just writing these words. There should be a rule that all phone calls should be short and efficient unless you are dating, and then make a commitment that it won't continue into marriage. There are way too many important things to accomplish as we go about changing the world, and the last thing we need is another interruption.

Barb: Since Chuck is not relationship oriented he doesn't understand my telephone conversations. He may have a goal to get off the phone but that isn't necessarily my goal. Sometimes it is, but even then I want to make my phone partner feel comfortable, understood, and valued. Chuck doesn't always understand my motivation.

Chuck: One time just before I left my home office to visit a client, I had a conversation with a woman radio station representative concerning some time she wanted me to buy. I said it wouldn't fit, but I appreciated her letting me know about it. When I got home, Barb gave me an "urgent" phone message from the woman saying she had more information to give me. I took the note and started downstairs to my office. Barb followed me for a few steps and said, "Aren't you going to call her back?"

I said, "I talked with her this morning and told her the idea wouldn't fit."

"But I *promised* her you would call her when you got home."

"There is no reason to call and waste my time, I have already given her an answer." I of course called for Barb's sake not the rep's, but I felt I had already taken care of the situation. There was no need to call back. Barb was so concerned about the relationship she had with this woman who was a total stranger that she was not about to let me ignore her.

You won't be able to believe this next bit of news I am going to tell you. It is almost too much for my heart to talk about, but maybe it will prevent some people from trying this barbaric act. It's called a couple's wedding shower where they invite *men* to interrupt their life and attend. I know it's hard to believe, but trust me, I've been to some. First of all, the only thing that would save the day would be something to eat, but all they have are wimpy salads. Just last week we had a couple of guys faint at a couple's shower. The hospital said the two had a severe case of malnutrition.

One of the barbaric customs in this odd ritual is sitting in a circle for a couple of hours and passing around foo-foo panties, dishes, and flower seeds made into bunnies. They also have one joke nightie that the new bride wouldn't wear on a bet after she gets married. The men are miserable. During the last one we went to, I leaned over and whispered to Barb, "Why do they invite the guys anyway?"

She whispered back, "I don't know. It would be more fun without them, that's for sure." So let's hit the streets with our placards and resist this menace and stop it in its tracks before it ruins the lives of too many more people (men).

I had no idea the TV remote (clicker) was a relationship thing. I just know that men are more gifted in this area of life than women are. The rule in our home is that whoever gets into the TV room first is chief clicker for the evening. As I look back on a recent episode we had with the clicker, only one member of our team (me) had this understanding. Even though I make my living in advertising making commercials, I don't like to watch other people's commercials—so I zap. I can watch three ball games, a car race, an archaeological dig on the Discovery channel, and a new country video on TNN—all at the same time. It's a matter of giftedness, and only men can do this.

Barb: Chuck can watch all this at the same time but tells me he can only concentrate on one thing at a time and I have to get his attention before he hears me. Now don't you think this is a contradiction?

Chuck: Men can't help being gifted in this. God designed them that way. But this is the *only* time we can concentrate on more than one thing at once.

Gifts allow you to do superhuman things, and this is the case with clicking.

Now since Barb is a woman, she does not have this gift. She has no feel for when to zap and when to stay. If you can imagine this, she will stop on two people sitting at a table talking and want to see them finish a sentence. A little boy is crying, and she will want to stay and see why. There is an ambulance scene, and she wants to see if they make it to the hospital okay. There is someone with cancer, and she wants to see if it is terminal. She lingers at a schoolroom setting, a lover's quarrel, or a hundred-year-old black-and-white movie that you can't see for the scratches. A more gifted chief clicker like myself knows these are not worthwhile subjects. We stop on important things like an alien attack on the space base, a war battle, another football game, skydiving, or the latest swimwear fashions. Now here we have to be very discreet. The speed of zapping has to be constant among all of these important subjects. Barb swears she perceives a slightly longer hesitation as I cross the swimwear fashions. I may be losing my edge with age because you should be able to maintain a consistent pace without anyone noticing an increased interest in one subject over another. As I say, it relates to giftedness and not everyone can do this.

One time we decided to watch the World Series. Since I had been in the TV room first, it was clear that I was chief clicker. I had clearly fulfilled all the requirements for chief clicker for the evening. I was happily flitting around five hundred channels waiting for the World Series commercials to end, when Barb began to make comments, "Go back one. Stop there. Let's watch part of the news. That looks interesting. WAIT! STOP! Go back to the dog that's dying!" It suddenly dawned on me that just because I had the clicker in my hand, I was not chief clicker. One of the two people sitting in the room seemed to have very definite ideas on what programs to stop on—and it wasn't me. I had flashbacks then to the thousands of times this had happened in the past and I hadn't noticed. So with my best Christ-like attitude I carefully laid the clicker on the end table by Barb's chair and began to read. She says my attitude wasn't very good, but I clearly remember being very calm and controlled. It just seemed logical to me that whoever needed to be "right" as to what programs to stop on should also physically man (or woman) the clicker. She thought—get this—she thought we were having a *relationship* and doing the clicking together. I felt it had nothing to do with a relationship. It was the logical outcome of who needed to make the clicking decisions most, and it appeared to be Barb who had this great need at that moment. So I did what any loving husband would do. I gave her the clicker. She got up and "huffed" (my word) out of the room, hurt. Later when we talked about it, she said I have forever destroyed the "fun" of doing the clicking together as a loving couple. "Never again" would we ever be able to click together. We had lost a precious relationship. That was all news to me. I just thought it was logical that the person getting into the TV room first was chief clicker for the day. I didn't have a *clue* it had anything to do with our relationship.

Barb: Using the clicker together *is* a relationship. We used to have so much fun with the clicker. When we would go into a hotel room I would quickly get the clicker and hide it under the mattress or else put it in my purse and take it to dinner with me. Then he would wrestle me for it and we had a lot of fun over it. One time we were in a Residence Inn and Chuck was in the bedroom lying on the bed grazing through the TV with the clicker. I stood at the door with the clicker from the living room and each time he would stop on a program I would click it one forward. He couldn't figure out what was going on.

So now we are at home where he suddenly becomes "king of the clickers." When the king clicks, no one must say a word. I didn't know he had taken on this persona. We had been watching the World Series and also some early football games. We hadn't seen any news for some time so I just suggested maybe we could watch the news instead of clicking past it each time. Chuck never lets anyone finish a sentence, so you hardly know what's going on as you pass by. I did not think it was unreasonable to ask to watch the news. But since he was in his king mode and because he withdraws rather than speaks, he put the clicker beside my chair with a bad attitude. I noticed his body language and thought I'd go to bed rather than sit there and feel badly. Besides, I wasn't going to touch that clicker.

The next morning he came to me and asked what happened. That's when I told him that he had just ruined a relationship. It wasn't really about the clicker at all. It was about sharing and enjoying one another *while* he is clicking.

Chuck: The problem with this explanation is how can we enjoy each other while we are watching someone dying of cancer, or visiting by the lake, or being rushed to the hospital? The idea of the clicker is to watch uplifting things like aliens eating the local population. Now there is something that can tear at your heart.

Well, since you're now "family" by reading this book, I'll tell you the *rest* of the story. I'm in a twelve-step clicker program. We meet in a hotel in downtown Seattle. We sit in a circle and only know each other by first names. The first thing we have to do is admit we have a problem. Then we have to admit we have *hurt* someone with our problem. Then we are to look for a higher power's help in overcoming our problem. They give us a guy to call in case we ever have the urge to click again. Like most addictions, one click and we're back on the sauce.

Both Barb and I have done lots of radio and TV interviews concerning our books. When I do them alone, I much prefer a woman interviewer than a man. She looks in my eyes, listens to every word I say, reacts to what I am saying with a related question, and makes me very comfortable. On the other hand, a man usually reads from the question list, or doesn't listen to what I am saying. I might finish a sentence with, "And so I met Barb at Washington State University during my senior year." He then asks the next question on the crib sheet, "Did you ever go to college?" I did an interview a few years ago with a well-known afternoon host who was broadcasting from a local fair. He would ask me a question and then get up and get some coffee, come back, ask another, and then go talk to the next guest. He'd come back, ask another question, and rustle through his briefcase. I can do okay because Barb and I talk about marriage for hours at our seminars, but usually his next question was so disjointed and unrelated to what I was saying that it was almost funny.

Men already have too many distractions that cut into family relationship time. But there is a greater danger that has only begun to be felt, and that is the Internet. A year or so ago there was a headline in one of our daily newspapers asking a question along the lines of: "Should we let children into cyberspace?" My immediate reaction to myself was, "Do you want your kid to find a job? Of course they will need to be computer literate. In business we depend more and more on e-mail, desktop publishing, and the Internet for daily commerce. And computers are increasingly part of our lives at home.

I thought of headlines that might have screamed back in the early 1900s when Henry Ford started building Model A's. "Should we let our children have a car?" In the body of the story the readers were no doubt reminded of the dangers of the rumble seat Henry was putting in back of the Model A's where couples could sit close together and do who knows what. They might even drive their cars into the country unchaperoned. The boys might take their cars on a trip and be snared by loose women when they stopped for lunch at some drive-in along the way.

Yes, our children should be ushered into cyberspace with the same cautions we exhibit with magazines, TV, videos, and films. And it's fun to see that most young kids are computer literate these days, including my six young grandchildren. One of my most treasured memories lately is seeing my precious five-year-old Cameron in front of our computer sucking his fingers on one hand and working the mouse with the other hand.

The *real* danger I am talking about is that more and more husbands are spending an inordinate amount of time on the Internet instead of relating with their wives and family. And pornography is so prevalent and accessible on the Internet it will overtake the girlie magazines in popularity soon, if it hasn't already. It is all so private. Another trap of the Internet is that time goes by so quickly. I'm on line as a relationship advisor for a Christian web site, and people send me questions about marriage, kids, and every other subject you could think of. I love it. I'm honored these people would trust a complete stranger for advice on the personal problems they are having. When I get a stack of questions, I'll take some time and answer each one. Sometimes I will start in the morning, and it's after dinner before I am finished. A great deal of time is consumed without my really being aware of it.

And there are so many fascinating things you can find on the Internet. I needed a caboose picture, and so my son Tim clicked around and finally found one and downloaded it for me. My printer went out a year or so ago and a computer guru friend of mine came over to see if there was something he could do. I had long since lost the instruction manual, so he went on line, traveled to Minneapolis to where the manufacturer of my printer was located, and walked right through the front door into the room where the file cabinet was located that held the manual for my machine. He opened the cabinet and then the file. He found out what was wrong, and in a mouse click was back in Seattle with the answer.

It's still too early to see if this interest in the Internet will ease off as men get more used to it. But my guess is that in just a few years, time spent on the Internet away from the family will be right up there with finances and sex as the major causes of problems in marriage. I bring this up to caution husbands to ration your Internet time and give your wife and family their proper priorities. Remember, we men are into goals, and our wives are into relationships. It's so easy for us to be distracted from the most important things in our life.

Now let's examine another thing that affects a woman's self-identity—the home.

9

I DIDN'T KNOW
BARB WAS A CHAIR

Chuck: Conflicts are inevitable in marriage. In fact, it is amazing so many marriages work out, rather than fail. Marriage puts a man and woman together as husband and wife with different gifts, different values, different parenting, and different cultures. Then add the fact that men and women are apparently from completely different species, and I think you can see the problem. This fits with something we have already talked about—the "completion" principle. God made men and women different on purpose, by design, and with forethought, so when they got together they would make a stronger unit than either one of them individually. Both would bring differing gifts to the relationship, and both would be helped and blessed by being God's team. Barb's and my forty-plus years of marriage proves it can be done, but it takes work. There are some hurts and tears once in a while, but you can take my word for it, it is well worth it.

I believe many marriage conflicts come from the man not understanding how closely a woman's self-identity is tied in with how her home looks. All men know is that not too long after the honeymoon is over we can't do one thing right in the home from our perspective. We men simply don't know the living room chair we just spilled chocolate syrup on was our wife.

I know one husband who wanted to refinish the cupboard doors in their kitchen. His wife was all for it. They couldn't afford to hire it done, so the idea was to do one door at a time—at least that was the *wife's* idea, but she failed to communicate this to her husband. One day when the wife was gone, the husband, who was into efficiency, took *all* the doors down and stripped them with paint remover. Then he got very busy in his work, and it was a few months before all the doors got back up. He was sorry he couldn't get them done as quickly as he thought he could, but his wife was *frantic* because everyone coming to visit was able to see all of her "insides" hanging out. The good news is that the couple did not get divorced. In fact, I think Barb was very gracious after the initial shock was over, but it was years before I really understood what I had done to her.

Barb: When we first came to Seattle in 1958, we moved into a home where we were given permission to paint the rooms and take the money off our rent. I told Chuck I wanted everything off-white. He told me he thought that was dumb.

Chuck: I didn't say it was dumb. I just couldn't imagine anyone having all the rooms off-white.

Barb: I think the word you used was dumb, but we were young then and didn't know better than to say things like that to each other. Every room of the house opened onto the large, connected living and dining room. I wanted to please Chuck, so I let him pick the colors. I did get to paint all the woodwork white, but he picked a bright harvest gold for the living and dining room.

Chuck: It reminded me of a sunset, and that reminded me of God. I can't see why that was so bad.

Barb: One bedroom was a spring pink.

Chuck: A baby girl had just joined our family, so I chose pink for the color. I guess this is proof that the firstborn never gets any breaks because it didn't occur to me to make a blue bedroom for my son Tim first. He had been with us a couple of years. The problem with firstborns is they always come when you can't afford enough bedrooms. Tim had already shared space with my "shop" in his bedroom when we were in the army, so it just seemed logical he was taken care of. Now a new baby had arrived, and it also seemed logical to honor her with a pink bedroom.

Barb: Next to it was a light spring blue bathroom.

Chuck: Blue always reminded me of blue skies. That reminded me of God, and I can't see why that was all bad either.

Barb: Further down on the left was a spring blue kitchen.

Chuck: Refer to my feelings stated above with regard to the blue bathroom.

Barb: At the end of the living room we looked right into another bedroom. This one was painted the brightest apple green you have ever seen.

Chuck: Reminded me of apples, nature, and God.

Barb: This happened before the days of "color draping" so we didn't know my coloring is autumn. The spring colors were okay but not all so close together.

Chuck: I thought the house was beautiful, and besides those were the colors I could get on sale. Does the White House in Washington D.C. have every room white? Of course not. There is the Green Room, the Blue Room, and the East Room is gold. Besides, I was raised on a farm where you used the paint you had on hand regardless of whether it was *right* or not. I remember painting the seats of our outdoor bathroom. We called it the halfway-house because it was half way from the main house to the chicken coup. One time, my uncle Clarence came in from work and sat down on the newly painted seats. I had forgotten to put up a sign. I can still remember vividly a picture of my grandmother taking the paint off my uncle's posterior with turpentine as he mumbled some words that I probably shouldn't put in a book like this. He was so patient with me. I don't know how he did it.

Barb: In our next house I made sure we painted everything off-white and used pillows and furnishings for accent colors. We don't believe the man should choose the colors or furnishings for the home because it is the extension of his *wife's* personality not his. The home is her workplace. This is where she spends most of her time and energy even if she works in the marketplace. This is where people will come in and comment on *her* decorating not her husband's. This also means when my home has leaky faucets or broken pipes, I don't feel right.

Chuck: Barb is also uncomfortable when the garbage needs emptying. I don't think you women are persistent enough when it comes to deciding whether the garbage pail is full or not. There's an ancient proverb that sheds light on this: "Wise man say, always room for one more thing in garbage pail."

Men honor this proverb, women do not. Barb will have me take the garbage out willy-nilly when there is clearly room for another couple of facial tissues or a large orange peel. In order to conserve a man's strength for more important things, I believe women should be more creative. What I think they should do is take the garbage pail out from under the sink and jump up and down on the contents for a few minutes. Then replace it under the sink. People pay hundreds of dollars for compactors, and I just didn't think we had money to throw away when it was something we could do ourselves. This would have created space for tons of extra garbage, rather than spending my sunset years taking out the garbage pail every ten minutes when it clearly could hold some more. I think women give up too easily.

Barb: I believe this difference in the husband's and wife's view of the home is God-designed rather than cultural, hereditary, or environmental. The reason I believe it is that in the book of Genesis God tells the man that he is to be the *provider,* and He tells the woman in the book of Titus she is to be the *keeper of the home.* It can also be translated *guardian of the home.* So, even if she is working, as the Proverbs 31 woman worked, she still has the feeling that if all is not right at home, *she* is not right.

When I worked for Chuck at his advertising agency, my mind was always on what had to be done at home. Did I have the ironing done? Was the wash done and put away? Did I have the right food in the cupboard so if we decided to "pick up" for dinner, Chuck would have his can of chili or tuna fish?

Remember when I mentioned Chuck bought equipment for the business, rather than carpets for the house? It wasn't until we learned this principle that we understood why we disagreed. When he said he was buying the equipment for *me* because it was for the business, it was true. He was *providing* for me. But oh, how I wanted to get my home fixed up to reflect my own taste and personality.

Chuck: What we were doing—and Barb really hasn't quite gotten a full understanding of it yet—was dividing our priorities between wants and needs. For instance, we *needed* a new camera, we wanted a new rug. We *needed* a new recorder, we wanted new curtains. We *needed* a new stereo, we wanted to have the porch painted. See how that divides up? I'm not sure why Barb didn't understand that.

Barb: For years Chuck not only bought exercise and business equipment, he also purchased countless tools. And each time he would buy another tool, he would exclaim that I just didn't know how wonderful it was to have the right tool. Then suddenly after thirty years, I realized the same could have been said for the things I needed in the home. I may be slow, but I'm sharp!

We have a red velvet chair in our home. We had a number of conflicts over this particular chair because our dog Muffit loved to sit in it tucked in alongside Chuck's leg. A hairy red chair did not express who I was. Chuck had a hard time understanding this, so the offense was repeated. Then he read Dr. Dobson's book *What Wives Wish Their Husbands Knew about Women*. That was where he learned about the home being the extension of my personality. Until then he thought a chair-was-a-chair-was-a-chair.

Also, do you men realize the home is the woman's workplace? And we cannot begin our work until we have picked up everything you have left out all over the house? An illustration came to me one day as we were doing a seminar for a group of coaches and their wives. I asked them how they would like to go out on the football field every day before practice and pick up their wife's slips, bras, pantyhose, and other whatnots before they could start work. Of course everyone laughed, but that is what it is like for us when the family leaves things around the house for us to pick up.

For years, each time we expected guests I would go into the bathroom to straighten and add clean towels. Then Chuck would come home from work and I would have to go into the bathroom and clean and straighten the towels *again* before the guests arrived. I asked him who he thought straightened up everything after he finished in the bathroom. It had just never occurred to him to ask. But now that he knows who does it, he carefully wipes down the sink and makes sure he hangs the towel right. I don't know why I didn't think to tell him about this sooner.

Chuck: Over the years it became quite plain that our home is where Barb found most of her identity. I became involved when something I did or didn't do altered the image she was trying to build. Barb and I have separate bathrooms in our home. She has been complaining over the years that I didn't get all of the soap out of my washcloth after I had finished getting ready for my day. She said she could "stand it in the corner by itself," which is probably true. But since we rarely invite guests to tour my bathroom, the chances are slight anyone would be offended by a washcloth in a stiffened condition. In fact, the only one who has ever been offended in over forty years of marriage by a tour of my bathroom is Barb. Since it seems my washcloth reflects on her self-image, I have been under a great deal of pressure to do a better job of washing all the soap out of it. The problem is how can I become a success in life if I spend until noon every day getting the soap out of my washcloth?

I've also been under pressure not to leave dirt on the towels. A few months ago Barb bought me a brand-new towel and washcloth set and presented them to me with the strong admonition that I keep them both fresh and clean. Well, you'll be proud. They are as fresh and clean as the day she brought them home from the store. That's because I've never *used* them! I call them my *ceremonial* towel and washcloth. I have *another* towel and washcloth standing behind the bathroom door that I use for my morning routine. Now our guests won't be offended needlessly when and if they ever stumble into my bathroom.

Barb: Here's how it really is. Chuck's washcloths get as stiff as a board. Sometimes I've ironed them to try to keep them folded. I finally realized it was because he was not washing the soap out of his washcloth. I've soaked them in vinegar water and washed them without detergent, but nothing seems to revive them again. When I bought new towels, I asked him if he could start washing the soap out of the washcloth. Instead of doing that, he decided he would not use them at all. He hung his old towel and washcloth on the back of the bathroom door. That way he didn't have to change a thing. I thought that was a pretty good idea. At least the new washcloths would stay soft.

And now about the dirty towels. Once I went into the downstairs bathroom where I had hung some clean, white towels. The towels now had large black stains on them from someone (not me) who had wiped dirty hands on them. I carried the towels out to Chuck and asked him if he washed his hands in the sink or on the towel? He said, "Everyone finishes with the towel!" We laughed about it, but that didn't make the stains come out. So I kept putting the same stained towels back for him so others wouldn't get ruined, too.

Chuck: The real problem is women don't know what the purpose of a towel is. You'd think it would be very obvious a towel is to wipe the last little bits of grease and dirt and grime off our hands so we can come to supper. Barb notices every little grain of sand or millimeter of dirt on the towel. It never occurred to me we husbands were never supposed to get them dirty. We thought that was what towels were for. I know, ladies, your husband should try harder to get his hands clean *before* he uses the towel, but if he messes up, just look at those dirt spots on his towel and washcloth as proof that he is working hard to support the family. Okay, how about the fact that he is too busy to do a complete washing of his hands? Okay, so his self-esteem is not tied up in the towel. I'll try to teach him why he needs to be careful. Therefore, I'll suggest he wipe his hands on his pants. That should take care of the problem.

Barb: Chuck is always making excuses for men. I think men should love their wives enough to *want* to keep dirt off the towel as part of his service to her.

While we were still learning a lot about marriage, we purchased a very large home on four wooded acres. When we moved in, Chuck had many goals and most of them included me. We were not a team at that time, however, because he was making a series of financial investments against my advice and the investments were failing. I had a resistant spirit and did not want to do everything he was dreaming about, and that included some of his plans for using the house. He was inviting everyone in Seattle over for meetings. His idea of a successful evening was to have a hundred people over. My idea was to have a candlelight dinner for eight. I just couldn't seem to make him hear where I was coming from.

Things had been fairly even through the years, but when we moved into the big house, we found out we were two different people. I started to hate living in that house. Having a nice home means nothing if your relationship is not good. I kept trying to tell him how I felt, but he just didn't hear me.

One of the things he liked to do was have the Seahawks football team and the Mariners baseball team over for a tennis-swim party each year. This particular year I was extra tired because I needed to have surgery. He wrote me a note saying I could decide whether or not to have the teams over, and as usual he said, "Don't go to any trouble. Just have it catered." I am just a farm girl from Wenatchee and I had never used caterers before. In my home we always did our own cooking. Besides, I had already tried a caterer once and he had put his steam trays on my oak dining room table and dripped hot water all over. And when he poured coffee, he didn't use a napkin to stop the drips, so the cream-colored carpet was a mass of spots. I didn't want anything to do with caterers again. (Now that I have had more experience and know some wonderful people in the catering business, I have learned what a great help they can be.)

Chuck: Hindsight is always in perfect focus, isn't it? Now, with the advantage of looking back at what happened, I can see clearly where we went wrong. How we could have been so blind escapes me. It was so obvious. Right there under our noses. We missed the very solution that would have prevented all our marriage stress. We could have hired *women* caterers. They wouldn't drip things all over the tables. That simple act would have prevented all the rest of the marriage struggles we have experienced. Remember *women* caterers when you come to this crossroad in *your* marriage.

Barb: As we talked about caterers, Chuck said again I had a resistant spirit, and I did! I didn't reply to his note about deciding whether or not to have the teams over because I had chosen not to. It was during this time Chuck was having some hard times at work, and I had decided to fast and pray for him. On the day I was fasting he came home and asked me again about having the parties. It was evident I really didn't have a choice, so I said I would do it. With a pounding headache from skipping coffee as part of my fast, I went out to the kitchen to start baking. Then he saw me in the kitchen and was mad at me for doing too much!

Chuck: I sound like a real beast, don't I? It was surely not the intent of my heart to give Barb a bad time. I just felt God wanted us to use our large home to entertain his people. It wasn't that Barb was against this. She wanted to use the house too. We just had different expectations. In addition to having our athlete friends over, I visualized sharing the facilities of this beautiful, large home with people who could not afford this type of privacy and convenience. As Barb has mentioned, her vision was having three or four couples over for a quiet, intimate dinner by candlelight. We had never talked about our expectations and visions, so the resistance we felt from each other was all under the surface. We had no idea what the problem was—at least I didn't. I now know I was stretching her energy level beyond the maximum. I really don't know how she survived those days, and I'm so sorry I caused all that pain for her.

As far as I was concerned, when we had a group in, all we had to do was zip down to our friendly supermarket and pick up some cookies, some peanuts, an orange or two, and we were in business. That way we didn't have to do all that third-world-war-type baking and slaving, vacuuming and dusting, cleaning up desks, and so on. I didn't want to play games with our guests. They needed to see me just like I was—messy. Why all this fuss just to have a few hundred people over? I just couldn't understand the problem. It was almost as if Barb didn't want it to appear that anyone *lived* in the house. If that is what she wanted, we should have just put up ropes like they do in George Washington's home. Our guests could then have gone from room to room hanging onto the ropes and saying, "That must be where Chuck and Barb have breakfast." "Look how neatly he hangs his clothes." "They even go to the bathroom, and look at that beautiful towel and washcloth in Chuck's area. They look brand new!" If we had kept our guests behind ropes, it would have prevented anything from being messed up.

Barb: Chuck had not learned yet that our home is an extension of my personality and reflects who *I am*. Caterers and supermarket cookies were just not *me* and would not reflect the type of cooking and serving I wanted done. I wanted to serve our guests personally. Chuck shows love by taking people to dinner at a restaurant. I wanted to do something more personal.

As Chuck sensed my resistant spirit, he would say, "I just feel it is the Lord's *will* that we have this group over." I hated that! The Lord had not mentioned one word about it to me!

One time we had a dearly loved couple staying with us. They had gone out to dinner with some friends, so Chuck and I went out to a restaurant on our own. Chuck and I had a big conflict that evening, but because we were at the restaurant we had to be discreet, even though our emotions were running high.

As we drove up to the house that night, we noticed our friends had already returned. As we sat in the car for a minute, Chuck told me how swamped he was at work, and he couldn't go in and entertain. He just had to go back to work.

I had been taught the value of word pictures by Gary Smalley (who together with John Trent has written about this in their book *The Language of Love*), so I decided to try one out. I asked Chuck, "How would you feel if I told you it was the Lord's will for you to come in the house and entertain? *You would hate it!* That's how I feel when you tell me it's God's will to do something I just don't feel I can do." Because I had pictured something with which he could relate, he understood and he has never said "the Lord's will" phrase to me again.

I painted another word picture for him that night. One of his favorite people at Safeway was having a retirement party the next week and Chuck stayed up nights to work on a "This Is Your Life" presentation for his friend. He used slides and multiple screens with lots of humor and good background music. This was his way of showing love to his friend. As we were talking about using caterers, I asked him how he would feel if I asked him to have one of his employees do the slide presentation. Even though he knew they would do a good job, it wouldn't be exactly how he would do it. "That's how I feel about caterers," I told him. Not once since that time has Chuck insisted on having caterers. He understood perfectly what I was feeling. The principle of word pictures is to relate a problem to their world so they can identify with what you're feeling.

One of my friends described herself to her husband as a wilted daisy with petals dropping off one by one. Gary Smalley uses the example of a wife who described herself as a car with ripped upholstery, four flat tires, peeling paint, no oil in her crankcase and an empty gas tank. Most husbands could clearly identify how she felt. This works the other way, too—where a husband could give his wife word pictures—but it's usually the man who needs the picture since he's not as gifted in observing feelings.

Chuck: I still run into occasional lapses of memory concerning Barb's identity being firmly associated with the home. For instance, I get in trouble when I don't wipe all the water molecules off the sink when I am through. I thought that was what sinks were for—to hold water. Or sometimes after I'm finished having lunch at the kitchen table, I'll just brush the crumbs onto the floor where no one is going to notice. And besides, someone is going to sweep the floor one of these days. What's the rush?

Barb also has all sorts of weeds growing around the house in pots.

Barb: They are silk plants.

Chuck: They look like weeds to me. But I just won a recent battle of the weeds. The only win I can remember, but it was significant because my eyesight was the potential victim. One night recently I started to get into bed and reached over to turn on my bed lamp and got a handful of leaves. She now had the lamp *behind* the weeds, and just a few dim rays of light made it through the foliage. So I moved the lamp back to where it was closest to the bed, and the weeds graced the wall. It looked great. I agree with her right to have weeds anywhere she wants, so I kept them on the same table—just in a different position. The next night I found the weeds had moved in front of the lamp again, and I switched them with the lamp. The battle went on for a week. Finally the weeds disappeared and I can see again.

Barb is also into baskets, ceramic jugs, and things, and she puts them all on the kitchen table. I have to take thirty-two pots of flowers, seventeen candles, and a copper kettle off the breakfast table before I can read the morning newspaper. Oops, it just occurred to me. I'll bet I forgot to put them *back* before I went to work this morning. Excuse me for a minute while I go upstairs and apologize.

I'm back. I thought as long as I was upstairs I would finish making the bed I sleep in. I know that sounds strange for a married couple to sleep separately. As younger married people it was something we saw our folks do, but *we* would never violate the marriage bed in that way. That is until something happened. I didn't plan to tell you this, but since you're family it won't be a big shock to your system. I snore. To me I don't see a problem with this, but Barb does. Something about her never getting any sleep. She wants me to get my throat cut. Well, maybe not quite that drastic, but they do have a laser thing that cuts the Septuagint so it doesn't flop over the occidental or something like that. The problem is I still make my living doing radio commercials, business consulting, and seminars. I don't think my clients would appreciate a raspy, guttural voice talking about their terrific values this week. I just don't want to take the chance. So I have to make the bed when I get up in the morning.

Another problem. Even though it is my bed, Barb has 743 pillows strewn all over it: white ones, red checked ones, flat ones, and poofy ones. The first time I saw the arrangement I thought it looked pretty casual. I found out quickly the casual look was carefully designed. Every one of those 743 pillows has a specified position, and even though she is fairly relaxed when we're by ourselves, if we plan to have anyone over, the red checked pillows being fourteen millimeters out of whack from the white pillows is a major problem.

Even though Barb would like me to make the bed perfectly every day, she has adopted my principle of adjusting that I try to teach my women friends. We men should try hard to make the bed right, but we're going to mess up once in a while since our self-esteem does not come from having perfect pillows. So my suggestion is to adapt the principle of adjusting. This means when I make the bed and see Barb at breakfast I will say, "I made the bed, and you can *adjust* it." Which means putting the pillows in the middle. This principle applies in other areas as well. When I help with the dishes, I say, "I filled the dishwasher, but you can *adjust* it." Which means taking all the plastic articles out of the bottom half and putting them in the top half so they don't melt. "I cleaned up the living room, but you can *adjust* it." Which means not only to arrange the magazines on the coffee table equidistant from each other by size and date, but to pick up the magazines I missed that had fallen *under* the coffee table too.

Barb: I'm so thrilled when Chuck helps me around the house that I just overlook it if it isn't done the way I would do it. Overlook means I don't say a word to him about it. If and when I adjust it, I try to do it when Chuck isn't around. He won't notice anyway. He'll just think he did a great job. Now just for fun, even though he knows not to, he puts the plastic on the bottom of the dishwasher. He wants to keep me on my toes and make sure I'm alert.

Chuck: Before I read Dr. Dobson's book about wives and began living in understanding with Barb, I thought a faucet was a faucet and a gutter was a gutter. I had no idea it was mixed up in Barb's personality or self-esteem. I don't know if you have rain gutters where you live, but they keep filling up with leaves at our home in Seattle. My idea is to let them get filled up until there is no room for any more, and the new leaves will then just fall to the ground. Barb's idea is to *clean* the gutters at least once a year. I hate cleaning gutters, and my nature is to get halfway through and give it up until the next time I don't have anything better to do. After I learned that Barb didn't feel good when the gutters were full, it helped me grit my teeth and finish the job even though I really didn't feel like it at the time.

Barb has a *thing* about leaves. She can hear each one click as it leaves its mother branch and flutters to the ground. Every time a leaf falls, Barb wants me to go out and rake it up. My idea of using the Lord's time wisely is to wait until February after all of the leaves have fallen and then rake them all up at one time. Who cares if we are up to our waists in leaves. They make a soft landing spot if we fall, and this is important at our age because our bones are so brittle. But since Barb feels messy if there are leaves all over the place, guess what happens? We rake up the leaves.

And then there's the patio. It gets rained on quite a bit, so the green moss thrives. Barb wants me to go out there and kill all those innocent mosslings. All I can think of as I am murdering mosslings is the mossling families that will be sitting down to dinner and wondering where Grandpa mossling is. He is one of the ones Barb made me do away with. Just because they make the patio slippery and threaten our houseguests' safety is no reason to take this drastic action. However, when I found out that *Barb* is green if I don't kill the moss, I go ahead with the job.

Because the leaves, gutters, faucets, and mosslings never make my top twenty priority list, I have some note paper on the refrigerator where I list Barb's goals. Every time I get something to eat, this list stares me in the face telling me about all the things that need to be done to make Barb feel better in her home. I'm committed. I *want* to please her. When something is number one on *Barb's* list, then it automatically becomes number one on mine, too. I really do care, and this is one of the ways to show it.

And ladies, if your husband does not get to your list fast enough, here's a practical hint. Let's assume one of your kitchen faucets is leaking and you don't feel good when it leaks. Sometime when your husband is in the kitchen reading the paper, say to him, "Honey, thanks for working so hard to support the family. I know you haven't had a minute, and I wanted you to know you don't have to worry about that leaky faucet over there in the sink. I'm going to fix it and save you the trouble." Then go to the garage and get a hammer, chisel, punch, and crowbar. Put a wash cloth on the faucet (so you don't scar it), and begin pounding on it (lightly) with the crowbar, hammer, and chisel. Pretty soon your husband is going to look up and say, "Wait a minute. That's not how you fix a faucet." Now *he* goes to the garage for a pipewrench, screwdriver, and rubber washer and fixes the faucet *right*.

Here comes the hard part. You know perfectly well how to fix a faucet properly, but you have more important things to do. I want you to put on your best Southern Belle expression, and pretend to be amazed he is so talented. You praise him, honor him, lift him up, tell him how wonderful he is, and take him to bed. All right, you don't have to do the bed part right then, but invite him for a romp soon. After this happens a couple of times, he'll probably change all the faucet washers in the *house* for good measure and while he's at it, unstick a few drawers, fix the screen door, and paint the house. I think our second greatest need as men is praise, and it's also nice when you take care of our *first* greatest need, too.

It's scary, but when I talk at seminars or women's groups I joke around about a man's greatest need. I always say, "In case you don't know what it is, see me afterwards." Of course, I'm thinking *everyone* in the room knows what I am talking about. They don't. I have a number of women come up afterward, a bit hesitant, but wanting to know what I was referring to. No wonder we have a water shortage in the country with all the cold showers men have to take.

You've probably wondered once in a while why your husband fixes the neighbor lady's faucet before yours. Your neighbor knows the praise principle. She tells him how talented and wonderful he is and then tells you what a lucky woman you are for having such a talented husband. Be honest with me. I'll bet sometimes the best he can expect when he fixes *your* faucet is, "It's about time."

Speaking of plumbing, I found out the toilet seat has two roles. First, it is an object that must be down at all times, and second, it is a relationship. I had no idea it was an essential part of our marriage. Barb says a woman always thinks about her husband: what food he likes to eat at home, what he likes to read, and his favorite restaurant when he goes out. Therefore, Barb thinks it is only right that in the middle of the night after he finishes in the bathroom he should be thinking about his wife and put the lid down. Ladies, we are lucky even to make it *to* the bathroom half asleep. Or if it is during the day we are very busy trying to make a living for you and don't have time to spend our last years worrying about whether the seat is up or down.

By the way, we men get a bad rap on the toilet seat. What did the first woman we lived with (our mother) tell us about the toilet seat? Put it *up*. Put it *up*. Put it *up*. What did the next woman we lived with (our wife) tell us about the toilet seat? Put it *down*. Put it *down*. Put it *down*. Ladies, it's hard for us men to change in midstream like that. We're just not that adaptable. And some wives are sneaky too. They will buy that fuzzy toilet seat back that makes the seat fall down automatically when someone leaves the room. Ladies, I don't think you have any idea how awkward it is for us to stand there with one foot holding it up. We had two guys fall and hit their heads on the tub just this week. It's very dangerous.

We have wooden chairs in our kitchen. Barb had expressed worry about the wooden legs scratching the hardwood floor. I put that bit of information on my to-do list. A few weeks later I stopped by the hardware store to get some of those pads that protect floors and make the chairs scoot well. Barb was gone the day I finally found time to put the pads on the chairs. When I turned them over, I found some idiot had put *corn* pads on the bottom of the legs, if you can believe that. *Corn* pads! Yuck! So I sanded them off with my power sander and put on the high-power Teflon-coated superskid pads that were specially designed and carefully crafted to protect floors. I was so pleased I had solved the problem for her. Not long after that she scooted one of the chairs and came unglued—not the chair—Barb!

Barb: When we moved into this home, the hardwood floors were beautiful. I asked the former owner how she kept them that way. She told me she used corn pads on the bottom of the chair legs. So I bought them at some expense and put them on. They protected the floor beautifully.

Then one day I moved a chair and it seemed to *scrape*. What was going on? When I looked, I couldn't believe it. All my corn pads were gone and in their place was a half-round plastic-looking thing. I knew Chuck had been at work. I knew he wanted to do something very special for me, but he did not understand the principle of corn pads and hardwood floors. I thought about it for several days before I approached him. I said, "Chuck, I know you wanted to do something very special for me, but I don't think you know why I had the corn pads on the chairs. The Teflon scratches the floor while the corn pads protect it. I'm so sorry, but do you think we could change back to something that won't scratch the floor?"

He felt terrible but immediately said, "I should do what I teach—not get involved with your areas."

We don't have corn pads anymore. I bought some little rug circles that work better anyway.

Chuck: It was my own fault. I had stepped in where only fools dare to tread—in the details of the home where any mistakes mess with Barb's self-image. In fact, as you will learn in the next chapter, men are not the best in noticing details in *any* area of our life, including the home. One time as we spruced up our house and grounds, I noticed the asphalt driveway coming down the hill had lots of dark Seattle moss on it. I thought I would surprise Barb and clean it up. I had gotten into trouble with Barb a few times in the past with my power washer. It does splash mud around just a tiny bit, and I admit the first time I used it I didn't clean up as much as I should have. This time I would be especially careful.

Barb: Chuck was so excited about his new power washer. He loved getting the patio clean and it *did* look great. There was only one problem. The patio brick floor was sparkling clean, but the patio furniture, flower pots, and ceiling were dotted with dirt. He had not noticed. Then he went around to the front of the house and enjoyed cleaning the sandstone floor of the front porch. I was standing inside close to the door, when suddenly water started bubbling up under the threshold and into the carpet. *I hate that power washer!*

Chuck: So Barb has never really trusted me with the power washer ever since. I have cleaned the moss off the patio a few times without her noticing any damage, but I really blew it with the driveway.

Barb had lined the driveway with flowers of some kind—red ones with some white ones mixed in. They looked like the flowers I had seen at our local hardware store at five for a buck, so I didn't really notice the flowers like I should have. I suppose subconsciously I felt if I were to hurt a couple of the flowers with my power washer, we could replace them easily at the store.

So I proceeded to wash the driveway, and it went great. You could eat off the cement it was so clean. Then Barb appeared a little earlier than I had planned, and I hadn't finished my cleanup yet. She commented on how nice the driveway looked, but said, *"You have destroyed everything else!"* Now that was not an accurate statement. The garage was still standing. So was my little office, and the trees were still intact, so I had not destroyed *everything*. Why women exaggerate so much I'll never know.

Barb: Sometimes Chuck does not value the same things I do. His goal was to get that driveway clean, but anything around the driveway was inconsequential. He knew I had wintered over the geraniums and nursed them back to health. But he didn't *know* it. Not only did I have geraniums I had kept all winter but also many I had bought. He failed to realize it was August and you don't buy plants that size for five for a dollar. In fact, they never are that inexpensive. But as I say, he didn't value them as I did.

So "the ole power washer" came out, and as he washed the driveway (that part of the drive was cement) the sand kicked up and buried all the flowering plants nearby. When I saw them I nearly fainted. I didn't say anything at that moment but Chuck tells me my eyes said it all. When he came to me I told him the driveway looked great, but he had destroyed everything around it.

I *love* having things cleaned up, but not at the expense of everything around. I don't want to ruin one thing to fix another. Chuck seems to focus only on what he is doing at the moment.

Chuck: As I looked around the area where I had power washed, I did see two or three millimeters of mud on a couple of the flowers. Barb said they were *covered* with mud. See, there again she was exaggerating. I could clearly see a couple of the petals on some of the plants as plain as day, so they weren't completely covered. I think she was being a little too sensitive, but I still felt terrible. Here I worked so hard to please her and make our home presentable for her, and I got in big trouble for not noticing some flowers. In fact, so much emotion was expressed that I thought maybe our marriage was ended. Barb spent the next day or two dusting off her precious flowers. I didn't know this, but I guess she had nurtured some of those flowers for *three years*—taking them out in the summer and putting them back in the garage during the winter. And one of them was a direct descendent of the nasty sturtiurm that George Washington had taken with him to Valley Forge. At least it felt that it was that important. I didn't really notice the flowers were in harm's way when I started power washing. I'm not into flowers. One looks just like another, only some of them are different colors.

One of the things that confuses me about the house is that Barb will put things for me on the landing by the stairs that go both up and down. I just step over the things and mumble that someday I am going to trip, and Barb will be a widow. She wonders why I don't take some of the stuff with me on my way upstairs or downstairs, instead of just stepping over it. But I don't know whether the stuff is going upstairs or downstairs. How do I know what the stuff is there for? Maybe she is just storing it for a while. Besides, my hands are already full so it's impractical to suggest I do this. A true Snyder never makes two trips. This means I try to bring all fifteen bags of groceries in from the car trunk at one time. Or balance the twenty-nine boxes on the way to the storage room. She thinks I just ought to know which way the things are going when she puts stuff by the stairs.

Here's another strange thing about women. I've already mentioned a woman's self-esteem is connected with what *we* wear and how *we* look? Remember the "Are you going to wear that tie?" episode? I was shocked to find out how I dressed affected her image. Not too long ago we were going out and she said, "Wear what you want." So I thought I would wear my Mariners shirt, everyday pants, and tennis shoes. I ended up wearing a white shirt, sports coat, good pants, and dress shoes. I thought she said, "Wear what you want." Once I found out that Barb's *image* is at stake with what I wear or don't wear, I gladly went along with the program. It's just a little confusing to be told, "Wear what you want," and end up in a tux.

I do want to please Barb in all this, but because I feel criticized if I don't have the right things on, I have asked her not to come at me so hard when she has a suggestion about my clothes. So one day as we were planning to go out she said, "Won't you be cold without a sports coat on?" (No, I'll be warm enough.) "Are you sure you won't be too cold without a sports coat on?" (No, I'm sure I'll be fine.) "You would *look* better with a sports coat on." (Oh, I would *look* better. No problem, glad to wear one.) I know this seems like a terrible effort, women, but believe it or not, men are quite fragile, and you have to be tender with our egos.

I think all this worry about how a husband looks may be the only real tie-in we have to evolution. There isn't any good evidence to support this theory, but there *is* something that worries me a little bit. Does your wife ever pick specks off your coat collar, or adjust your eyebrows, or straighten your tie, or pick something out of your ear? Have you ever gone to the zoo and watched the mother and wife monkeys picking fleas off their sons and husbands? It's the same thing. Tell your atheist evolutionist friends. They'll be excited with this new revelation.

We men need to realize women are just made differently, and since we now know her self-esteem is tied up in how her house looks and how we look, we should no longer go out with a scruffy beard, dirty Levi's, or the wrong tie. We should grieve when we break a plate. We should be careful when we take the chair out to the garage. We should try to keep our towels reasonably clean. We should remember to wipe out the sink when company is coming. We should make the bed like *she* would make the bed. We need to pay more attention to the details of life and try not to leave our clothes lying around. If your closet is a mess, at least keep the door closed so people won't see what a sloppy housekeeper *she* is. Keep things painted and fixed. Create a goal list for your wife on the refrigerator, and commit yourself to working on the projects she thinks are important. Be careful with your power washer. Make sure the gutters are clean. Check for hairs on the chair after you and the dog get up. Put trays or saucers under the plates and cups when you eat over a rug. Take off your muddy shoes when you come into the house. Keep her side of the garage orderly so she can come and go easily. In fact, why don't you put this book aside for a few minutes and write out a list of the things you could do that you *know* would please her. Post it on the refrigerator, and express your commitment to getting the things done in a timely manner. Encourage her to add to it whenever she wants. *Ask* which way the boxes by the stairs are going instead of stepping over them. In short, become her servant, and then *stand by*. What usually happens is your wife will notice your efforts to please her, and she will begin to meet more of *your* needs. The Bible says in Ephesians 5:28b, "A man is really doing himself a favor and loving himself when he loves his wife!" So do yourself a favor and love your wife. I know from first hand experience how well this works. Sure I fail from time to time. We all do. But when the focus of my heart is to please God and please Barb, *I'm* the one who gets blessed.

Now let's flip the coin and talk about where we men get *our* self-identity.

10

CHUCK IS ALWAYS
IN THE BASEMENT

Chuck: Men get most of their self-esteem and self-worth from their job or career. My work history starts on my grandfather's farm way back before you were born. As a twelve-year-old I began driving the wheat truck in the field. My uncles had to put a mattress on the seat so I could see out of the windshield, but I would still have to scoot down to reach the clutch pedal. If anyone was watching me from the side of the road, they would see me disappear every time I went to shift gears. I never went very fast, so it wasn't all that dangerous. I enjoyed driving the tractors and combines and the weekends when I could go into town to see my grandparents.

When I got in from the field, I milked the cows and fed the pigs, horses, and chickens. I gathered the eggs and weeded the garden and picked the fruit. I didn't think any of this was a big deal until later in life. At the time I thought *all* twelve-year-olds had this much responsibility. I have tears in my eyes as I write how grateful I am to my grandparents and uncles who gave me the priceless gift of trust.

Even though I made mistakes and caused my uncles grief from time to time, they always treated me like a grown-up. One day I shot Charlie, one of my grandfather's prize hogs, right in the side while he was sleeping. I had a Red Rider BB gun and loved doing target shooting around the farm. Charlie grunted and died, and I was terrified. There was no way I could explain myself when my grandfather found his dead pig. That evening just before I had gathered up the courage to tell him about my awful deed, I saw my grandfather feeding the pigs, and Charlie was munching along with the rest of them. Looking back, of course, Charlie thought the BB was some fly biting him and didn't even wake up. It was a good lesson, though, and from then on the animals were safe. At least from me.

My uncles were something else, because they would butcher the pigs and steers for meat. I won't even describe some of the things I saw and felt because I agonized so much over the process. There was nothing wrong with it. The animals didn't know what hit them, and therefore experienced no pain. The Bible says God has given us animals to provide food. But it still traumatized me as a small boy, and the memories are still vivid today. Come to think about it, I guess I did enjoy the pork chops and steaks.

My uncles even hurt Bambis and Thumpers during hunting season, too, if you can believe that. I never did acquire a taste for venison. I've not been an adventuresome eater. My family thought my taste was all in my head, so one time Barb and my son Tim said they were going to fix me some venison in a way they *knew* I would like. I was willing to go along with the plan as long as I could spit it out quickly. At dinner they served the venison to me, and I *liked* it. I said, "It tastes just like pork." Of course it did. It *was* pork. They were playing a joke on me to prove my taste was in my head, and I passed the test with flying colors. It gripes them even now to remember how they thought they had me for sure.

Probably the most wonderful thing about the farm was the hired girls my uncles brought out to the farm during the busy harvest season. They would help my grandmother prepare the meals, do the dishes, housework, and shopping. It was such a delight to come in from the harvest fields to such visions of loveliness. They looked terrific, smelled great, and once in a while my heart leaped within me because our elbows touched at the dinner table. Meals were about the only time I saw them because we worked from dawn to dusk. By then we were so exhausted we went right to bed when we came in from the field, so we could prepare for an early rising the next morning.

Go buy a farm. What a beautiful place to raise kids and teach them responsibility. When the animals needed feeding or the fields needed plowing, I was never able to say, "I'm tired," or "I don't feel like it." I knew the cows, pigs, horses, and chickens would tattle on me if I didn't get them fed, so I did it regardless of whether I felt like it or not. What a heritage that was to help me be successful in my work later in life. If you can't buy a farm, find some old people my age who have a farm, and adopt them. Ask them to keep your kids on overnights once in a while in return for painting their house, fixing their car, or letting them borrow your camper. Your kids will never be the same.

When I first began thinking about what I wanted to be when I grew up, I decided to be a veterinarian. I loved kids and animals, so I thought it would be a fun job. I even practiced filling animals' teeth at the "happy hunting ground" down in the draw behind the barn. Here is where the animals were taken when they had died of old age or other natural causes. The whole landscape was littered with bones of all types. I would bring some skulls back to the house and work on the teeth with my electric drill. I even tried my hand at taxidermy, stuffing some small animals, but the problem was I had to kill them first. That wasn't something I enjoyed, so I soon gave that up.

I already told you about going to Washington State University to study veterinary medicine and ending up playing in a country band and changing my major to communications. Way back in the olden days when I was in college, every male had to put in two years of military service. I decided to go through ROTC so I could be an officer and not have to crawl around in the mud like the enlisted men had to do. I decided I would go into the air force, but the line of applicants stretched all around the college gym. There were only three guys in the army line, as I remember, so I opted for the army. I know you can understand that. I saved at least an hour by not waiting for the air force line to go down, and I had a busy life and had lots to do and couldn't be wasting my time standing in line.

I went to boot camp at Fort Gordon in Georgia. That's another book with memories, but at this time I'd rather leave them alone instead of digging them up. It wasn't horrible-horrible, but since I learned only recently that one of the characteristics of my learning style is to dislike authority, it explains why I didn't have a perfectly wonderful summer. But I survived and felt good about myself that I had gotten through the pain.

I suggested to the army I would do my best work for them if I was stationed at Fort Lewis near Tacoma, my hometown. Of course, the army decided I could *really* help them in Fort Bragg, North Carolina, just about as far away from home as I could get. I was assigned to the First Radio, TV, and Leaflet Battalion at the Psychological Warfare Center. It was an unusually cold southern winter's day when I reported for work at the battalion. I spent most of the day by the stove, since no one seemed to know what I was supposed to do.

I can't even remember what I did those first few months, but soon a position opened up for me to serve as the Public Information Officer for the Psychological Warfare Center. I applied and got the job. What a difference. Rather than supervising the enlisted men picking up pine cones or making new rake marks under the barracks, I now had almost a real job. I had a couple of sergeants to help me, and I proceeded to make our "Bird" colonel commander famous in the camp newspaper. I guess I did too good a job, because after six months or so I was sent back down to the battalion. I was told that the "Star" (a one-star general) who commanded the base had his nose out of joint because this "Bird" was getting all the publicity.

So I was made training officer for the battalion—a second lieutenant in a major's position. That brought all kinds of challenges because here all of a sudden was a second lieutenant telling the company commanders what to do, and they were captains. This was one of my first learning experiences in being a servant. As I served these officers and the men in the battalion, they seemed not to worry so much about giving me leadership.

Since I was the training officer, I was in charge of the planning for the field exercises. Even we officers had to participate in yucky things like the infiltration course where trigger-happy troops parted your hair with tracer bullets as you crawled through the dirt. I also scheduled gas chamber exercises where we learned who had the defective gas mask. I suggested to our commander that we hold the exercises in October instead of September, so we wouldn't have to worry about the men getting heat stroke in the hot southern sun. He agreed that was a good idea. I did have a love for the guys, but I guess I'll have to confess my main motivation for changing the field exercises from September to October is that I got out of the army in September. While I missed the good times they undoubtedly experienced, I just had better things to do than ducking tracer bullets and breathing tear gas. I just didn't quite understand the army's need for having the pine cones spit-shined, so I decided to find my fortune elsewhere. I just hope they don't make me take army over again when the government reads this book in the Library of Congress.

Finally the day came to be discharged. The physical was a little bit different from the one at my induction. There were a number of us in a room, and I remember a tired old sergeant saying things like, "Can everyone hear me?" (Yes.) "Then mark your hearing okay." "Anyone sick?" (No.) "Mark temperature normal." It was great! I was getting out.

So I was now out of the army and unemployed. There was a new TV station going on the air in Seattle, so I decided to put in my application and wait. During my waiting time we stayed with Barb's folks and I worked in the apple packing shed thanks to my uncle-in-law who owned the place. One of my most vivid memories was taking my lunch break in the car, drinking hot chocolate, and listening to Paul Harvey. I *still* taste hot chocolate when I hear Paul Harvey. The work in the apple shed was boring and hard, but I now had two kids to feed, so I put my shoulder to the plow and survived.

Occasionally we would drive over the mountains from Wenatchee to see my parents in Tacoma. One time while we were there, Kit Spier called from KING TV and wanted me to interview for a floor director job. KING TV was the top station at that time, and I was very excited to be considered. They told me another man would be competing with me for the job, but I would take my chances. I painted sets, cued actors, set up props, and worked on remotes. I was thrilled to be in the exciting world of television. I was so excited, I offered to do *extra* things. And when I had to work a little overtime, I didn't complain.

One of the worst jobs I had was working on a boxing show called "King's Ring." The station carpenter built a ring out of four-foot by four-foot logs (it seemed), and we had to drag all the logs, ropes, and tarps out of storage each week and set up the ring and then take it down again all in one night. It was a real hassle. One of my duties was emptying the boxer's spit buckets, and I took that in stride with all my other duties. I'm told, however, that the man competing with me for the job complained about working overtime, didn't do anything extra, and for sure refused to empty the spit bucket. So I got the job. I guess my spit bucket work convinced them I was the better man.

I remember so clearly my first full day on the job after I had won the position. Here I was standing beside a TV camera with one of my idols just a few feet away—Charles Herring. I couldn't believe a farm boy from Coulee City would be working with the most popular newscaster in the Northwest. I was in shock for days. He treated me just like a *person*.

One of my first assignments during the news was to put an Alka-Seltzer tablet into Mr. Herring's glass of water so it would be fizzing nicely when he held it up to go to the commercial. The director would go to a tight shot, and I would crawl in on my hands and knees and reach up and put the tablet in Mr. Herring's glass. One time the director got busy and forgot to go tight. I was new and didn't know a long lens from a short one, so I crawled in to do my duty right in front of the entire Northwest. I didn't get fired. It wasn't my fault, but it did make for some fun memories for everyone.

Ted Bryant and Casey Gregerson were also working at the station. They were in the TV and Radio Department with me at Washington State University, and both were popular on campus. Now they had made it big, but they were very friendly and seemed to be happy to have me there, even though my greatest claim to fame was emptying spit buckets.

Another one of my idols was Stan Boreson, a kid's show host. We hit it off right away. I began appearing on his show as a singing Victrola. We wrote our own songs and had a marvelous time. We would meet about 3:30 P.M. each weekday afternoon to prepare for a 5:00 P.M. live show. Talking, laughing, and planning, we had a show on the air by 5:00 P.M. that seemed to appeal to all ages. I took Stan's place as host once in a while during his vacations. This was a terrific learning experience to prepare me for doing my own TV commercials and programs later.

Then I was made producer/director. That was a wonderful challenge. It was the type of job that needed specific gifts. You had to learn to do things at the last minute and take the pressure of being live. This meant fixing things when they went wrong during the show, making sure the actors were ready for their cues, getting the right music ready, seeing that the sets were in place, cueing up the correct commercials, and hitting the network on the second. I loved it. It fit my personality perfectly.

I especially loved directing the news because we were always on the edge of disaster. At thirty seconds before air time Chuck Herring would hand me a script I had never seen, and the photographer Phil Sturholm would take the news film that I had never seen to master control. The news pictures I had never seen would be placed on an easel in the studio, and at 6:30 P.M. sharp we rolled the theme and Charles Herring was in control of almost every TV set in the Northwest. There was little competition at that time since there had been a freeze on new TV signals coming on the air.

I get excited about it all over again as I write these words, but I wasn't seeing my kids enough. Since the newscasts were in the evening, I went to work around 3:00 P.M. before the kids got home from school and came home around midnight or so and was still asleep the next morning when they left for school. So when a chance to direct some of the daytime shows came up, I took it even though it was not as exciting or satisfying as directing the news. I did that for a few years and then began doing filmed documentaries. I learned so much under my boss Kit Spier and my friendly cameraman Ralph Umbarger. We made some award-winning films, but in time I got tired of the travel, "Dag" burgers three times a day, and late nights editing film to a hard deadline.

Then a chance at middle management came up, and I took that opportunity. Jack Fearey was my boss and I loved him dearly. I'm sure he had been involved in my promotions along the way, and I walked up in his footsteps. My job as operations manager was to oversee everything that was not "live" in the studio. This included the networks, movies, commercials, announcers, the station logs, and the shipping department. I worked hard and enjoyed all my working relationships.

However, after three or four years I noticed my work never got done. The things I put in my "out" basket at night were in my "in" basket the next morning. The network would never do what it said. The movies would never arrive on time. The commercial films would always break. I might as well have been in a steel mill because I had gotten out of live TV which was my first love. I guess I was slated for upper management sometime, but I didn't like what I saw as far as a time commitment. My boss was in early in the morning and stayed late at night. His boss did the same. Since my family had a higher priority for me than making money, I decided to leave. I really felt God calling me to move on. It was very hard to explain "God's will" to my friends at KING TV.

I didn't have much of a message then. I was a Christian, but had never been taught the practical aspects of the Scriptures, so I had a "head" message rather than a "heart" message, and the "head" message was boring, at least to me. So I didn't say much. But after I left, one of my friends from the radio side, Frosty Fowler, told me how much influence I had had on his life while I was working at KING TV. I don't think I ever said a word to Frosty about the Lord, but somehow the message came through to him, and eventually he became a wonderful man of God and a Christian broadcaster.

So after leaving the TV station, I began my job search by having lunch with the head of an advertising agency for whom I had produced commercials while I was a director. I had taken Advertising 101 at Washington State, so I assumed that was enough background to look for a job in the field. I asked him if he knew anyone in town who needed some help. He said he didn't know of anyone, but *he* needed some help, so I went to work for him.

My primary job was to write and produce commercials for a retail supermarket account. Though I had directed lots of commercials at KING TV, I had never written one. But why let a little thing like that hinder anything? So I started writing commercials. The problem was they never pleased my boss. He was kind in his criticisms, but my scripts just didn't hit the mark in his opinion.

Most of the things we talked about for the supermarket were similar to what we did last year: the George Washington Birthday sale, or Christmas hams, or Easter turkeys. So I began taking last year's copy that my boss had written, updating the price and turning it in to him for his approval. He *still* rejected them. His own copy! Okay, there's more to this than my inability to write commercials. Obviously he just needed to be in control, so I could relax and serve him in other ways.

It was still hard never to do anything right. The lighting on the ketchup wasn't bright enough, the lettuce was a little wilted, the sign wasn't straight, the music was too loud, the meat was too red, and so on. I suppose most of you have had someone in your life you couldn't please, so you know how hard it is to keep-on-keeping-on. I would go home in tears at times feeling defeated and discouraged. I wanted to leave, but the Lord seemed to be saying in my spirit, "Stay there, I have a plan for you." So having no peace to find something else, I stayed and tried to survive.

God's direction caused me to do some strange things like leaving a promising future with the TV station and *not* leaving a stressful working atmosphere at the agency. I'm sure you face difficult decisions in your life, career, home life, and relationships, too. I found the more time I spent in the Bible finding out about God's character, the more relaxed I could be living through the difficult circumstances surrounding my decision to change jobs. As I got to know God better I found he had a perfect plan for my life regardless of whether it made sense to me or anyone around me.

So having no peace to leave the advertising agency, I continued to work hard even though I wasn't getting the affirmation I really needed to feel like I was accomplishing anything. Then one Sunday morning I got a call from the owner's wife asking me to come by the house. I did and she told me the owner had died. I found a half-written commercial in his typewriter. I finished it and wrote commercials for the next eighteen years for the account.

Not long after the owner died, I purchased the agency from his wife and was in business for myself. It would take another book to tell you all the details of the next eighteen years. I had a wonderful advertising manager at the supermarket I now represented. Andy Attaway was his name, and we are like family to this day. I owe him *so much* for putting his trust in someone who just showed up for meetings once in a while when the owner of the agency was out of town. I will be eternally grateful, Andy.

After a couple of years I received a call from another national retailer. The voice on the phone asked if I would take their account for Seattle-Tacoma. I said, "Sure." Now this is *not* the way things work in the advertising field. Usually a client lines up four or five agencies and has them give big presentations, grinds the agencies down on price, and then chooses the one they think would fit best. Here was this national store chain asking me to take their account, and I had never met *one person* at the company. Later I found out that Phelps Fisher, one of my friends from KOMO TV, had mentioned my availability to the retailer and had said I was a man of integrity. I tried to be honest in everything I did, and I was glad someone noticed.

Once in a while a radio or TV station would make a mistake and overbill me for some air time. They would then send me a refund check. It would have been so easy to deposit that in the Chuck Snyder account and praise the Lord for his marvelous provisions. But I would quickly add a note to the check and send it on to the advertising manager. One time I received a duplicate check from the supermarket for $250,000. Obviously they would have found this slight oversight in due time, but I quickly attached my note and sent it back. I think over time this spoke to them about my honesty.

So I began working for my new client, and then he called and asked if I would take western Washington for them. I said, "Sure." Then he called and asked if I could take the entire state for them. I said, "Sure." Then he called and asked if I could take the five western states for him. I said, "Sure." While he probably didn't know it, my client's calls were because God wanted us to be able to pay for the large home we told you about earlier in which to entertain his servants when they were coming through town.

I worked for this account for about six or seven years and then with an investment we had made in a limited partnership with our friends George and Liz Toles, we paid off our home. The *month* we paid off our home, the account moved its advertising to California in a consolidation move. God had supplied the money to pay for his house. Then when it was paid for, God decided He had some other things He wanted me to do, so He sent the account to California.

If I had not known God personally, had not experienced his marvelous peace and love and contentment, and had not seen his handiwork in every aspect of my life, I would have been devastated by the loss of this account. Sure, I was disappointed because it meant I had to cut down my staff a little bit. Yes, I enjoyed working for them and seeing their success. But God had another plan, and I knew Him well enough to know His plan was perfect. My job was simply to relax and let God work.

Then about ten years ago, I didn't survive a management change at my supermarket account, so I had to go out of business. There was no way I could quickly find enough business to replace two of the largest accounts anyone had in Seattle. We put our large home on the market because we couldn't afford the maintenance without a good cash flow, but it took eight years to sell, and we used all of our retirement and IRAs to live on during that time. This will be the subject of another book one of these days, and in that book I'll tell how God and I regularly wrestled over how long He was taking to sell the home. All He had to do was find *one* person in Hong Kong or Japan. Surely

He got over there once in a while. Some mornings at the breakfast table I would say to Barb, "I have no purpose." She was amazed. Focus on the Family had just published my latest book. I was doing marriage counseling with five or six couples a week, doing some speaking, coordinating the Mariners chapels and Bible studies, and working with a couple of small advertising accounts.

I have to explain that what I really meant was, "I'm not making a *living*." I didn't consider living on savings as supporting my family. I had tried to get some more accounts, but nothing worked out. I tried a number of different ways to make money, but they all fizzed out. I don't care if a man is a Christian or not. He gets most of his self-esteem from his work. Often when someone is out of work, well-meaning people will say things like, "Just trust the Lord." I was trusting the Lord, but I had zero self-esteem because I felt I was worse than an infidel, as the Bible calls someone who is not supporting the family.

We had lots of people stopping by to see the house, but something unusual always happened. One couple in Hawaii wanted to give us *more* than the asking price and then got a divorce. A bed-and-breakfast place couldn't get zoning. It was almost like Lucy and the football where God would set it up, but just as I ran up to kick it he would take the ball away. By the way, don't be worried. The Lord and I have such a tight relationship, he understands *fully* what I was going through. He doesn't get depressed or angry when I question whether he is paying attention to my problem. He grieves with me and tries to give me some hope.

It reminds me of the time when our secondborn grandson Connor was about one year old. We were sitting out on the patio when a big mosquito landed on his arm. His mom swatted the mosquito and Connor started to cry. As far as he knew, he had done something wrong and was being punished. How do you explain mosquitoes to a one-year-old. That was exactly God's attitude with me. He saw the future clearly. He knew the reason he wanted to delay selling the house. He knew I felt terrible about using our pension and IRA funds to pay $26,000 in property taxes and other inflated costs for a large house we could no longer afford.

I think the Scripture that had the most impact on me during this horrible time (horrible from my perspective) was Romans 8:26. All my life I was brought up with Romans 8:28 which told me that all things that came into my life worked together for my good and God's good. When I found Romans 8:26 it was very comforting.

"By our faith—the Holy Spirit helps us with our daily problems and in our praying. For we don't even know what we should pray for, nor how to pray as we should; but the Holy Spirit prays for us with such feeling that it cannot be expressed in words. And the Father who knows all hearts knows, of course, what the Spirit is saying as he pleads for us in harmony with God's own will. [Now we get to the familiar Romans 8:28.] And we know that all that happens to us is working for our good if we love God and are fitting into his plans." (Romans 8:26–28)

The comforting thing to me here is that God realizes sometimes we don't have a clue how to pray. It isn't our lack of faith. It isn't because we have sin in our life. It is because the time is not right for us to know God's complete plan. However, the Holy Spirit knows what God wants for us, and he prays in words we can't even understand—but God does. The Holy Spirit knows God's "Chuck" plan, agrees with God that this plan is good, and then prays in accordance to this knowledge. He and God agree what will happen in my life and why. Then everything that happens in my life has been filtered through the Holy Spirit's prayers and God's hands, and is for my good and God's good. That's quite an awesome team to have on our side when we go through questioning times. Then add the fact that God's Son Jesus Christ loved me enough to give his life for me, in spite of knowing I would make mistakes and question God's wisdom and complain and whine about things not going my way.

Barb: This was a hard time for both of us. For one thing, having your home on the market for that long can be very wearing. I did not feel I could relax. I never knew when the next buyer would want to come by. We had showings by appointment only, but no one told me the realtors would sit at the head of the drive and call on the car phone saying, "This is the only time my clients can come." It was very difficult.

I felt I had to be *up* for Chuck. After all *he* was the one who had lost his main client. As we came to the sixth year, I realized *I* had lost our main client as well, and I needed Chuck to support me, too. I am not one to be depressed, but I started feeling that way more and more. Chuck asked me to tell him what was wrong, and I told him I couldn't put it in words. But as he kept probing, I suddenly could verbalize that I needed to feel supported, too.

It was at that point that I believe Chuck relied on the Lord more than I had ever seen him. He became strong for me and strong in the Lord. I admired him so much.

Chuck: I don't know how Barb made it through this period of our lives. My whole world had collapsed. I was trying my hardest to find new clients, but nothing worked out—except ministry opportunities. I wasn't in ministry full time, so my self-esteem depended on providing for my family which I was not doing. It wasn't my fault, but I couldn't get away from the feeling that I had done something wrong and God was delaying the sale to teach me something. Maybe he was, and someday I'll find out exactly what it was. So I'll just have to trust him that it will all make sense in time.

Chuck Swindoll has had such an impact on my life, even though I have only met him briefly a couple of times. He has been a major player in my spiritual life as I've listened to his tapes over the years. He talked about a cycle the Jewish people went through in the wilderness that sounds like the wilderness I went through with the house. He pointed out that when things went well for the Jewish people, they would look *up* to God. Then they would look *ahead* in anticipation that the good times would continue. When the bad times came, the people would look *down* and feel sorry for themselves. Then they would grumble and complain and look *back* (to the food of Egypt). Then God would rescue them and they would look *up* again.

I don't know why God puts up with us, but he does, and he loves us very much. I would be *stupid* not to put my weight down with someone who sees the future as if it was already the past. He loves me. He prays for me. He wants the best for me. What more could I possibly want from life. Knowing this just drives me into the Word again with new fervor, so I can get to know God better and better. We can't trust someone we don't know when hard times come. Maybe this will give you women an idea of why we men are so focused on work.

Most men are goal oriented with an emphasis on accomplishing, counting, amassing, competing, building, and setting records. Most women are relationship oriented even if they are in the marketplace. Sure, there are some relationship oriented men and things-driven women, but the tendency is for a man to get much of his self-esteem from what he does for a living. Men compartmentalize their lives more than women. Here is my work, my wife, my kids, my hobbies, my shop, my golf club. A woman, as we've mentioned, tends to get much of her self-esteem from her home and relationships with kids, grandkids, women's Bible study, friends, business women's fellowship, and her parents.

Jimmy Johnson, the ex-head coach of the Dallas Cowboys, was the only person to play on and coach an NCAA championship football team and also win a National Football League title. He had just won back-to-back Super Bowls and had the world at his doorstep. He had a ten-year contract and everything was wonderful. But he said one time when he was being interviewed, "At times I get antsy. At times I get bored. And I do like a challenge." I think he reflects the attitude of most men. They can accomplish everything in sight and still not be content or satisfied.

Now let me say something to wives whose husbands are trapped into working long hours. Sometimes we men choose this, but there are times when we are building our careers, or the company is temporarily shorthanded, or the only openings are on the night shift where we have no choice. We went through this when I was directing the evening news at the TV station. Barb explained to the kids that I would be home if I could. I was just trapped into working evenings for now and the family adjusted. This is going to be a tough call for you, because so much of a man's identity is wrapped up in his work. Most men could easily work fifteen to eighteen hours a day at something they really enjoyed. Their relationships would not survive nicely, but they would hardly notice if work was their passion. It's a balancing act.

One man came into my life who had to be at work by 6:00 A.M. Pacific time so he could do sales work by phone in New York. He was still at the office at 6:30 P.M. His wife complained that he worked all the time, and I agreed. I asked him why he couldn't take off at 3:30 P.M. when New York shut down. He had never really thought about it. I was able to be his third party and help him with his priorities.

Work can easily be "the other woman" if your husband really enjoys what he is doing. Somehow he needs to hear what God's priorities are for a man, and how important your need is for a relationship. You can't really tell him yourself. It will take someone else to make the point with him. Even the Bible warns wives not to try to teach their husbands anything. It just doesn't work. Seek out a Godly business man at your church or among your Christian friends and see if he could help. Or get our audio tapes so we could talk to your husband on his way to work, and explain what we feel God wants a man's priorities to be.

Now let's talk about who can remember details the best. I'll give you a hint. It ISN'T the man.

11

IT WAS TWISP!
IT WAS WINTHROP!

Chuck: One of the critical differences between men and women is the fact that women tend to be very much into the details of life, but a man is fortunate to be able to remember where he put his pants. It is this fact of life that has enabled me to solve one of the great mysteries of the Bible.

Women played many key roles in Bible history. There was our Lord's mother Mary, Deborah who was a judge, and many more. A woman even wrote one of the books of the Bible but does not get the credit she deserves. The great Bible scholars have debated for centuries about who wrote the book of Hebrews. Well, they can rest now that I have solved this great puzzle. It was Priscilla. She was Aquila's wife and one of the apostle Paul's key helpers.

The reason I am convinced a woman wrote this marvelous book is the deep subjects she covered, and the way she included all the myriad of details we need to know to put this book in perspective. She talked about God's glory, God's relationship with his Son Jesus, angels, the new heavens and new earth, signs and wonders, Christ breaking Satan's power, Christ as High Priest, Christians as God's House, Israel's rebellion toward God, God's promises, God's rest that he has prepared for us, God's Word as a two-edged sword, his all-knowing nature, God's understanding of our weaknesses, the duties of the Jewish High Priest, animal sacrifices, Christ's obedient nature, the nature of baby Christians, the milk of the Word versus the meat of the Word, the fairness of God, spiritual dullness, God's promise to Abraham, oaths, the hope of our salvation, Melchizedek's role in God's plan, tithing, genealogy of Levi,

God's New Covenant with man, the old system of priesthood that doesn't work, gifts and sacrifices, how to build the tabernacle, God's new agreement with Israel, rules of worship, the contents of the Ark, the priests' duties in the Temple, rituals, the role of the Holy of Holies, last wills and testaments, the role of blood in the Temple, eternal security, the Law's foretelling of Christ, the message from the Holy Spirit, forgiveness, the doctrine of salvation, the unpardonable sin, God's justice, suffering, how to do God's will, faith, trusting in God, Moses against Pharaoh, the Red Sea miracle, how the saints were murdered, and many more wonderful issues outlined in the greatest detail throughout eleven long chapters. Then she gets very practical and gives us many suggestions as to how to live our everyday lives in the final two chapters of Hebrews. Then at the very end she says: "Brethren, please listen patiently to what I have said in this letter, for it is a short one" (Hebrews 13:22).

If this was a *short* letter, I can't imagine what her *long* letter would be like. Earlier in the book she says: "There is much more I would like to say along these lines, but you don't seem to listen, so it's hard to make you understand" (Hebrews 5:11).

It's obvious what her problem was. As stated in the first verse I quoted, she was talking to the *brethren* rather than to the sisteren. The sisteren could have sat still longer and paid more attention than the brethren could.

This reminds me of when Barb and I do women's marriage conferences. The women all come with their notepads and are even there a little early. They don't want to take any breaks. They groan when we have to stop for lunch. They don't want any free time. They just want to learn.

Men are wired differently. They can only sit just so long at retreats. They have basketball games planned at the breaks and during the noon hour. They need free time in the afternoon for volleyball and horseshoes. There's no way you women would know this, but there is a nerve going from a man's behind to his brain. At about twenty-eight minutes a small alarm goes off in his brain that alerts him to the fact he has been sitting a long time. Sometimes he is forced to reset the alarm because the pastor or retreat speaker is going more than twenty-eight minutes. We do this by pulling our left earlobe and holding our breath for twenty seconds. We don't get another twenty-eight minutes, however. The alarm now goes off every *five* minutes. So, ladies, it is crucial to get your husband out of the seminar or preaching session as soon after the first alarm goes off as you can. His brain will explode after the alarm is set more than four times, so you can see how important it is that you know this fact of anatomy. Don't bother looking at the charts in the doctor's office. This particular nerve is hidden behind a bone, and not too many people know about it.

I believe Priscilla wrote Hebrews. Tell your friends. There's no doubt about it. She thought thirteen heavy, detailed, long, deep chapters were short, and she couldn't keep the brethren's attention. It fits exactly what we experience today.

Barb: As Chuck mentioned, men are usually into the big picture, and women are usually more into details. When the family moves to Kansas City for the new job, the husband is going for the goal—the job. It's his wife who remembers to pick up the kids from school, sell the house, and turn out the lights. The man just wants to get going toward his goal. This can be a cause of conflict if both partners are not aware of what's happening. The man feels threatened because he failed to remember the details, and the woman will panic because there is so much to do before they can go.

This is what happens. The man comes up with a big goal. He's all excited and all he sees is the goal. The woman can usually see how to *get* to the goal and what the pitfalls are. She asks things like, "What about this?" "Have you thought about that?" or "We already have one." When I would make these statements or ask questions, Chuck would say, "You don't have any confidence in me." He was just thinking about the end result and I was thinking about how he was going to get there. I'm sure men feel we women are popping their balloons when we ask about the details and give them our opinions.

Chuck: It *does* feel like you're popping our balloons. When I present a dream to Barb she tells me all the reasons why it won't work.

Barb: No, not why it won't work. I just want to know if you've thought about this detail or that detail. I was just wondering!

Chuck: My problem is I back off too soon. I need to do a better job filling her in on the details without getting defensive. I've asked her just to let me dream without adding too many details. When I reach for the phone to call the contractor, *then* she can give me her opinions.

Barb: Not every couple is the same. In some marriages it is the man who is the detail person. But in general we have observed that women are into details and men into goals. Here's what happens when we get in the car to go someplace. Usually I will have the trip all planned out in my mind as to what streets I will take. Chuck just starts out. He doesn't really know how he's going to get there. He just knows he's here and eventually wants to be there.

Chuck starts out to go to work when we should be going to church. He goes north when our destination is south. He turns right out of our driveway instead of left. It's especially bad when we have friends in the car and I don't want to look like a backseat driver, or like I'm telling him what to do.

Author and counselor Dr. Henry Brandt tells of the time he found himself going the wrong way on the freeway after declining his wife's direction advice and then his struggle as he tried to figure out a way to get the car turned around without his wife noticing. Chuck says he does pretty well when I'm not in the car, but I wonder how he makes it anywhere.

Chuck: It used to bother me to have Barb say, "Why didn't you turn there?" or "Why are we going in this direction?" or "Shouldn't we have taken that exit back there?" Finally I realized I *wasn't* the best navigator in the family, and I turned all of that over to Barb. I told her I would be writing commercials or building furniture in my mind while I was driving, and it was up to her to make sure we got to where we were going. This is not an exaggeration; one time she coughed and I turned right. The street to the left was blocked.

Women seem to have this pressing need not only to pay attention to details but to get them *right!* I had no idea Barb had that need. I would be telling a story at dinner with some friends. All of a sudden Barb would interrupt with a detail I had missed or gotten wrong. She says she thought during our early years of marriage that I was lying. Then after adding a couple of corrections, she would take over the whole story while I sat there steaming inside. Who cares if I did get my details mixed up a bit. At least I got to the right point.

One of the people who worked for us was planning a vacation and asked me about the sights to see in Twisp, a small town in eastern Washington we had visited.

Barb: It was Winthrop.

Chuck: It was? Okay. Winthrop. I suggested she and her husband eat in the local hotel because all the old miners in the community had breakfast there, and it was colorful to see them in their Caterpillar hats and hear them banter back and forth. When she got back from her vacation this person told Barb how much they regretted not having had time to eat in the hotel Chuck told them about. Barb asked, "What hotel?" I guess the hotel I was talking about was in *another* small town—175 miles away. When you've seen one small town hotel you've seen them all. How could I remember a piddly detail like that? A hotel is a hotel.

Barb: The trouble is Chuck not only doesn't get the details right, but he *adds* details to make his story work. He changed the tulip farmers at the LaConner Hotel to old miners for his Winthrop story. It's beyond me!

Chuck:: Tulip farmers or miners. They all wear hats and look the same to me. I doubt whether the people hearing my story would care—but Barb cares, and that is important. The way I learned to handle Barb interrupting my stories was to look at ourselves as a baseball broadcast team. Dave Niehaus does the play-by-play for the Seattle Mariners, and he might be reporting that Dan Wilson was rounding second on his way to third. Right then Rick Rizz, the color man, would *interrupt* and say Dan was batting .289 and leading the league in catching defense. He lived in Seattle in the off-season and liked pizza. Did Dave get all threatened when Rick interrupted and say to him, "Would you shut up?" Not at all. Rick was adding some very important details. So now when Barb and I are out for dinner, I just consider myself doing the play-by-play with Barb adding the color, because she has this strange need for all the details to be accurate.

Barb: Why were you so threatened when I added the details?

Chuck: Because it made me feel like a two-year-old who had to be corrected all the time. I felt like I had failed again. I couldn't even tell a story right.

Barb: That wasn't the intent of my heart.

Chuck: It wasn't?

Barb: No! We women just want to get the details straight. It has nothing to do with you. I just don't think the story is as good when the details aren't right. Friends who were with us and know what happened will be with us again when Chuck tells the story. When it's not the *real* story, I get embarrassed and so do they. But if nobody knows the real story, and you realize your husband *can't* remember it, and you know he really *isn't* lying, you can relax and let him tell his stories any old way he wants, even though it won't be how you would tell it. Sometimes Chuck mixes up his stories and then comes to a dead end. He looks at me and we both laugh. He *does* try to remember details that really matter to me, though.

Chuck: When I don't get corrected the first time I tell a story, I assume I got all the details right. It is a shock to me to find out years later I'm telling it wrong. What we men have to understand is just how important it is to women to get the details right.

For instance, the husband comes home from work and asks, "Is dinner ready?" His wife says "I went to the school to get Cliffy, but he wasn't where I usually pick him up. I was worried so went into the school office and sure enough he had skinned his knee, and the nurse was fixing him up. Then I stopped by the supermarket to get some ground beef for tomorrow and ran into Kathy and she told me what a hard time they are having selling their home, and I got back on the freeway—but I shouldn't have—because I ran into that construction that has had things torn up for a week. Then I stopped at the corner to get a paper, and ran into Mrs. Rice—she's the one who sits way down front on the left side of the church and runs the Awana program. Well, she reminded me of the Awana dinner Saturday night, so I'll need the punch bowl up from the basement and no dinner is not ready." Her husband really didn't need all of those details. What he wanted to know was whether he had time to change his clothes or check the headlines before he was to put in an appearance in the kitchen. This is not a put-down of women. It is simply saying that the details of life are more important to the average woman than they are to most men.

Or here's the worst thing. The husband will come home and his wife asks, "Notice anything different?" The husband knows instantly he is in big trouble because he has missed something. "Got a new davenport! I love the color."

"No, we didn't get a new davenport."

"You had the place painted, it looks terrific."

"No, I didn't get the place painted. I got the drapes cleaned." He didn't even know they *had* drapes, let alone whether they were dirty or not. He surely did not notice they had been down for two weeks at the laundry.

Or another time she might ask, "Notice anything different?"

The husband says, "Got a new davenport." No, she has cleaned the cupboards, and now the cloves are next to the celery salt.

Or he comes home and she asks, "Notice anything different?" He mentions the davenport and the paint job, and she says she got her hair done. The problem with Barb's haircuts is her hair stylist cuts her hair with a microscope. He goes, "A snippy snip here, and a snippy snip there—that will be 30 dollars, please." Her hair is one billionth of a millimeter shorter and I'm supposed to notice. Wives, your husband needs hints like, "Notice anything different about my *hair?*" and "Don't you think the drapes look better cleaned?" Giving him hints will help keep him out of trouble.

Barb: I think sometimes a man remembers what he *wants* to. Way back in the olden days Chuck used to fix black-and-white TV sets to earn a little extra money. He knew which tube handled the audio, which was the high voltage tube, and which one controlled the horizontal hold. He even knew the names and numbers by heart, but he couldn't for the life of him remember to put the plastic dishes in the *top* of the dishwasher or remember which way Beverly's dress went on. I went to church early one day when Bev was small and left her for Chuck to dress. When she got to church she not only didn't have her dress on right (Chuck thought buttons always went in front) but she wasn't sliding down the slide very well because she didn't have any panties on. Maybe this has something to do with the brain surgery a man gets right after the wedding ceremony.

What's true about this for Chuck and me is also true in many marriages. It's our different perspectives on the little things that can make us both uncomfortable. Most men tend to be more stable when it comes to the big things— handling earthquakes, disease, disasters, war—but can go out of their mind if their nail clippers are missing. Chuck has been known to go out and buy ten flashlights or five pairs of scissors or six sets of nail clippers, just because the one he usually uses is missing.

Most men tend to have their eyes set on the end result down the road and don't want to be bothered by disruptions and details, while women seem to be able to handle the little details and interruptions of life. It's a good thing because there are so many of them.

While it's true men have trouble with details and tend to see the end result, it isn't because they can't remember if they want to. There is an ability in our brains called the reticular activating system. This causes us to tune in or tune out anything we want. We have moved to a community on Puget Sound. Train tracks run along the shoreline and we hear their whistles now and then. When we first moved here we heard every one. We don't notice them anymore. And the ferry boat docks close by and toots its horn to warn it is approaching. We don't usually hear that either. That's because we have decided *not* to hear them. They are not important to us. But when we were raising the children, I purposely tuned in to their voices and doings. I was instantly aware when something was wrong. And when they were babies I jumped out of bed at their first cry.

Our granddaughter Brooke has had a choking problem since she was little. Once when I was with them Brooke's mother suddenly said to me, "Brooke's choking!" and ran to her aid. She had decided to tune in to hearing that sound.

So you can tune in or tune out anything you want to. When our husbands say they just don't hear the kids at night it's because they have decided *not* to hear them! And sometimes I think when they don't hear *us,* it's because they have decided *not* to do that either.

Chuck: I'm afraid we men would have to plead guilty—at least most of us. This is probably why we miss so many of life's little details. I think our claim of, "I just can't remember," falls a little flat when we are overheard talking about details that *are* important to us. It's fun to listen to old baseball players replay the events of the 1971 World Series. "I came up to bat. There was a guy at first and third and two outs in the ninth. The pitcher was throwing smoke, but he was also mixing in a change and getting guys out. The count was 3 and 0. Then he threw the change. 3 and 1. Then smoke. I couldn't catch up with that pitch. 3 and 2. I thought he might throw another change but decided to look for the A train, and there it was. And there it went. Over the wall."

I remember the summer when Barb and I were in Wenatchee waiting for our first job. I got up early and played the Three Lakes Golf Course all by myself. I remember clearly being in a ditch on my tee shot. There is a road on the right side of the first fairway that is distracting. Then there is a sharp dog-leg to the left. Then on the back nine there is this hole that is elevated. I think it is number thirteen. You have to hit a perfect shot to make it stick. As I remember, the pin was close to the front edge of the green, which of course made it almost impossible. But I took a five iron and put the ball pin-high. I remember how excited I was. I almost wished there was someone else there to witness this fabulous shot.

We've talked about some of the differences between men and women such as their temperaments, cultural upbringing, and heredity differences. But did God design women's and men's brains differently? This may be the case concerning the wiring of our brains. There have been several books written about this, and the radio program *Focus on the Family* has had some programs concerning this difference. I don't pretend to have all the details, but it appears that the brain in a boy baby is bathed with a hormone early in its development, which destroys many of the interconnecting fibers between the two hemispheres of the brain. A girl baby's brain does not experience this, so she is born with a full set of interconnecting fibers. One of the things this does is make a man more one dimensional. That doesn't mean he can't use both sides of his brain. It simply means he usually uses only one side at a time. He might be figuring math problems, learning a language, or examining details with the left side of his brain. Or he might be painting a picture, listening to music, or writing with the right side of his brain. He moves back and forth depending on what he is working on.

One example of this comes on Monday night during the football season. Let's say I'm watching the Seattle Seahawks maul the Dallas Cowboys (a little fantasy never hurt anyone). It is an important game and I am really into it. All of a sudden I am vaguely aware of a disturbance in the room. And all of a sudden I discover Barb is trying to communicate with me. I always advise wives not to try to talk with their husbands until halftime, but here is Barb trying to get my attention to tell me the roof blew off, the cat had nineteen kittens, a child is trapped in a tree, or some other piddly household detail. She finally gets loud enough to break through my concentration on the game. You see, I don't know I am married, or have three kids, or a cat, or a roof, or live in the United States. All I know is if our running back doesn't make third and long we are in big trouble.

Then suddenly, I am aware of a noise in the room just in time to hear my wife say something like, "You never hear anything I say" or "You don't love me anymore." I love her, and if that ever changes I will let her know. Right now I'm watching a football game and cannot communicate and watch at the same time. The last thing I hear as my wife huffs out the door is, "Well, if you didn't hear me, you can just forget dinner!" I'm innocent. I didn't even know she existed.

Or there are those times when I am reading the paper at breakfast. I don't even know Barb is out of bed yet, but all of a sudden I glance up and she's sitting at the table saying something like, "Isn't that right?" or "What do you think about that?" Again, I didn't even know I had a wife. I was into my paper.

Here's the way to solve this problem, wives. This will be worth the price of the book itself. When you want his attention for something, just take his head in your hands and look into his eyes. They will be glazed over a bit, but don't panic. Then say something like, "Testing, testing, Barb-to-Chuck, Barb-to-Chuck." Then his eyes will unglaze, he will see that you exist, and you can tell him anything you want and he will hear you. Just don't expect him to hear you automatically because your mouth is opening and closing. Make sure you have his attention before you speak.

When Barb and I go to a Mariners baseball game she takes her hand work. During the game she does her cross-stitch and talks to several of the player's wives. She knows who's angry, who's pregnant, and who's lonely. She knows the score of the game and where Rick the peanut guy is—all at the same time. All I know is if Junior doesn't get on base, we are going to lose the game. This is because I am just working on one side of my brain at any given moment, and Barb is working on both sides of hers at once. That makes her more aware and sensitive to what is going on.

Brain damage might also be the reason husbands can't find things easily in the cupboard. Say a wife asks her husband to get the kumquat juice from the cupboard. He goes to look for it but comes back empty-handed and reports, "It isn't there." The wife drops what she is doing and goes to the cupboard. She moves something, and there is the kumquat juice. He didn't know he was supposed to *move* anything. What he is looking for should be right there on the front row.

The problem is sometimes the husband reports a no-find, and the wife goes to look and can't find it either. Instead of being in *that* cupboard, it is in *this* cupboard. Rather than apologizing, most wives degrade the husband for not looking around a little more. Or, worse than that, tee-hees and giggles and makes a big joke about her telling him it was somewhere it wasn't. That's enough to drive you nutty. It's World War III when *we* don't find something, but when *she* can't find it either, it's the comedy hour. Sounds like a double standard to me.

Barb: I guess the difference is that Chuck makes a habit of not being able to find things. It can be right in front of him—it could reach out and touch him—and he still doesn't see it. But it's true. Even though it's not very often, sometimes I give him wrong directions, so it's kind of funny.

Chuck: I don't know if the love of sports has anything to do with brain wiring, but I suspect it does. You hear coaches say over and over, the pitcher wasn't *focused* on the game. The hitter did not *focus* on the ball. The wide receiver didn't *focus* on the football. The whole team lost their *focus*. Ladies, when your husband is watching sports on TV, he is trying to be an example of *focus*. He wants to do a good job of paying attention to the details of the game so when you ask him what the score is, or who scored the goal, or what the pitch count is, or whether the defense is a 4–3 or 3–4, he will be able to tell you instantly and satisfy your need for details. I don't really expect you to understand why he gets all excited about one tenth of a second in the one-hundred-yard dash. Just accept it, and you'll be happier for it. Go shopping or something. He won't know you're gone.

Because of our advanced age, Barb and I love to watch *Capitol Gang, McLaughlin Report, Washington Week, Equal Time, Reliable Sources,* and those type of TV programs. I remember my grandfather always listened to Gabrial Heater and Walter Winchell in the afternoons. We had to be very quiet, and we couldn't talk to him as he sat in his old rocker glued to the radio set. So we sit glued to our TV sets as we see Fred Barnes, Mark Shields, Al Hunt, and John McLaughlin give us the scoop on what happened in our world that week.

I remember one week prior to the Super Bowl, which is of course one of the most spiritually meaningful times in a man's life. The game had been hyped every day, in every newspaper, in every sports report, on every network station, as well as on all the sports cable channels. There were 750 million people around the world all tensed up as the great day approached, and this is as it should be.

The TV reporters spoke to all of the players and coaches to see what they had planned for this great event. We heard from the ball boys who would be giving the winning coach an ice-cold shower on the sidelines. We heard what kind of potato chips are *in* this year. It was an exhausting week for all of us, but it was important we have this background before the big weekend arrived. Las Vegas printed the odds as to which team was the favorite. All the newspapers had big headlines comparing the strengths and weaknesses of the two teams. The team names were on the lips of all informed Americans as they began to decide which of the teams they thought had the best chance of winning and who deserved their support.

Then came Friday evening. This meant we only had one more day of agony before we could see maybe one of the greatest events in the history of mankind—excluding perhaps the invention of the printing press and the discovery of fire. It also meant the Capitol Gang would bring us up to date on what was happening in the world. Of course the most important item on the panel's agenda is always covered first, so Al Hunt asked Margaret Carlson, the only woman member of that august panel that day, who she thought would win the Super Bowl. She threw up her hands and said, "Who's playing?"

There, ladies, is the basic reason why there is so much friction between men and women and why we don't communicate even though we are both speaking English. Here is the most important event in the universe other than creation itself. Billions of our precious dollars have been spent promoting this critical phenomenon, and she doesn't know *who's playing!* What planet has she been *on!* Now I'm not saying all women are this deaf and blind to important events like this. I know there are women who *love* to watch the Super Bowl. There's a woman in Chicago, one in Tokyo, one in London, and a real fanatic in Chico, California, but those are the only ones we know of right now. Is it any wonder so many marriages are on the rocks?

We men get so much abuse and criticism from women for wanting to watch sports on TV. What you ladies don't realize is that it *isn't our fault* we look at so many games on TV. It's the *announcer's* fault. People like Brent

Musburger talk about an upcoming Florida-Miami football game and call it the *game of the century*. Now who in his right mind would want to miss the game of the century.

And those promos for the upcoming Monday Night Football matchup yell at us, "Don't miss next week when the greatest matchup since Moses and Pharaoh takes place. Exciting bone-crushing action as two magnificent teams battle it out on Monday Night Football!" Blooey, pow, crash, sparks as the helmets hit head on, and we have to catch our breath because of all the excitement and anticipation. What red-blooded, patriotic American is going to pass up the greatest matchup since Moses and Pharaoh? It glues us into our chairs as we await this once-in-a-lifetime event.

I've read where it won't be too long before we have five hundred channels available to bring us all the sports happenings of the day. Ladies, I think this portends a great danger for the human race. When we get five hundred channels, the men of the world will not have time to have sex with their wives because of all the sports and other important things on TV. That means the human race will go right down the drain. I hope someone can think of something to solve this crisis before it is too late. You might try passing in front of the TV set in one of your Victoria's Secrets outfits, but I really don't hold out much hope.

Well, back to the basics. The greatest thing we can do for each other is allow our mates to be different instead of fighting the differences. We all need appreciation. Your husband does for sure. But he also needs to appreciate you, too. Often! You have killed yourself working all day at home, or have come home from the office to a dirty house, fixed dinner and did the dishes, picked up clothes and toys, and put the kids into bed, battled PMS and a cranky neighbor. You have deadlines at church or for the school, and he wonders why you haven't gotten the flowers planted yet, or why dinner is late. He has not approved of you, or acknowledged all the yucky things you've had to do all day. Then he wants more. I know this is discouraging, sometimes to the point where you just want to give up. On the other hand, if he were quick to help you around the house, give you a hug once in a while, grieve with you over your busy schedule, praise you for getting so many things done and wonder, "Is there anything else I can do for you?" then you would do anything for him.

My point in all this is we must be quick to communicate approval and praise to our mates just for being a good mother, or a husband working so hard to provide for the family. When we each focus on trying to build the other person up, then *both* our needs are met in the approval area, and our marriage is stronger. When we think the other person has just performed his or her *reasonable* service and don't say anything in appreciation, then the marriage relationship suffers.

We expect our mates to be just like us. We assume they will show love in exactly the same way we do. We expect our mate to act and react like we would in every situation. Men don't communicate like women or share their feelings like women or respond like women. We forget that men and women are *supposed* to be different according to God's plan, and our job is not just to endure the differences, but we need to try our best to *appreciate* the other person's gifts and acknowledge the fact that God gave your mate to you on purpose. It wasn't a mistake.

Now let's investigate a part of the marriage relationship that is a mystery to a group of people who make up about half the population. They are called *women*. Most of you don't have a clue why our next subject pops into your husband's mind at least daily, sometimes hourly. It's called *sex*.

12

HUPOTASSO WHOOPEE!

Chuck: Now let's talk about something that affects everyone, but NO ONE wants to talk about it...especially in the church. Sex was God's idea. It is pure and holy within a marriage relationship. I have no idea why Christians are so uptight on the subject. Probably because our culture has contaminated this beautiful part of the marriage relationship so much. It is the icing on the cake of marriage and is designed by God to be enjoyed by married couples.

Barb and I participate in this wonderful experience too, but because of our busy schedule and advanced age, I suggested to Barb that maybe we should restrict sex just to holidays. Because Barb is a planner and likes to have a schedule, I worked up some dates she could put on her calendar. So here's a typical January for us in case you would like to use this list as a guide for your own life. Here are some of the holidays we celebrate.

January 1	New Year's Day
January 2	Celebration of the first white sale in U.S. history
January 3	The invention of glass
January 4	The birthday of the *Mona Lisa* painting
January 5	Einstein's birthday
January 6	The invention of paper
January 7	Guttenburg's first printing press put in service
January 8	Four-minute-mile record broken
January 9	First white man to reach the North Pole celebration

January 10 First laptop computer reaches the market

January 11 Nat King Cole's anniversary

January 12 Ricky Skaggs's first appearance on Grand Ole Opry

January 13 Moss day in Stockholm

January 14 Battle of Hill 203 in Korea

January 15 Texas declared a state

January 16 First computer megabyte discovered

January 17 Anniversary of Ulysses S. Grant's fifth year of sobriety

January 18 The nation's first schoolhouse in New England opened

January 19 The birthday of the artist who *painted* the *Mona Lisa*

January 20 The first lawn mower invented

January 21 Battle of Hill 204 in Korea

January 22 Five-minute-mile record broken

January 23 The invention of glue

January 24 The annual hut cleaning day in Ubanga, Africa

January 25 The invention of marbles

January 26 False teeth invented

January 27 Battle of Hill 205 in Korea

January 28 Toxic pickup day in Phoenix

January 29 Org paints his first cave in France

January 30 First calendar chipped out of rock in Babylon

January 31 Charlie Johnson's Edsel stock went up

I won't take the time to list the other months of the year, but if you need some guidance on bringing order into your life for this important activity just let me know.

Ladies, I want to talk with you about the most important thing on your husband's mind. There is one guy in Billings, Montana, who likes Monday Night Football better and one guy in San Francisco who likes ice skating better, but for most husbands the greatest pleasure he has in his life is the physical relationship with his wife.

On the other hand, one of the great mysteries of life for a man is why our wives are not as excited about the sexual part of marriage as we are. In fact, it appears to us like our wives would be content to go the rest of their life without this experience. In fact, she seems bothered by a man's focus on sex. In fact, she thinks we are beasts or animals or worse.

Take the "Ann Landers" column a few years back where she reported that 72 percent of the women she surveyed would rather have a hug from her husband than go to bed with him. Actually that figure is probably low. But I like to look on the positive side of things. That means 28 percent of you women out there attack your husband in his workshop. You don't have to raise your hands. I know who you are by the smile on your husband's face.

As I mentioned in my book *Men: Some Assembly Required*, sex was *God's* idea. He thought long and hard about whether to give Adam or Eve the primary responsibility for this part of marriage. He finally chose Adam because in his foreknowledge he knew if he trusted Eve with this important work, she never would have thought about it! The Bible would only have one book in it, because the history of mankind would have been written about Abraham, Isaac, and Jacob, then—poof. The end of the human race would have come quickly because Eve had so many other things to think about.

On the other hand, Adam was focused and one dimensional, and he expressed his eagerness to take care of this critical part of God's plan for mankind. God in his foreknowledge knew Adam would do a good job. When we men want to go to bed a little early once in a while, it is *not* for ourselves. It's for the *destiny of mankind* and the *preservation of the human race!* What a noble and soul-stirring burden for man to carry. We want to be in strict obedience to God as we carry out his mandate to preserve the human race from going down the drain because the woman is so busy. Ladies, are you convinced yet? I didn't think so.

All the comments we make will be made in the context of a monogamous marriage, which according to the Bible is the only time sex between a man and woman is blessed by God. And a reminder that we are just talking about tendencies when we talk about differences. There are always exceptions, but we want to deal with what most people normally do. So it appears to us that most men think about sex often. And for the most part (maybe new-century women are exceptions) women rarely think about physical sex, except as part of a loving, caring marriage relationship. While the first thoughts of a man are about sex, the first thoughts of a woman are usually about the relationship, and how she is being treated in other areas of her marriage. Someone has said men make love to *feel* good and women make love *when* they feel good. That means the whole relationship has to be going well before the woman feels like going to bed with her husband.

Affection and conversation seem to be higher on a woman's list of needs than sex. If the man is not honoring and valuing his wife in areas other than sex or taking time to be a conversational partner, she feels neglected and doesn't respond to her husband when he wants to go to bed. He looks at sex as an event. She looks at sex as a relationship. The problem is a woman needs an emotional relationship in order to have a physical relationship. A man needs a physical relationship in order to have an emotional relationship.

Barb: Women need to know they are valued for more than sex. Kindness, gentleness, helpfulness, conversation, and loving words are what spell intimacy to a woman. Sex is a relationship that is continual in a woman's eyes. We are responders, and the very makeup of our bodies attests that we have a hard time responding to someone who is just being nice to us for that moment. It's very difficult.

Let's say the wife has been busy all day taking care of little ones and doing the laundry and cleaning. She has prepared a good meal ready to serve when he gets home. She has been waiting all day to have some adult conversation and is excited when her husband gets home. The first thing he says is, "Why is the house such a mess?" Then he wonders what she has been doing all day. He doesn't see the clean clothes in his dresser drawers nor does he know the house wasn't a mess before the kids got up from their nap. Now he sits down to dinner and complains about it. Next he's so tired from working all day he wants to read the paper and watch a little television. She still has to wash the dishes (with a heavy heart) and give the children their baths and put their pajamas on. He is still sitting in front of the television. She finally sits down to relax, and he says, "Coming to bed?" He has that twinkle in his eye, yet he hasn't been interested in her or the kids the whole evening. She thinks, "No way am I coming to bed. I'll sit here until he's asleep!"

Chuck: Gives her a headache, doesn't it?

Barb: You bet. It's hard to respond to someone who hasn't cared about you all day—maybe for weeks. I know he's shown his love by working to support her—and he has—but we need a friend *and* a provider. Just like he needs more than a housewife and mother for his children.

Chuck: Since the husband doesn't have the big picture on all this, and he senses his wife is not as interested in their physical relationship as he is, he decides to have dinner with the secretary at the office to get some recreational companionship. He's not looking for sex. He is looking for someone who is fun and thinks he is wonderful. He does things with her without feeling too many expectations. This *other* woman finds someone who will meet her needs for affection and conversation. Someone who will listen to her and authenticate her feelings. He feels like Mr. Wonderful out in the world but Mr. Jerk at home.

Now, hold your cards and letters. I'm not suggesting it is the wife's fault if her husband falls in love with his secretary. It's called sin, and God will hold him accountable for it. All I'm saying is if we as marriage partners pay close attention to the top needs of the other person and do our best to fulfill as many of those needs as we can, then the likelihood of our wife or husband running off with a boss, or coworker, or neighbor, or secretary is less. Why would you run off with someone else when your needs are being met at home?

But when the woman is offended because her husband wants to go to bed all the time, and the man is offended because his wife is never enthusiastic about sex, then there can be stress in this part of their marriage.

Now, on the other hand there *are* some women who are the initiators in the sexual part of their marriage, and it is their *husbands* who have the headaches. I've met a few, but there aren't many. Because I want to stick with the tendencies most of you will relate to, I'll assume most women think their husbands are animals.

One of our biggest problems as men is all the pornography in our path every day as we go about our normal business and living patterns. I don't even mean the overt sexual displays in magazines like *Playboy* or *Hustler*. I'm talking about opening the morning paper and seeing a page of bra ads. Sex is the theme in most secular magazines because it sells copies. It is the dominant theme in our culture.

I don't know if you've noticed, but even *Popular Mechanics* has gotten the message. Have you ever seen the boat manufacturers' ads that always have a man riding the waves in his boat with a knockout boating companion who is ready to burst out of what is laughingly called her bathing suit. And the pictures are very, very small. It takes a magnifying glass to really appreciate the lines—on the boat. I have to up the power on my magnifying glass constantly as I get older and my eyes get dimmer. (Barb, this is not true. I'm just trying to make a point so other people can relate. I don't even *have* a magnifying glass, and even though you know I hate boats, I need to keep up with the latest innovations in case someone at the men's Bible study I teach is in the market for a boat. So please don't cancel my subscription to *Popular Mechanics*.)

Even though I'm a committed Christian husband, and try to be as pure-minded as I can, my eye always stops at the girl in the bathing suit who is standing by an oil filter in the truck maintenance manual. I don't believe it is possible to get to the point where a man does not notice a beautiful woman. Unless a man is blind or homosexual or over 120 years old, he notices a beautiful woman as she goes down the street. The trick is not to go around the block to see her, or leer as she goes by, or find out her route to work, or observe her every day. That would be sin from God's point of view.

Christian men have the same wiring as non-Christian men. We just have a different set of instructions. We don't subscribe to *Playboy* or *Hustler*. We don't sneak looks at skin magazines down at the barber shop. We don't have Showtime or HBO or any of the other movie channels in our home. First, we don't want to expose our kids to that sort of thing. Second, we are not able to handle all the nudity without sinning in our mind. We must run from temptation.

A man can appreciate a beautiful woman, but God tells us not to *keep on* looking. That would be lust and is against what a man of God should do. But don't have false guilt for noticing. Blame that on your God-designed wiring, and then be totally under the Holy Spirit's control so you won't be tempted to sin.

To most men a woman is simply the most beautiful thing in the universe, and I don't mean necessarily in a lustful way. Yes, our culture has contaminated this, but I believe there is a definite element of appreciation. God designed men to be visual, but we have to control it and keep our thoughts in the realm of *appreciation*. Now, ladies, after you quit laughing about a man's appreciation ability, please pay attention again. Yes, a man *can* appreciate a beautiful woman without sinful thoughts. But we are not to *keep on* looking at a woman because that easily becomes lust.

Early in our marriage I would point out beautiful women to Barb. I thought she would appreciate my good taste. Instead, she was threatened, thinking I felt there were other women more beautiful than she was. This wasn't the case at all. Barb wasn't even involved. I was commenting on a stand-alone, one-of-a-kind situation that had nothing to do with Barb. I just appreciated God's design. I don't know if Barb has ever fully bought my appreciation of God's design theory, but she finally relaxed and just asked that I not mention anything to her about my appreciation.

Barb: I hated it when Chuck talked about other women. It was a habit of his life and I got tired of it. If I did the same thing, he couldn't and wouldn't stand for it. Each of us needs to know that if we were ever choosing a marriage partner again, we would choose each other. Talking about other women does not show value to our relationship. In fact, it tells us that we don't measure up and the other woman is what he would really like.

I know Chuck is not blind and I'm not blind either. But are we going to love and serve each other in a way that makes the *other person* feel loved, or are we going to be self-centered?

Chuck: This is one of those areas between men and women where we may never understand what's going on. I can surely see why women would feel like we are shopping around when we make comments on how nice another woman looks. I was young and didn't understand all I know now about how much a woman's self-esteem is tied into her husband's approval. I can see why Barb might think noticing another woman would be threatening. I believe, however, it is more the way God designed us. He made us more visually oriented than women are. But when does looking at a woman appreciatively become "looking at a woman lustfully," which Jesus called sin in the Sermon on the Mount? We owe it to our wives to control our eyes and keep our mouths shut and make sure she *knows* she is the only woman in our life—which she is. But she doesn't feel like that's the case when we talk about other women—even in appreciation.

Bill Gothard changed my life and gave me many practical ways to be obedient to God. He suggested a man avert his eyes downward when any luscious creatures happened along his way. I tried that when we were in Hawaii one time walking along the beach. It didn't work too well. We incurred some unexpected hospital bills because I kept banging into palm trees with the top of my head as I kept my eyes down as Bill Gothard suggested.

Because of the extra medical costs, Barb decided it was okay for me to look where I was going. This worked a little better, but even though I believe I have convinced Barb I'm a one-woman man, once in a while she will test me. We will be walking on a beach and Barb will tease and say, "That was a nice bathing suit, wasn't it?"

I reply, "What suit?" and we proceed on our walk. I have to be careful because once in a while I will blow it by replying, "You mean the purple one?"

One of the great pressures on a man is to come up with the right answer instantly. I have no idea what she was reading, but one time Barb asked me if I was a breast man, a bottom man, or a leg man. I quickly said, "I'm a Barb man," and the issue was dropped. Oh, what a minefield we men walk. I hope our wives appreciate all the stress we are under.

When men get married, they assume they will have unlimited sexual opportunities with the woman they love. All of a sudden there are pregnancies, cycles, fatigue, relationship problems, ignorance on his part of how to be a good lover, and boom—the couple goes six weeks without coming together. The man has a little pressure gauge, and when he goes very long without a sexual release the gauge moves into the danger zone and *cartoons* will turn him on. Or he'll see that beautiful silver silhouette of a woman's body on the mud flap of the truck in front of him and want to go home and look you up to do something about this urge he has.

Men think sex comes naturally, but most men are completely ignorant as to what a woman needs. They have no idea that a woman heats up slowly—like an iron—and then cools down slowly. You women already know your husband is designed like a light bulb. On! Off! He's snoring before you have had a chance to get your mind off dinner. You ask, "Who was that masked man, anyway?" And when he doesn't satisfy you (mostly because of his ignorance) you are confused and hurt and more reluctant to try it again next time. When he never touches you except when he wants to go to bed, you feel like an object and he wonders why you aren't more enthusiastic. Someone has said sex begins in the kitchen. Most men don't know this. So we both get on edge. The man is afraid to get too huggy and romantic because he worries his wife will think he wants to go to bed. The woman is afraid to get too huggy and romantic because she *knows* he will want to go to bed. The solution to this is good old-fashioned communication. The man could say, "I just want to be close to you. But don't worry, I'm not trying to drag you to bed. I just want to enjoy being with you."

I don't think there is much debate—at least in male circles—that sex is a man's greatest need. I also think it is obvious a woman's greatest need is a *relationship* with her husband, where sex is a culmination of their oneness and fills a need in both of them.

Now let's talk about some practical ways you can meet your partner's needs in the sexual area. First of all, there is nothing sinful with any aspect of the physical part of marriage. The only caution is to do only those things that are comfortable for *both* partners. Hopefully you both will be creative in this exciting part of the marriage, but you must agree together on the details, so neither person is uneasy. God is very clear. He honors the marriage bed. "Marriage is honorable in all, and the bed undefiled…" (Hebrews 13:4, KJV).

I'm not sure why women are more uneasy with sex than men are. Maybe it's because they are more vulnerable to sexual harassment and abuse in their growing-up years, and this has made them wary. Even men in our culture today are more on guard in everyday men-women relationships, especially in the marketplace. This is a confusing minefield for single men because a majority find a wife in a work situation. Therefore, sexual interest is normal and a part of life. However, these days sexual interest on the part of the man is many times called sexual harassment, and it complicates this delicate system.

A man can't say to a woman (other than his wife), "You look great." It would be naturally accepted the other way around if the woman were to tell a man *he* looked great, or was handsome, or whatever. The problem is if we men don't notice how good you look, you are offended. You spent two hours in the bathroom this morning making the repairs. But if we *say* something, you are still offended. It's really tough to know what to do.

On the other hand, I can easily understand how men have blown it in the past. It's one thing to comment on a beautiful dress and quite another to comment on body parts. I'm just afraid these abuses in the past will cause both sexes to back off from the admiration and attention we all need as we go about our day.

I read about a man who was taken to court because he thought he was getting signals from a woman saying, "I'm available." He evidently gave her gifts which she accepted. He took this as a further clue she was open to his attentions. He made a more overt move, and she sued him for sexual harassment. When is it harassment, and when is it what we used to call *courtship?* There's a difference between a man misreading signals and deliberately forcing himself into the situation. I'm sorry this is so complicated. All it does is promote further misunderstanding between the sexes.

All of this game-playing of course applies to unmarried men and women *only* and should not be a part of our life if we are married. God has clearly stated the rules with regard to husbands and wives.

> But usually it is best to be married, each man having his own wife, and each woman having her own husband, because otherwise you might fall back into sin. The man should give his wife all that is her right as a married woman, and the wife should do the same for her husband: for a girl who marries no longer has full right to her own body, for her husband then has his rights to it, too; and in the same way the husband no longer has full right to his own body, for it belongs also to his wife. So do not refuse these rights to each other. The only exception to this rule would be the agreement of both husband and wife to refrain from the rights of marriage for a limited time, so that they can give themselves more completely to prayer. Afterwards, they should come together again so that Satan won't be able to tempt them because of their lack of self-control. (1 Corinthians 7:2–5)

One time I sent out a survey to do some research on men and women relationships. One of the questions I asked on the survey was whether men would like their wife to be more available for quickie sex in front of the fireplace, in the sleeping bag, in the closet, or on the roof. About 90 percent of the men who responded said they would like the woman to do this once in a while.

The other 10 percent did *not* fill out the question. I assumed this meant their wives were *already* doing this, and they were of all men most blessed.

One man, however, sent back the survey and took me to task for asking a "sick question." He obviously thought sex was bad or dirty or something you shouldn't enjoy. I was sad, because God invented sex, and it is wonderful, healthy, and very satisfying when it occurs inside a marriage relationship. I'm angry at the way the churches in my background have treated this subject. If we can't talk about sex with our Christian brothers and sisters, we force people into the world to talk about it, and there are all kinds of minefields out there. Many of our kids have to learn about sex from their peers in school and are handicapped with all kinds of wrong information which plagues them well into adulthood. Both men and women need to educate themselves as to what their partner needs sexually and to understand some of the other aspects of their physical makeup such as PMS. If a husband doesn't understand the cycles in a woman's life, he can easily misunderstand some of her words and actions during certain weeks of a month.

Barb: I used to have a terrible time with monthly moods. I probably had one week that I felt well during the whole month. We were at a home fellowship for our Sunday school class and someone asked me if we got the magazine *Moody Monthly.* Chuck overheard the question and replied, "Do *we* get *moody monthly!*" It got a big laugh from everyone, because most of us were going through the same thing.

But I must tell you that when I added Vitamin E to my diet, the moods lifted and life was easier—not only for me, but for the family.

Chuck: Now I realize sex on the roof or in front of the fireplace is not always practical in a marriage. I know the fear of pregnancy freezes women up sometimes. To help in this regard I suggest the woman take care of the birth control details if at all possible. I know this sounds one-sided, but you women pay more of a consequence for casual sex than your husband does, and I would like you to be in control of the situation. Then when you have all the children you want to have, I suggest the husband go in for a vasectomy. I know that's scary for men. They think their voices will go up ten octaves, or their beard will fall out, or they'll become a eunuch or something. But take it from a satisfied customer that a couple becomes more relaxed than they have ever been in this part of their marriage. It makes sex sweet and free and wonderful for both parties.

Not everyone will agree, but I do *not* suggest that younger women have their tubes tied or whatever is done (I don't understand all the plumbing aspects of this) because it is the man who dies first: in wars, accidents, workshop tragedies, and from heart attacks. If a woman marries again after her husband's death, the new man in her life will probably want them to have children of their own.

Our culture suggests we solve the birth control problem with abortions. Non-Christians have no problem with people living together and having sex without a marriage commitment. Even some Christian women have been caught up in the thinking that if she is available sexually, in time he will want to get married, have a commitment, accept Christ, and everything will be okay. The problem is the woman is the one who is hurt the most in a sexual relationship outside of marriage. When she finally brings up the word *commitment,* he takes off. He was getting everything he wanted—physical and emotional closeness—so why would he want to make a commitment, too. The woman is then left emotionally shattered and wonders what went wrong.

If we would only do things God's way, things would work out much better for everyone. God says a man and a woman should have no sexual relationships outside marriage. This protects from sexual diseases, and there would be no illegitimate births and no need for abortion. There would be no divorce, so kids would always have their natural parents to nurture and care for them. The man would serve the family and die for it, giving up himself like Christ does for the church. Every kid would have two sets of grandparents who would invest time and resources into those precious little lives regardless of whether they did a good job cleaning up their rooms. The parents would give loving discipleship to their children in order to make them into useful citizens. Even our culture, when presented with this scenario, has to admit it does sound good.

Why don't we see this more often? I suppose the main reason is because of sin and selfishness in human beings. My heart goes out to the millions of women who have had husbands reject them for another woman. I weep with the millions of single Moms who have been abandoned and are trying desperately to do a job that only two can do well. Maybe talking about the ideal situation is like throwing salt in bleeding wounds, but that surely is not my intent. I just want to point all of us once again in the direction of obedience to God's principles that would make our lives so much more fulfilling. I realize hardly anyone is in this ideal situation in our day, but maybe we can start the pendulum swinging back to doing this marriage thing with God's principles in mind and stop passing the sins of the fathers and mothers on to the next generation.

Well, that's just about all I know about this complicated subject, except for one suggestion for you women. Just once before your husband dies, send the kids to the neighbors, cook his favorite meal, light some candles, and meet him at the door with nothing on except a tiny apron (be careful you don't surprise the UPS man if he knocks). Look and smell like you did on your first date. Then let nature take its course and delight in each other just like God intended. Yes, I know you sometimes meet him at the door in your nightgown, but it has *feet* in it. You have to be more creative than that! But be sure to do this only once during his lifetime. His heart simply could not stand the strain if you were to try it more than that. It will be an evening he will savor the rest of his life.

I already mentioned the verse from 1 Corinthians where it says that if the married couple refrains from sex for prayer and fasting, they should "come together again" after that is over. Other translations say come together "regularly." I looked up the word *regularly* in the Greek. It is Hupotasso Whoopee! Meaning three or more times a week. Now don't blame me, ladies. Look up the Greek for yourself. Barb says I could never keep up the pace. I say she has never tried.

Now that we've taken care of sexual communication, let's look at communication through talking. Once again, there can be some differences between husbands and wives.

13

I THOUGHT
BARB LOVED TO ARGUE

Barb: Remember the expression "opposites attract"? But after you're married for a time you'll find what attracted you the most about your mate in the beginning now becomes your greatest irritation. He or she is just *not like you!*

When it comes to communicating, Chuck and I are nothing alike. God has created different kinds of communicators ranging from very expressive to nonexpressive with varying degrees in between. Chuck and I are at the opposite ends of this scale. This difference may not show up in regular conversation, but it certainly shows in how we handle conflict. Usually a nonexpressive person will want to walk away from conflict, while the expressive person wants to talk about it, find out what's wrong, and be friends again. The nonexpressive does not want to talk about it and believes if they don't, it will go away. They feel if they just let it alone, everyone will remain friends. The expressive *knows* it won't go away, especially for them.

An expressive person knows right away why they feel the way they do. The nonexpressive usually has no idea what they are feeling. All they know is they are angry. They may even try to hide it and can even hide it from themselves. It is never good to pretend you are not angry and stuff your feelings. The trouble with stuffing is that the feelings are stuffed alive, not dead. They sit down there in a warm dark place fermenting and pretty soon you have an explosion. On the other hand, to let your anger out in a way that hurts others—like expressive people often do—is not good either.

As you may have guessed, Chuck is the nonexpressive and I am the expressive. Betty Coble from Chuck Swindoll's former church taught us a word picture using the game of tennis to describe how expressives and non-expressives communicate in a conflict. In tennis the ball has to go back and forth over the net in order to have a game. It is the same thing with communication. Words have to go back and forth to have a conversation. So I would send a ball (a sentence) over the net to Chuck, and nothing would come back. I would send another ball over the net, and it wouldn't come back. Then another and another, and pretty soon I would be slamming them over the net as fast as I could. Finally Chuck would "feebly stick out his racket" and hit one back (he'd tentatively send back a feeling), and I would run up to the net and smash it right down his throat. And even if I didn't smash it, I would half-volley it, which means to hit it immediately after it had bounced up to about four inches off the court.

For eleven years Chuck did not tell me I had done anything wrong. When we would have a conflict, he would just get silent and say it was his own little problem, and I believed him. Knowing what I know now, I should have kept questioning him, but I took him at his word. I didn't know anything about playing games—saying one thing and thinking another. I really did think he had his own little problem, and he would be better later. I was too naive to realize that *I was his own little problem*. If he had just talked to me about how he felt, I would have done anything for him. As it was, I thought I was the most perfect wife to ever walk the face of the earth. Even though he didn't do this intentionally, it really wasn't fair. If I didn't know what was wrong I couldn't do anything to help the situation. He must have been super human to have lasted for eleven years.

I got my first clue something was wrong as we had dessert one evening with some friends. I guess I interrupted him for the last time he could possibly stand it, and he showed his anger in front of our friends. (I'm sure I was just adding a needed detail!) He didn't get mad out loud, because that's not his way. He just pulls his neck up in a certain way and does something with his lips, so I know by his body language something is wrong. He also got silent and did not enter into the conversation anymore. I used to tell him that he disappeared. His body was there but he was nowhere around. Of course I knew everyone had noticed. We had made a pledge never to show anger to each other in public, and here he'd gotten angry at me for everyone to see. It surprised me, because Chuck rarely showed his anger, even at home.

Chuck: I really don't think anyone noticed. Oh, maybe the women did since they pick up on things like that, but I thought I covered myself pretty well. Part of this came from my childhood where I got the idea somehow that anger was wrong, so I didn't express it. In Barb's family they got angry, but became friends again quickly. I kept my anger for days. I've had to learn to express my anger in constructive ways, but for me it's not an easy thing to do.

Barb: Sometimes, even though I'm the expressive one, I don't have energy to work out the problem verbally. Once we were on our way to see the Mariners baseball team in spring training, and I got into the car and told Chuck I had turned on our home security alarm with the red light showing and now I wondered if it would go off. "Yes, it will," he replied and jumped out of the car to catch it before it called the police. I sat there for a while and then decided to go in and help him. I didn't have my keys, so I rang the doorbell. Chuck says I rang it with a bad attitude.

Chuck: I was on hold with the alarm company. I couldn't get the system to quit asking the police to come, and the doorbell began to ring. Not with a ding dong, but with a loud ding dong dong. I had cut myself shaving, and my audio recorder hadn't worked properly as I recorded my commercials earlier that morning. Here I was with the house coming down around my ears, and Barb is *donging* the doorbell. Well, I'm afraid I lost it and became angry and aggressive and blustered.

Barb: I had been stuffing some feelings, if you can believe it, and I took all Chuck's blustering very personally. We didn't have a wonderful weekend, to say the least. We were polite to each other, but we were still both angry and the fun was gone. When Chuck and I are having a conflict, I usually pursue and Chuck withdraws. Each of us perceives something the other does not intend. Chuck used to say about my verbal responses, "Remember when you stuck the knife in, twisted it, and blood dripped down my front?" When did I ever do that? It was beyond me how he could even think such a thing. Then I was startled to see in Norman Wright's book *The Christian's Use of Emotional Power* a page that had nothing else on it except the phrase, "To disagree is not to attack." Finally I understood Chuck's perception of being attacked. And I thought, *No wonder he never wants to discuss anything.*

We heard a saying once that fits here. When a man gives his opinion, a woman takes it as an opinion. But when a woman gives her opinion, the man takes it as a command. This also might explain why Chuck and most husbands do not like to discuss things with their wives.

Chuck: Talk about misperceptions. When we were giving each other our opinions, Barb would say, "If I let you know how I feel, will you *punish* me [by becoming silent]?" I loved her. I wasn't trying to punish her. She loved me. She was not trying to attack me. It was just our view of the situation during conflict.

Barb: When I came to understand how Chuck felt, I tried to back off and come at him softer. I think it was part of letting his tennis ball bounce and come up real high (getting all his feelings out) before I hit it back. In other words, Chuck wanted me to think about what he'd said for a while before I responded. Two seconds seems like an eternity to me in that situation. It's hard for me to be quiet. When Chuck understood I felt punished when he withdrew, he did his best not to do that anymore. So most of the time he has chosen to talk to me even when he knows our talk will end up in a conflict or difference of opinion.

Chuck: As a nonexpressive person, I need a little time to get in touch with my feelings. I'm not like Barb, and I don't instantly know why I am upset or angry. So when Barb begins slamming words over the net at me, I let them go because I'm not ready to talk just then. Barb and all the rest of the expressives in the world can't imagine someone could be angry and not know why. But it's true. If she presses me too much for answers as to why I am upset, it just makes me more upset. I'm frustrated because she seems to be able to handle conflict toe-to-toe, and I want to run away. By the way, being expressive or nonexpressive is not a man-woman thing. It's a personality difference. In some marriages the husband is expressive and the wife is nonexpressive.

Over the years living through this, we found out I needed some time, and Barb needed some hope. Every time we had a conflict, she would *attack* (my word) and I would *punish* (her word) by withdrawing emotionally, and sometimes physically from the situation. I just don't know why I'm so angry. I just am and I feel terrible. We finally got to the point where we would pause in our exchange, and Barb would say, "I suppose you can't talk right now."

I would say, "No, I really can't, but let's have a date Thursday night, and I'll be ready to talk about it." I can get in touch with my feelings eventually, but I need some time to mull over the situation. It's hard for Barb to wait until Thursday. In fact, when we talk about this in our seminars, some expressives from the audience will complain they just wouldn't be able to wait until Thursday. I remind them that both the expressive and nonexpressive are compromising in this. Barb would like to talk about it right now and be friends again quickly, but she compromises and gives me until Thursday to get in touch with my feelings. I *never* want to talk about it. I was hoping it would just go away, so *my* compromise is agreeing to talk *at all* and suggesting a date on Thursday to talk about it.

So I go out to breakfast with myself the next morning. I take my notepad and try to come up with some reasons why I was upset. By the time breakfast is over, I have three points to my feelings. Barb can hardly wait for Thursday to come so we can solve our miscommunication. I equate this whole process to vomiting. I hate to get to it, but I *do* feel better when it is over. If you can afford it, get together at a restaurant. In this way you are not interrupted by kids, phones, dogs, and doorbells.

We still had another thing to learn about the Thursday date. At first Barb would ask me why I was upset, and I would pull out my notepad with my three points on it. By the way, if you can relate to how I feel, be sure to take your notes. Your more expressive mate can reduce you to a puddle of blood just by a raised eyebrow and outtalk you big time, so you must have notes to keep you on track. So I have my notes and Barb asks, "Why were you angry?"

I look at the first point on my notepad and say, "I was angry because…" and I would give her my first feeling.

She would pounce on it, evaluate it, cut it up, crush it, and mash it. She would add some "How could yous" and "What were you thinking abouts." Then she would ask, "Anything else?"

I had two more points to my feelings, but after getting beat up over number one I would say, "Oh no, everything's cool. No problem." There *was* a problem. I had only gotten one point out. I stuffed points two and three, and she thought everything was fine. I would stuff a couple of points today, some tomorrow, and some on Saturday. Pretty soon I would blow up over burnt toast or something. I would have way more anger than the situation warranted. Neither of us knew what was going on.

Barb: Often the nonexpressive will feel the expressive person is nagging about something. The expressive is just trying to talk it through, but the nonexpressive imputes something negative and subconsciously wants to avoid the discomfort of talking. The expressive goes ahead and brings up something that needs to be talked about and resolved, and the nonexpressive feels hemmed in and doesn't want to talk.

By the way, have you ever noticed that men are not usually accused of nagging? Even the Bible speaks of the quarrelsome or contentious wife who is "like a constant dripping." I've chosen a better word that fits what men do— they *badger*. They talk about the same thing over and over and over again until you agree to do it, even though you may have doubts about it.

Chuck has often used badgering when he wanted me to agree with some goal or idea he had. He just wouldn't quit talking about it.

Chuck: Hold it! I need to explain that I'm in a no-win situation on this. Barb has asked me not to surprise her with my goals and ideas, so I've begun to write notes. Now my problem is getting the notes back with Barb's written comments. Barb hates to make decisions and is uncomfortable getting involved in my world-changing plans. So she doesn't send back my notes, hoping I will forget about the latest big idea. However, I've decided if I don't get my notes back with her comments, I should just assume she is excited about the project.

Barb: No, no, no. I'm the one who thinks if I don't answer the notes, Chuck will forget about them. I hope his ideas will go away. When our daughter Bev was thirty-five years old I found a note from Chuck in my stack of papers. It read, "Okay if I make Bev a potty chair? I think our Success Story over time will pay for it. Glad Tim is walking. See you tonight. I love you! Chuck." He dated it April 17, 1959! Chuck just wanted to make his point that I don't get his notes back to him in a timely fashion.

Chuck: Instead of joining her husband in a lifetime quest for great new ideas and projects, I'm sure Barb had dreams of marrying someone who would sit on the porch and rock with her the rest of her days. I honor that. I take ten to fifteen minutes off every summer to rock with her. But how can I quit talking about new ideas when they can benefit the world so much?

Barb: Now back to the subject at hand. I work so hard to get Chuck to talk that when he finally does, I evaluate everything he says. Like, "How could you possibly think that?" Or, "I think you're wrong!" Or some other choice little tidbit. Of course, this closes him right back up again. I didn't know Proverbs 18:13 which says: "He who gives an answer before he hears, it is folly and shame to him."

I have had to learn to be a better listener. Our daughter Bev has taught me a lot about listening. I thought I *was* listening to her, but she didn't think so. When I asked her how I could show it more, she said I could ask questions about what she is talking about. I think that is a real key, because it lets the other person know you have heard them and are interested in what they are saying. Sometimes I'm guilty of thinking about what I am going to add to the conversation, rather than focusing in on the other person's words and feelings.

Of course our emotions are running high during times of conflict, so even after knowing all this, it is still hard for me to put into practice. I still want to jump in with both feet and have my say—like this morning.

Chuck: I thought it was last night.

Barb: Probably both! At least it wasn't in the car on the way to teach a seminar on communication. That's usually when we have had the worst communication difficulties. You see, just because we have had some successes in this area does not mean we no longer have problems. We still have our unique temperaments and personalities, and it takes lots of work and commitment to go *through* the process of learning to communicate, rather than just walking away as so many couples are doing these days.

Our biscuit story illustrates Chuck's need to have some time to think things over before he can talk about them. When I worked with Chuck at the office, he would call across the hall and ask me what we were doing for dinner. Sometimes I would say I had something in the Crock-Pot. He would say, "Oh, you don't want to cook. Let's go out for dinner." And since I was usually tired, I would welcome the dinner out and would put the food I was going to have away for another day.

When our daughter Bev came to work for us, that meant I could be home with more time to cook. Chuck would still call me from the office each evening and ask what we were going to do for dinner. When I would say I was cooking, his voice would fall, and he would sound disappointed. I never understood why. He *used* to like my cooking! This went on for a whole year. When I asked him if he liked my cooking, he would say yes. But there was something in his voice I just couldn't figure out.

One Sunday I was too tired to go to evening church, so Chuck went alone. We had gone out for dinner on Friday night, and I had not used the chicken I had thawed. I thought I would make him biscuits and gravy, fried chicken, and salad, and he would really be pleased. He would really like this dinner. When he came home, he came up behind me as I was rolling out the biscuits, put his arms around me, and asked why I was working so hard. *That proves it!* I thought. *He doesn't like my cooking. Forget the gravy!*

At dinner he didn't eat any of my biscuits. Now I knew for sure he didn't like my cooking. I wanted to talk about it right then, but because of all that we had been learning about giving Chuck time to get in touch with his feelings, I decided not to. Later when we went to bed, I asked the Lord, "Should I talk to Chuck about this?"

I heard in my head, "Leave it alone."

I said, "Chuck!" (I was really obedient, wasn't I?) I asked him if he had eaten anything on the way home, and he said no. I pointed out to him he had not eaten my biscuits! He said he hadn't noticed any biscuits. I told him I was making them when he hugged me in the kitchen. He had seen me put them in the oven! I was really upset and again talked to him about not liking my cooking. He insisted he did, and asked why was I making such a big deal out of this. There must be something more going on to make me so angry.

There was! I was reading a book about a man who had a worldwide ministry but was neglecting his family in favor of the ministry. Even though his wife was sick in bed with a nervous breakdown, this man left his family to go and wait in Hawaii for more money to come in so he could get on with his ministry. Then he would write home and tell about all the people who were coming out to hear him speak. If Chuck wasn't controlled by the Lord, he would be just like that man, I thought. In fact, in the past Chuck *had* put ministry above my feelings. He had changed, but I was identifying so strongly with the wife's situation I forgot about how Chuck had changed. I was getting more and more angry at Chuck while I was reading the book. So that was in my heart when the Lord told me to leave it alone and I ignored God's still small voice and had it out with Chuck. We had a hard discussion that night. I had caused a crisis.

Here's another principle—most of the time a crisis makes the nonexpressive person start thinking.

So the next day Chuck called and said, "I know why I don't always want to eat at home for dinner. The phone is ringing, you're up and down doing dinner things, and we just don't get to visit like we do when we go out."

I said, "Oh, I'll go out to dinner with you anytime!" Wasn't that wonderful and simple?

We've learned that when you know how the other person feels, you can handle it. It is *not* knowing that is so hard. Proverbs 13:10 says, "Through presumption comes nothing but strife." Both of us have to keep from reading into what the other person means.

Chuck: Reading into is called *subjective thinking*. When the subjective person reads into what the other person is saying, he or she usually assumes the worst. An example of this was the time I was preparing some cheese for a snack. I like it melted in the microwave. I cut a piece of cheese and was putting it on a plate when Barb said, "Boy, that's a big piece of cheese." Since I have been wrestling with an extra twenty pounds for a long time, what I heard was, "Listen, chubby, you don't need all that cheese." She swears she only meant the cheese would not melt very well in the microwave. It would burn the edges before melting.

Barb: It took a crisis and a year of Chuck thinking about what I was asking him about my cooking to bring things to where we could talk about them and come to an understanding as to why he didn't want to come home for dinner. It was just more proof to me that nonexpressive people need time to get in touch with their feelings. Then after they *do* know how they feel, it's important for them to make a date to come back and talk about the problem. They seem to think if they don't talk about it, it will just go away. As we've mentioned, when people stuff their feelings, the feelings are not dead. It's like putting garbage in a closed container in a warm place. Sooner or later, after it ferments, it *will* explode. And often the explosion of anger comes when you least expect it and at a time when the anger does not fit the occasion.

Once I just tapped on the car window to get Chuck's attention, and he was instantly angry because of all the things he had been stuffing. I told him I didn't feel safe with him, because I never knew when the next explosion would come. I've mentioned Chuck has a quiet way of exploding, but I can easily read his body language and his silence, and I *know* he is angry.

Everyone needs to feel safe. I knew Chuck had me on a performance basis, but I wasn't sure what performance was causing the anger. He did not have unconditional love for me at that time. As long as I performed correctly, I got his approval. I did not have his approval when I did something that bothered him, and he let me know it in no uncertain terms even though he did not use words to tell me.

One time Chuck was on the phone giving directions to someone. I got his attention and added some details. He got furious. It was one of those times when his anger did not match the situation. Later he came upstairs and apologized, but I could not get over the hurt. He kept his hand on my shoulder (he had never done that before) and insisted we talk about it. Keeping his hand on my shoulder and staying there to talk showed me he valued me. It was one of the kindest things Chuck has ever done because I know how hard it is for him to remain in the conflict.

Chuck: Once again I sound like a real beast, but the phone thing was just a matter of my being more one dimensional like most men are. It's hard for me to do two things at once—like talk to a person on the phone and Barb at the same time. I hate the phone. I don't know why I even answer it. Barb knows all the details of our life anyway, and the calls are usually for her. Besides, she's the social director. I can't tell you how many times I have gotten in trouble by making unilateral decisions as to when and where we would be available for dinners out, or counseling, or other social activities. I finally got it through my head that we had to decide together whether the timing was right. Since she had a better feel for that sort of thing anyway, it was easier for us when we talked about it. I had been known to schedule a morning breakfast right after a very exhausting trip. It looked fine three months prior to the date, but as we dragged ourselves off our deathbed to keep the commitment, I could see the foolishness of my decision.

Barb: Again, personality differences play a part in how we communicate. Some people are nonassertive, some are aggressive, but the best is to be *assertive*. Our culture has changed the meaning of being assertive. Today we think it means aggressively standing up for our rights. But a better meaning is you tell me how you feel about a situation, and I'll tell you how I feel. It's done with pure motives. We want the best for each other.

When a nonassertive passive person disagrees, he or she thinks this way: "I have no power. I'm not worth much anyway. I really don't have a right to tell them what to do. It won't do any good anyway. It's better just to leave it alone. No one will listen to me anyway." There's a problem with this approach. By not asserting or expressing feelings, the nonassertive person stuffs his or her feelings, and later on (eleven years for Chuck) they will skip over giving their feelings assertively and come out in an aggressive, angry manner.

On the other hand, the aggressive person says, "It's all your fault. *You* are responsible for my feelings. *You* made me do that. *You* change. *You're* wrong." The aggressive person cares nothing about the feelings of the other person. When the anger of an aggressive person flares, everyone is in trouble.

There are many unspoken rules we bring into our marriages. One of our unspoken rules resulted in how each of us handled anger. Chuck's family did not have conflict—at least with words. In my family we were allowed to show anger with one another, speak it, and then it was over.

So when Chuck and I had a disagreement and talked it out, *he* thought we had failed while *I* thought we had succeeded.

In reality, conflict is neither good nor bad, it just is. It's how we handle our anger that matters. It isn't good for me to pursue Chuck and force him to talk when he feels he is unable to tell me what is wrong. On the other hand, it is not right for Chuck to withdraw and decide never to talk about it again. We had to learn how to serve one another in this area of our lives.

Body language is another important part of communication. During our hard times, I would go places in the car with Chuck. He would let me out but start moving the car forward before I had gotten completely out. Chuck was just saying through body language (car language) he wasn't pleased with me. I remember telling him, "I sure hope you find out soon what is bothering you or *I'll be dead!*"

Studies have shown that 55 percent of communication is through body language; 35 percent tone of voice; 2 percent intuitive; and only 8 percent words. If our body language and tone of voice don't match our words, then we have not really communicated. We have given confusing or even dishonest signals.

We might ask our spouse, "Is something wrong?"

They say, as they look out the other side of the car, "No, everything is fine!" Because their body language and tone of voice don't match their words, we know everything isn't fine.

I really think it's harder to be a nonexpressive. I've accused Chuck of controlling me, and he is mystified as to how he is doing it. In psychological circles it's called being a passive aggressive. In our relationship it works like this: When Chuck is ready to go or ready to get out of a situation—especially in a group—he drums his fingers on something, or stretches his arms and legs and moves around in his chair, or stands up, or eventually all three. His body may be there, but he is nowhere around—especially in a group. I've been asked so many times, "What's wrong with Chuck? Isn't he feeling well?"

"No, he's fine. He's just been working hard." Which is true, but basically he's just uncomfortable in that situation. I've asked him to be more *sparkly* when we're out, but it's just not that easy for him, so he gets quiet. Although, once again, if his goals for the time he is spending with someone include teaching or counseling, I can hardly get a word in edgewise.

Chuck: The nonexpressive carries much of the responsibility for the process of communication during a conflict. We are the people who want to run away and not talk. We need to make a gut-level decision to talk anyway—no matter how much we dislike conflict. The expressive person must create the crisis to give the nonexpressive the reason to talk. The crisis is saying, "Can we talk?" Or "Why were you so angry?" This starts the process. The nonexpressive then takes some time to get in touch with his or her feelings, and the couple talks on Thursday or whenever.

We always like to give practical solutions to problems, so here is how an expressive person and a nonexpressive person can solve conflicts and live in harmony. We call it quick listening based on James 1:19 where it says, "Everyone should be quick to listen, slow to speak and slow to become angry" (NIV).

This principle is a useful communication tool for all relationships; kids and parents, bosses and employees, neighbors, and especially wives and husbands. I first heard about this when I went to an assertiveness seminar. During the seminar, we had an exercise in listening. The idea was to pair off with another person we did not know and pick something from a list of subjects on which we disagreed. The seminar was secular so there were many subjects to choose from like abortion, the women's movement, affirmative action, nuclear deterrents, the environment, and people living together without being married.

Each person was given two minutes in which to convince the other person of his or her point of view on the chosen subject. We could do anything except slug the other person. Person A would begin and talk for two minutes about how he or she felt on the subject. Then Person B reflected back to A what he or she heard. B would keep reflecting until Person A said, "That's exactly how I feel."

Now it was B's turn to present his or her two minutes' worth. Then Person A reflected back the feelings until Person B said, "That's exactly how I feel." It was wonderful. I even saw people switch sides as they, maybe for the first time, listened to a conversation rather than just thinking about what they were going to say next. But I felt the rules were wrong, so I had to rewrite them. Some expressive like Barb must have decided to have everyone speak for two minutes back and forth. But that doesn't give us nonexpressives time to get all our feelings out before we're interrupted.

The first time Barb and I tried this at a restaurant, she said, "Just keep it short."

Barb: I couldn't remember everything he was getting wrong. So he gave me paper and pencil and said, "Take notes."

Chuck: So she took notes, and I got all my feelings out. Something amazing happened. After we were through talking, I had gotten out all my feelings on the table, and Barb had gotten all of her feelings on the table. Now I became William Buckley the debater. I was *very good* at this communicating-in-conflict stuff. Since all the details of our disagreement were out in the open, I could then say things like, "I didn't know that. Please forgive me. I didn't realize *that* was how you felt." At the end of that discussion we were best friends.

In the process of doing this we discovered the cause of much of my anger (and Barb agrees with this). I had not finished one thought in thirty *years*. In her desire to get the conflict solved she would speak too quickly or evaluate one of my points too soon. Then I would stuff the feelings I didn't get out, and anger was the result. With this "quick listening" technique we learned at the seminar, both of us were able to understand the other person's point of view completely. That doesn't mean we always agreed, but there is no anger or resentment or bad feelings because each of us has had a chance to say how we felt. Looking back, I can't remember a time when we have had lingering resentments or questions after doing this. I think every time we have done this, we came away knowing how the other person felt, and we were friends again.

For some of you it might not be quite this easy. You might have been harboring some hurts for years, and one time might not be enough to get everything out in the open. If at your date you find yourselves at an impasse, just agree to table the situation and try again next week. Most of the time, however, I think you will find just talking about it will defuse most of the heat.

I know this sounds like a technique, and it is. We *needed* a tool to help us communicate. This had a great impact on our life, and we hope you'll find it as helpful in your relationship.

Barb: Another thing that is *very important* is to be nice to each other during the time you are waiting to talk. Before we tried "quick listening" I was without hope that we could ever solve anything. No matter how hard I tried to be soft with Chuck, it always turned into another disagreement. So now that I have hope that we will talk in a way that brings resolve, it is no sacrifice to treat Chuck as if we had never had trouble in the first place. In fact, we both are kind to each other because we have nothing to prove. We *know* we will talk later. I can't tell you just how wonderful this *quick listening* has been for both of us. We finally found a way to communicate even in the worst of disagreements.

Chuck: Barb mentioned she thought it is probably harder to be a nonexpressive, and I can tell you from personal experience it's awful. I hate it when I get silent or withdraw. If I don't get my feelings out verbally, they will come out physically. My hands break out when I am under a great deal of stress at home or work. I also get headaches, backaches, and neckaches when I'm keeping my emotions in. I guess that's where the phrase "You're a pain in the neck!" comes from. People and problems can *be* a literal pain if we don't deal honestly with our feelings.

Some of the reading I've done suggests that many of the people in mental institutions are there because of not facing difficult situations in their lives. Many people with real physical ailments are in hospitals because of suppressed anger, bitterness, resentment, and other feelings they have stuffed. It's dangerous to be a nonexpressive. That's probably why God usually pairs us up with an expressive person like Barb, so they can help us get in touch with our feelings.

Even though we are writing this book, we still blow it once in a while. Even *Barb* has blown it a couple of times, if you can believe that! (In communication circles this is called *counterattacking*.) Now this is not something *you* should do, but I need to level the playing field just a little bit because she is so perfect. Really!

We were on our way to attend the funeral of a beloved aunt who had been such an inspiration to me in my growing-up years. Before I go on, you need to know Barb and I have this running patter where I tease her about various things. I will say, "We need to give Molly (our dog) more people food. I just cut my finger on her ribs."

Barb's response to my statement about Molly's ribs is, "She's so fat she can hardly walk!" or something like that. Yuk, yuk. Fun, fun. We both know the solution to Molly's problem is to cut out the snacks. But it's fun to tease Barb about it, and she gives me the proper response almost automatically.

Barb may be on her last gasp of energy. She will have taught two or three Bible studies during the week. Maybe we have done a couple of seminars. Maybe she has done some radio interviews. There has probably been a family birthday dinner at the house. The phone hasn't quit ringing, and all she can think about is having a little peace and quiet in her favorite rocker with her fifteen-foot-high stack of Bible study books. As she stumbles toward the chair with her eyes starting to go half-mast I say, "Oh, by the way, the such and suches called and they are coming to visit for a few days, but you'll have to entertain them because I have so much work to do."

Her proper response is to sigh and smile and plop into her chair saying, "Have a good time visiting." Yuk, yuk. Fun, fun.

Even as I write these words, she is preparing the house for a baby shower celebration for the extended family. I have just completed all the things on her list that I needed to do to help her get the house ready. Now I do her the biggest favor of all and get lost so I don't mess up the kitchen or something. That's why I'm down here at my computer talking to you.

I have always wanted a farm. I still would like to have a farm, but that requires getting a new wife, because the closest Barb wants to come to farming is having a black-and-white TV set at the Hilton. I just can't face training a new wife, so I have put the farm on my to-do list to accomplish after the Rapture. But I still tease Barb about a farm like I do the other things I've mentioned and get her time-tested response.

On our way to my aunt's funeral we passed through some of the farming areas where I'd grown up. It brought back floods of memories of those wonderful times. As we drove along, I put on my teasing hat and said to Barb, "I sure hate to think of our grandkids growing up without being on a farm with animals." Yuk, yuk. Fun, fun. Then *blooey!* Barb exploded. (Exploded is my word. Her voice just gets firm and goes up in pitch, but it sounds like exploding to my ears at least.)

"I don't *want* to live on a farm. I thought you *agreed* we would buy a house with a view. Now you are changing just like you *always* do. I can't depend on your word. I don't *want* a farm. Why are you changing your mind again?"

What happened to the Fun, fun, yuk, yuk? What happened to her proper response and her smile? All of a sudden she is threatened, and I'm in deep toxic waste. Then she violates all the principles we teach in our seminar on communication. She demands feelings and wants me to talk about why I had changed about wanting a farm instead of having a view of the mountains. I hadn't changed. I was committed to a house with a view, and I was teasing about the farm since we're traveling through farm country, just like I tease about Molly's ribs, and people coming over to visit.

At this point in our conversation my brain went dead. I thought I was teasing, but maybe I *was* mentioning it too much. I better think about that. I hadn't even *looked* at a farm in my preliminary search for a new home. Now, as always, when Barb is demanding feelings and whys, I needed some time to figure out what I did wrong, but she continued to demand feelings with more and more emotion. I continued stuffing my emotions because she can always outtalk me in a crisis situation. That made me even more frustrated and I reacted with even deeper silence.

I mumbled some trial responses, but she immediately pounced on them, and I quickly retreated. So we had lots of silence on the rest of the journey to the funeral. Every few miles she would sputter out something about how I *always* did this and *never* did that. She sounded like the old Model T Ford my dad used to have. I'm just sitting there in silence because I have no idea what just happened until I get alone and spend some time thinking. I am not going to be an effective debater of the issues until I've had a chance to think about what happened. Finally Barb said, "When you figure out how you feel, let's talk about this later." This was my cue to begin figuring out what I did wrong and make a date to get together to talk.

After I got home I wrote out a page of feelings and presented them to her during our quick listening time, and we managed to resolve the issues. It proves that even after over forty years of marriage, writing marriage books, and teaching seminars, we *still* have to work and compromise in this special relationship called marriage. Barb still hopes someday I will finally be able to communicate immediately without anger, or say, "Wonderful," when told about the wedding on Saturday during the NFL playoffs, or wipe down the sink, or pay more attention to details. And I'm working on those things, but I doubt if they will ever come easily.

I would have trouble giving you statistics on this, but I have a feeling that men have a harder time with marriage conflicts than women do. Since women are into relationships, they are more apt to want to go to counseling, or talk through a conflict. When a man is also a nonexpressive and gets silent and withdraws in a conflict situation, everyone suffers. When we withdraw or run away from a conflict situation, it shows little regard for the relationship. It's insulting and demeaning and leaves the other partner helpless and hopeless. I value Barb as the greatest person in my life besides Jesus Christ. I'm so glad we have the quick listening tool to help us talk back and forth in a conflict. It has given both of us so much hope.

For sure there are some women who are nonexpressives like me, so whether it's your husband or wife who withdraws in conflict, help them learn to communicate by being a better listener. If they attack in conflict, ask them to give you a little more time to get in touch with your feelings. Barb thinks the nonexpressive has the hardest job, but I really feel the expressive's job is harder because usually the nonexpressive is so fragile.

Barb: As I have said, conflict is neither good nor bad, it just is. It is okay to be angry, but the problem comes in how we handle our anger. Do you force someone like Chuck to talk when you realize he can't really tell you how he feels, and cause him to feel attacked? On the other hand, do you withdraw in anger when a person like me wants to talk it out and give no hope the problem will ever be solved? Remember, God is the author of marriage harmony. When we are obedient to the principles and commandments He has written in the Bible, then we have a chance to make our marriage everything God wants it to be.

Now let's take a look at one of the most cutting ways we hurt each other. The instrument of destruction is the tongue.

14

IT WAS ONLY
A HELPFUL HINT

Chuck: As I have mentioned before, because we have so many differences in a marriage, it's easy to look at our mate as *wrong* rather than just *different*. Earlier in our marriage both Barb and I tried to make each other into another one of us, and it didn't work. The way we often did this was by giving critical comments about our spouse's faults and differences. All this did was drive us further apart from what God had in mind when He designed marriage partners to be completers of each other. Hopefully by the time you finish this book, you'll be able to appreciate and even thank God for the differences He has designed in your husband or wife.

Matthew 7:1–5 shows what our focus should be in relationships and especially in marriage: "Don't criticize, and then you won't be criticized. For others will treat you as you treat them. And why worry about a speck in the eye of a brother [husband/wife] when you have a board in your own? Should you say, 'Friend, let me help you get that speck out of your eye,' when you can't even see because of the board in your own? Hypocrite! First get rid of the board. Then you can see to help your brother."

It's interesting to note the original language suggests the speck and the board in this passage are made out of the same material. This supports the idea we tend to sense our own weaknesses in others. If we have a pride problem, we immediately spot the egotist. If we have a sensual problem, we are aware of the sexual vibrations given off by another person. If we are lazy, we get irritated when others don't carry their load.

I also like the fact God chose eye surgery as his example, because the eye is the most tender part of our body. When a person gets something in his or her eye, I'm told a doctor clamps the head in a viselike arrangement and with a steady hand, carefully and tenderly lifts the particle out. That's a beautiful picture of how we are to take specks out of other people's eyes—carefully and tenderly.

Yes, there *are* times when God asks you and I to help each other with our blind spots, but at least in my experience, these times are quite rare. God seems to be more excited when I pay attention to my *own* weaknesses rather than dwelling on other people's shortcomings—especially any that Barb might have. Rather than worrying about her weaknesses, I'm much better off taking advantage of her strengths.

Barb: I don't have any weaknesses, remember?

Chuck: Oh, that's right. How could I have forgotten that? It's quite an awesome privilege having a perfect wife, but I still feel criticized once in a while. This is hard for wives when we take their comments as criticism. If a woman gives her feelings or makes a suggestion, often her husband will feel put down and a failure. He is hurt—chewed up, spit out, and kicked in the stomach. This is *not* what the woman intends. She just wants to give some helpful hints to make their lives better. She, on the other hand, is in a bind if she *doesn't* say something because he then continues the activity she doesn't like or is not good for the relationship. She feels hurt that he doesn't notice she is sad. She feels stabbed, wounded, unappreciated, and degraded. She's giving a helpful hint. He feels criticized. It's hard to get much further apart than this in the perception of what the wife is saying when she tries to give her opinion.

Barb: The age-old problem is how does a wife give her opinion so her husband does not feel like a two-year-old and that she is being his mother? When husbands tell us they don't like it done like that, or they do like it done this way, a woman will do her best to do what he wants. But when we tell our husbands how we like things done, and things don't change, we're caught in a trap. If we *don't* tell them again, nothing will ever change. There's a chance for a root of bitterness to start growing, and he's going to wonder why we seem distant. If we *do* tell them again, we're nagging, we're trying to tell them what to do, we're treating them like a two-year-old. Worst of all, we're trying to be their mother.

This isn't our motivation because we think they have just forgotten how we wanted it done. If they only remembered, they would want to please us like we want to please them. So we tell them again. Dr. Deborah Tannen in her book *You Just Don't Understand* says each time we wives tell our husbands to do something they put off doing it until it looks like *their* idea. When the request is repeated again, the woman gets accused of nagging!

While criticism is hard to hear, the intent to criticize is not always present. A wrong perception interprets the words as criticism.

On the other hand, remember the Lord tells us wives to build our husbands up and make them feel special. If we do enough of *that,* maybe our husbands won't take everything we say as criticism.

Chuck: One of the most helpful books I have ever read on criticism is called *The One Minute Manager*. The whole idea of the book is to catch people doing things *right*. All of us are prone to criticize, complain, and cut down the people around us. It's like noticing a black dot on a white piece of paper. We don't appreciate all the white paper. We just focus on the black dot. This idea of catching our wife or husband doing things right does not come naturally for us, so we need reminders. I suggest putting a little sticker of some kind on the mirror where you do your repairs in the morning. Every day when we men shave or when you women fix your hair, we would be reminded to praise, not tear down, the people around us—especially husbands and wives.

Wives, here are some suggestions as to what you could do. Your husband needs praise for doing things right. I think one of the reasons you don't always praise your husband for doing things right is because you feel it is his reasonable service. So what's the big deal. That's what he *should* do in the situation. The problem is that one of a man's greatest needs is to be approved of, admired, and built up. When he does something for you out of gut-level obedience to God and gets no praise, then in time he'll subconsciously feel, "Why do it? She doesn't notice or appreciate it." But from your standpoint as a woman, you thought it was what he should do, and it wasn't necessary to say anything. I suggest praising him when he goes to the wedding without complaining, or puts the plastic in the right place in the dishwasher, or helps you around the house, or plays with the kids, or goes to church, or spends time visiting with you. I hope you'll get all excited, because he is doing this out of obedience and his love for you, not because it comes naturally to him.

On the other hand, we men need to realize that when our wives give us some helpful little hints, they are not trying to dominate or "jerk us around," as one man put it. From the depth of their hearts they want to help us. They are shocked when we are hurt. That was not what they meant at all. After I realized it was natural for Barb to want to help me because she values our relationship, I began to feel *grateful* that Barb cared enough for me to be concerned about what I wore, whether I took my pills, how fast I drove, or what I ate. She's a wonderful partner, and I would not be anything without her love, help, and support. Now I'm not saying this comes easy. It is a process, and we men will always flinch a bit when we're told that something we did was wrong. Since women get most of their self-esteem from how their home looks, much of what we men would term *criticism* is a natural concern that women have about keeping their home in good shape.

I have an office in our home, and one morning Barb came down the stairs and we hugged. Then she backed up to me for a neck rub. We had given our marriage seminar for a church the night before; she had a big family dinner coming up; we were about to leave for a Pro Athlete's Outreach Conference; and she had her Tuesday Bible study to study for. So she was tense and ached all over. She said with a twinkle in her eye and a smile, "It must have been all my years of marriage with you that are causing my stress." I replied I could only remember two times when I was the one to cause her stress. One was back on June 15, 1984, and one on January 7, 1997. She has had a wonderfully stress-free life since then. However, some stress for *me* was about to happen.

I usually put the water on in the morning for coffee. If Barb isn't up by the time it is hot, I will also *make* the coffee. This particular morning I couldn't find the filters. Barb has two areas where she keeps supplies: in a large cupboard in the kitchen, and out in the garage. I scoured the two areas but found no filters. So I just ate my breakfast and was reading the paper when Barb came down. I told her we were out of coffee filters. She went over to the *cake mix* drawer and there were the filters. That's not even *logical*. It doesn't make sense to have coffee filters in the cake mix drawer. That would have been the *last* place I would have looked for coffee filters, but it seemed to make sense to her somehow.

Barb: It wasn't the cake mix drawer, it was the miscellaneous drawer. Makes sense to *me*.

Chuck: I didn't even know we *had* a miscellaneous drawer. Anyway, as I was in the process of making the coffee, she asked if I was washing out the coffee pot with soap in the morning before I made the coffee. I could faintly remember a discussion on this topic some years before, but it had not seared into my brain in any way. I always washed the coffee pot out with pure tap water but was not aware that I had to do more. When she asked me about washing it out with soap, my eyes rolled back in my head. I became dizzy. I had this sick feeling rushing through my system. I was faint, and my liver began to quiver. I was suffering what many husbands experience. I mentioned this malady in my book *Men: Some Assembly Required*. The medical term for it is RO. It is a horrible sickness that causes great stress to a man's heart, kidneys, liver, pancreas, thyroid, stomach, large colon, lymph system, and brain stem. Usually it is fatal, but not always. The expanded name for this terminal disease in the medical books is Rule Overload or RO for short. The husband can accumulate only so many rules, and then his brain goes *blotto*. Anyway, I now wash out the coffee pot with soap in the morning before I make the coffee. It usually takes me until noon to get all the suds out of that small pot, but I don't have anything else to do anyway. Actually, we have joined the elite by serving flavored coffee. I'm sure you have heard of mocha, and Irish cream for coffee flavorings. At our home you have your choice of Ivory, Borax, or Dial, and the pot is very clean.

Barb: Washing out the oils from the old coffee keeps the new coffee tasting good longer. And about Rule Overload. Chuck came home laughing all the way from his men's Bible study because the men had discussed the rules their wives had for them. I asked him, "Why is it when I worked for you and you wanted things done a certain way, it was *just the way we do business!* And when I have a certain way to keep my home running properly it's called *rules?*

Chuck: Here are a few more of Barb's rules:

RULE: *Don't wear pants with spots on them.*

I think the spots on my pants tell a beautiful story. It means I had a wonderful time with the grandkids the last time they came over. There's a bit of chocolate syrup, a smudge from a Tootsie Pop, some ink from the flair pen we drew pictures with, a bit of grass stain from the wrestling match, grains of sand from the sandbox, some moss from the swing set, and a little paint from the wooden animals we made in the garage. I believe anyone seeing those spots would just praise God that here is a grandfather who is having fun with his grandkids. It should be a matter of adoration, not criticism, but I change pants since I'm committed to Barb.

Barb: Chuck would wear the same pair of pants for weeks if I didn't mention he had spots on them. Also, if his hands slide into his pockets too many times between washings, I can't get the dirt stains out of his pants. I'm glad he changes his pants with a good attitude when I mention it.

RULE: *Be "sparkly" at weddings.*

Chuck: I probably offend many of my young friends when I'm honest about weddings. I've already told you how my whole *life* screeches to a sudden stop when I go to a wedding. No longer can I work on God's goals to change the world through a book or video or radio program I am working on. No longer am I accessible to the phone to help desperate people with marriage problems. No longer am I able to read God's Word and learn from it. No longer is *anything* possible, except to sit in a hard church pew and suffer. If they had any decent magazines in the pew, it would make things a little better. About the most exciting thing I've ever found was a booklet on the Miocene Council of 1320 and the discussion of the dispensational ramifications of the apostle Paul's trip to Troas. I'm surrounded by the ponderous thoughts of the ages, and Barb wants me to *sparkle*. She sees my body there but says no one is home. I fail more than I succeed at this, but I do try to be sparkly since I'm committed to Barb. And if you want to discuss the Miocene Council's thoughts, give me a call.

RULES: *Don't spray the windows with water when bathing the grandchildren.*
Don't use so much bubble soap in the grandchild's bath.
Put all the toys back after the grandchild's bath.
Mop up the four inches of standing water on the floor after the grandchild's bath.

Chuck: I don't even need to comment on this. You can plainly see how illogical these rules are, and how they take the fun out of life.

Barb: I don't need to comment on this either!

RULE: *Put gas in Barb's car if I use it.*

Chuck: Barb and I both have our own cars. I use mine for work and she uses hers mostly for family. When we ride together in her car, I usually drive, even though she is equally as good a driver. In fact, she's probably a better driver than I am, but this is the way we are comfortable. We were driving somewhere recently in Barb's car and she noticed the gas gauge was nearly empty. She berated me a little bit for not getting gas.

I said, "I never drive this car."

She couldn't believe what she was hearing. *"Of course* you drive this car. That's what you are *doing* at this moment!" I begged to differ. I was not driving the car. *We* were driving the car. I never drive Barb's car unless she is with me. For some reason she thought I drove her car. Driving the car means to me that I drive it by myself. I never drive her car alone. She's always with me, but I still got in trouble for not getting gas. This is not fair because I never drive her car! I'm being criticized for something I never do.

Barb: I didn't berate him. I just mentioned the gas tank was nearly empty. He took it from there and this has been one of our ongoing discussions. Does he drive my car or not?

RULE: *Don't cut anything out of the newspaper until Barb has finished reading it.*

Chuck: The problem with this rule is I never remember to cut out the cartoon or article I wanted to save until after the garbage man has come and gone with the papers. And besides, most of the time the other side of the article I want just has the Chicago hog prices on it, or an ad for seeking enlightenment through crystals or something. I know these are not things Barb cares about, so I take the chance and cut them out before Barb reads the paper. Now I realize this does not fit with my total commitment statements, but this is something I must do because we have lost so many wonderful items. She's resigned to this fact, but I'm very careful to show her the hog prices before I take the piece downstairs to my office.

Barb: Chuck is not aware, most the time, what's important to me. So I asked him just to let me know and I'll save the paper for him or I'll cut it out. But sometimes he goes ahead and cuts it out himself. He's more careful now, though.

Chuck: Some of the guys in the Bible study were criticized by their wives for having some old cars in the backyard. The women had forgotten that when they were dating they thought the cars were cute. Now they are *junk*. I think farm women seem to have an extra measure of grace from the Lord for some reason. When I was working on the farm growing up, I noticed every time a piece of equipment would break, my uncles would haul it up behind the garage out by the barn. I'm sure they wanted it close to the shop so they could fix it. But I guess they were always too busy, so it just sat there and rusted. As a young boy, I loved wandering around all those old cars and farm equipment. I think my uncle Clarence would be happier in the city now that he is slowing down a bit. I wonder if he would sell me his old place so I could bring some of the stuff home to put in my yard in Seattle. I know Barb would treasure those old memories of my growing-up years. I hope I can get the combines in under the trees. So what if I break off a branch or two. They'll grow back in twenty or thirty years. No big deal.

Barb: I'm so thankful Chuck didn't get into saving big junk. Now we live in a community with a covenant that says we *have* to keep our yards neat and tidy. Am I glad! I teased him a lot about the neighborhood covenant when we bought this house. He's lost his chance to be Uncle Clarence.

Chuck: I was feeling pretty righteous about this burden of rules we men have to carry, when Barb burst my balloon. She said a home is a woman's workplace even if she has a job outside the home. Barb asked, "Don't those of you in business have rules for people who work there?"

I told her, "Absolutely not." We let the employees do anything they want anytime they want to do it. There are no rules in business. We just ask that they make us a little profit and everyone's happy. I think she was a little offended, because I was making jokes about her rules. Well, at least they feel like rules to me. She said they are guidelines for making our home run smoothly and efficiently, and they help a husband to live in harmony with his wife.

I follow the rules because I'm committed to Barb, but there are some times I feel a little bit destroyed. It's not Barb's fault. She is just trying to manage a home, and one of the big obstacles in that process is *me*. Actually, the whole thing boils down to my *reaction* to her helpful little hints. She is beside the point. I am the one who needs to handle the criticism and take it in the way she means it.

Barb: It is not criticism. It's probably something I've asked Chuck to do, and he's forgotten how I wanted him to do it. So he calls it criticism.

Chuck: At least if *feels* like criticism. I know she doesn't do this to tear me down even though I feel torn down at times. Men, if our greatest goal is to love and serve our wife like God has asked us to, why is it we are not *grateful* when she tells us something that would help us serve her better? We are really honoring the Lord doing this. Why is it so hard to put aside our prideful desire for control, and look at our wife's opinions as ideas that would make our lives more fruitful and satisfying?

I wish every husband could do marriage right like you women seem to do it naturally. We husbands do make dumb mistakes from time to time. We *should* pay more attention to details and appreciate the home more. But the question I want to pose to you ladies is this: What do you *gain* from criticizing him? When you complain about what he wears, does, looks like, or eats, what do you gain? If you criticize him for playing too much, working too much, not coming home early enough, or not playing with the kids enough, what do you gain? When you express your concern that he is not the spiritual leader he *should* be, or doesn't talk to your mother enough, or hates weddings, or watches too much TV, or slurps his soup, or trims the wrong tree, what do you gain? I know what you *get*. You get defensiveness, silence, probably some anger, and withdrawal. He feels destroyed, inadequate, and goes to his shop or work to grieve. If you feel it is worth doing this to get revenge on your husband, then that's your decision. But I think you'll lose in the long run.

As I write these words I feel like I am being much harder on women than men, but I don't mean it that way. Men actually have the harder role. We have to give up our lives for our wives. That means we have to put aside all of our own desires and serve our wives. The problem is we men are not into relationships as much as you women are. We make more mistakes which generate helpful little hints from our wives. We get defensive, and you get hurt. I wish I had a good answer for this, but I remember one time in our Sunday school class we posed the question: How can a woman give her husband an opinion without him feeling like a two-year-old? There was great silence in the room, and it continues to this day. I don't have a clue how you can. I know that's not much hope, but the only answer Barb and I could come up with is that it *is* impossible—unless the man has enough of the Holy Spirit in his life to cause him to do what *he* should do as a godly husband.

One thing you wives might try is using the grandfather principle on your husband. I was thinking about this just yesterday when my precious grandson Caleb came over to visit. I can't think of *one* thing that would alter my unconditional love for him. He can't drop food too much, or spill his milk too much, or cry too much, or get too dirty, or too whiny, or need the same story read too much, or wreck the car, or get a girl pregnant, or go to prison. I would grieve over some of these things, but *none* of them would cause me to cut off fellowship and support and love. I would *always* be his—unconditionally.

Even though we men should be the initiators of God's *agape* love, here's a suggestion for you women. Why don't you unilaterally try this with your husband for just one week? Don't do it any longer than that, because he might have a heart attack. Pre-program yourself every morning to give your husband *nothing* but *unconditional* love for the entire week with no opinions on anything. And if you should blow it, ask his forgiveness quickly. Do you know what I think might happen? He might feel so good he just might begin meeting some of *your* needs. But remember, no expectations. He might not. He might just sop up your love like a sponge and want another week without giving you anything in return, but that's okay. God will bless you for a good try. If I were a betting man, I'd put my money on you having a wonderful response from your husband. No guarantees—but the odds are in your favor.

And here's another project. Too many times women don't appreciate what their husbands are *not* doing: things like *not* having an affair, or *not* having an alcohol or drug problem, or *not* beating the kids, or *not* hating Christ, or *not* working too much. What I suggest you do is list all the things he *is* doing right and praise him for those things. Usually a woman's list is long and their tears are real as they reflect on what they already have. My goal in all this, women, is for *your* needs to be met. But you can't do it through criticism even if your heart doesn't have that as a motive.

Okay, guys, here are *your* marching orders. To start with, you have to be Spirit-controlled. You must spend enough time in the Bible so its principles can invade every cell of your mind and body. That way you begin to do things God's way automatically, which is, of course, contrary to our human nature.

We usually think of ourselves first. God says put others first, especially our wives and children, no matter how they act, look, or whether they give us opinions.

The word picture I like is from athletics. The football coach works hard and long to get his linemen to block on instinct. He doesn't want them to think about fundamentals like foot stance and hand placement. The minute the ball is snapped he wants the player to fire off the ball without thinking and do the job. That's what God wants. He wants us to be so familiar with the basics of Christianity—love, joy, peace, patience, kindness, goodness, faithfulness, gentleness, and self-control—that when the ball is snapped (your wife gives you a helpful hint, or doesn't meet your needs, or someone cuts you off on the freeway, or your kids pull a dumb stunt, or your boss has an unrealistic expectation), you automatically react in a way that is honoring to God. You do the right thing without much thinking or analyzing. You react because God's principles are so ingrained into your personhood, you can't act any other way. And the greatest gift we men can give to our wives is God's love as outlined in 1 Corinthians 13:

A husband's love is patient.
A husband's love is kind.
A husband's love is never jealous.
A husband's love is never boastful.
A husband's love is never proud.
A husband's love is never selfish.
A husband's love is never rude.
A husband's love does not demand its own way
A husband's love is not irritable.
A husband's love is not touchy.
A husband's love never holds grudges.
A husband's love doesn't notice when his wife does something wrong.
A husband's love is never glad about injustice.
A husband's love rejoices when truth wins.
A husband's love is loyal.
A husband's love believes in his wife.

A husband's love expects the best from his wife.

A husband's love defends his wife.

God holds you and me responsible for the health of the home. In 1 Timothy 3:4–5 it says a man must manage his own home well before becoming a leader in the church. With Jesus' emphasis on the leader as a servant, I stretch this to mean we shouldn't even ask a man to sweep out the church unless his own family is well managed. How can he help the church family when his own family is not in order? It's a big challenge, but we can do it—because God will give us the strength to love and serve our family the way he loves us— unconditionally.

One of the greatest tools for married couples is a book called *The Five Love Languages* by Dr. Gary Chapman. He suggests there are five basic love languages: touch, meaningful time, serving, giving gifts, and encouraging words. The problem is we tend to talk to others in our *own* love language. A person with touch as a love language is usually a huggy person. They might reach out and touch you on the arm to make a point. They may pat you on the back or reach over and take your hand for a minute.

A person with meaningful time as their love language wants deep, intimate sharing of their life with another person by spending quality time with each other.

A person who serves likes to do things for people. They will help clean up the kitchen, pick up the chairs at church, mow the neighbor's lawn when they go on vacation, or bring you a hot cup of coffee.

Some people show love by giving gifts, and other people show love by encouraging words, saying things like "You did a great job today," "You're the best employee we have," "That solo was one of the finest I've heard," "I love the way you drive so carefully."

Dr. Chapman tells of a couple that came to him for counseling. The wife said, "My husband just doesn't love me anymore."

The husband said, "What do you mean? I wash the dishes while you're at work, take care of the kids when they come from school, do most of the cooking, mow the lawn, do the laundry, and keep the house clean."

She said, "Yes, but you don't *talk* to me."

He said, "Yes, I do. I say hello, how was work, what do you want to watch on TV?"

He was talking to her in *his* love language—serving. She was not feeling loved because her love language was spending meaningful time by talking and communicating. Some husbands are amazed their wives don't feel loved after being given diamonds, big houses, nice cars, fur coats, and other material things. His language might be giving gifts; the wife's language might be touching or talking. The idea is to find out what your mate's love language is, and then talk to them in that language, rather than in your own.

Be sure to read Dr. Chapman's book, and then take your husband or wife on as a project. Unfortunately, Barb has all *five* love languages, so that really keeps me hopping. But usually a person will have one way that makes them feel especially loved. This is a perfect antidote for criticism, and we recommend it very highly.

Now let's talk about an emotion that we all experience at one time or another. For some of us it is a very troubling area of our life. For others it can be as bad as murder, or it can result in divorce.

15

LOSING CONTROL

Chuck: I guess anger is one of the most common emotions we humans have. The cost of human anger is incalculable. It is beyond the mind's capability to comprehend the damage, hurt, sorrow, and agony that angry humans have inflicted on other humans. As I write these words, we seem to be having a rash of shootings in the country by angry people. Just this week an ex-boyfriend killed a mom and her three kids in a fit of anger. The average newspaper probably has forty to fifty examples a day of anger gone ballistic. Multiply that by the number of communities that have daily newspapers. Add in the holocaust, the genocides, divorces, hostile takeovers in business resulting in down-sizing which affects millions of families, world wars, tribal warfare, religious warfare—the toll is staggering.

On the other hand, God never promised us a perfect world. In fact, He made it very clear in the instructional manual He left us that anger, greed, immorality, lust, murder, trials, and tragedies will be the hallmark of the human existence. He gives us a way out, however, through the death of His Son Jesus. But anger is one of those lingering problems that will affect us personally and as a world until Christ returns to put an end to it.

Let me go back a few years and describe the time when I was learning the most about this emotion called anger. I had a small advertising agency that handled some large accounts. I had chosen to stay small and do much of the work myself with only a small staff. This had its upsides and downsides. The upside was being able to do more personal service for my clients, which I think played a part in keeping them as long as I did. The downside is the necessity to be involved in many of the details of getting the job done. Maybe this is primarily a management style. I have friends in business who do their best work by helping people do *their* best work. Others of us prefer to have a hands-on approach. I don't think either one is better than the other, but I do believe being in control of your own destiny does have some advantages.

I worked very hard at the office, and once in a while I would get bitter and resentful and feel overwhelmed. I wanted to keep our advertising business healthy in order to pay for the various ministries God had given us. All I really had to sell was me, and I wanted to serve my customers so well they wouldn't even consider looking for another agency. I did a lot of things free to show them I could give as well as receive in business.

Staying so close to the business, however, meant I had to be involved in much more detail than I would have if I had delegated all the client contact to an employee. Problems came when a client wanted to know something like, "Why are we paying a premium for drive time in Prosser when the city is only two miles wide?"

I needed to be able to give him an instant answer as often as possible and not say, "I'll get back to you." Keeping a healthy business paid for our ministries, so my clients came first and deserved my close attention. I worked hard at my secular work and made that a very high priority. I realized, however, that the things I do here on earth will only last for a time, and there are hundreds of opportunities to affect people for eternity. It was (and is) a constant battle of priorities.

As I reflected on my situation once in a while, I would think how nice it might be to minister full time some day. So at one of my regular business meetings with the Lord, I would suggest He find me a nice little gold mine close to the house, or maybe in the basement, where I could go and chip off what I needed that month to live, and then spend my time having counseling breakfasts, lunches, and dinners, writing books, and loving my Christian and non-Christian friends full time. The Lord would think about my suggestion for a few minutes and then remind me that some of the people I want to relate to wouldn't give me the time of day if they didn't know I experienced the same pressures they did like profit and loss statements, employee turnover, time pressures, pension plans, and overhead growth.

So after the Lord once again reminded me why he had me in secular business, I returned to my messy desk and once again put my nose into the day-to-day details of the agency. Meanwhile, I squeezed in early breakfasts, long lunches, and late phone conversations with the people I felt God had asked me to love for him. As the problems and challenges of the business began to mount and more and more people came into my life for me to love for Christ, the time pressures became almost unbearable. It got so bad sometimes that I resented the next person who just needed a few minutes of my time. Maybe they needed a "simple" slide presentation for their church, or some financial advice, or employment counseling, or help to find God's will for their life in some area.

I know God didn't want me to be bitter, resentful, and burned out, so I started cutting back on those things I found myself involved in—good things, but maybe not the *best* things at that point in my life.

It comforted me as I was buried up to my eyes in projects to reflect on what Christ said at the end of his ministry. He said his job was finished, yet there were lepers, blind people, and other hurting folks all around him. This suggested to me I should be very careful with my priorities to make sure I am working on the most important thing at any given moment. If there are some projects I don't get done, that's really God's problem. He will either impress on me to find the time to get them done, or give someone else the blessing. When I get all tied up in knots, I really don't do a good job at anything.

I'm especially touched by the story of Jesus Christ *also* feeling burned out at one point in His earthly ministry. Mark 4:35–41 tells about one day when Jesus said something like this to His disciples: "I am going to go across this lake and leave the crowds of people behind. I don't want anyone to follow me. Phil, Pete, see that no one puts a boat in the water because I am up to *here* with people and I need some *space! Understood?*" Okay, I put words in Jesus' mouth. But it does say he left the crowd behind and crossed the lake to get away. Does that offend you? For me that simply makes Jesus more real, and it's comforting for me to know that he knows how I feel when I'm overwhelmed. Jesus Christ also got angry and frustrated. Remember what he did to the money-changers in the temple? He also wept. Before he started his teaching ministry, I'm sure he worked hard at his father's carpenter shop. I'll bet he banged his thumb with a hammer. Picture this. There's Jesus working on a wheel for Octavius, the phone rings and it's Flavius wondering if his oxen yoke was done yet. Just then Rufus dropped by with a little suicide problem, and Jesus was late for a counseling lunch, and his lumber vendor with cedar from Lebanon was waiting outside to find out where to put his load of materials. I've *been* there, and I'm *so glad* my Lord has, too.

One time as my anger, frustration, and bitterness were increasing daily because of time pressures, there came a Saturday when I had no immediate deadlines. I had only one person coming over for counseling. It was almost a free day, and I relished the thought of puttering around my workshop or playing some tennis. Maybe I would read a book or do some of the other 119 projects I hadn't been able to get to.

That day the sun came out, brighter than usual for Seattle. After breakfast, my sweet wife Barb approached me with some projects to do. We had invited a group of people over for the next day. I was to bring up the tables, put chlorine in the pool, clean the filter, lay out the pickle-ball court, prepare the barbecue, clean off my desks, pick up junk in the basement, sweep out the garage, sort my books into piles, and a few other things on her list. Maybe you don't have piles of books in your life, but both Barb and I read before we go to sleep at night. She is very organized and when she starts a book she usually finishes it, so she only has one or two books by her bed. As I mentioned earlier, I usually have lots of books going at once and will read them depending on my mood. They are all stacked by my bed. If I want to stay awake, I read a spy novel. The kind where the hero escapes from the jaws of the shark just as the airplane crashes into the sea barely missing him just as the natives start throwing spears at him from the river bank and the poison gas gets thicker as the alligator catches his scent. Or if I want to go to sleep, I'll read a history book. I love history, but it's a little dry at times and off to dreamland I go. Sorting books into piles on Saturday is something I can handle. No problem.

Then Barb threw in the ringer. She also wanted the pie cherries picked from a tree we had in our backyard. For eleven of the twelve years we had lived in our home at that time, the squirrels had eaten every cherry before we had a chance to get out to pick them. They would even crawl along the branches upside down to get the last ones. But this particular year the little monsters were asleep or on vacation or something. Who knows? Anyway, the tree was loaded with cherries, and there wasn't a squirrel in sight. There is something chemical between a woman and a tree because Barb has this thing about fruit being picked when it is ripe. As far as I am concerned, those cherries were to feed God's furry little friends, and we were meant to buy what we need at the supermarket. There's a Scripture on this subject in Proverbs 12:10 that says: "A good man is concerned for the welfare of his animals."

I think this makes it very clear the cherries should go to the squirrels. Anyway, there they were—luscious, red, fat, ripe, juicy cherries, crying out to Barb, "Pick us!" Where are you, you dumb squirrels? Why haven't you done your job this year? Now, I realize some of you cherry pickers can't relate to what I'm feeling. You and Barb want the cherries to put into pies we can't eat anyway because we're too fat. I couldn't believe I was being asked to sacrifice my precious Saturday for something like this! But I got the dumb ladder, the stupid bucket on a wire that hangs on my belt, and climbed this ridiculous tree to pick some idiotic cherries that seemed to be splitting their seams laughing at me. From my standpoint, it was stupid for me to use the time for which I had longed and prayed—just a little extra free time from the pressures of work and ministries—to do what I *had* to do rather than just once doing what I *wanted* to do. Here I was picking dumb things that Barb could buy at the supermarket for seventy-nine cents a pound, and as far as stewardship is concerned, I could sit at my typewriter and make many times that amount in the same period of time. It just didn't make sense.

I can also hear all of you fruit pickers taking me to task for wanting to waste fruit. It wasn't wasted. The squirrels ate it. It was fantastic nutrition for them. Besides, we were taking care of God's creatures as Proverbs instructs us to do. God does not want us to be cruel to His animals, condemning them to a long cold winter without proper nutrition.

That Saturday brought a fitting end to a whole week of anger and frustration. I won't bore you with all the details, but it was terrible. I had so many expectations and so little fulfillment! My typewriter broke down, two of my employees had traffic accidents, the copy machine broke down, I couldn't find essential films and tapes, and Saturday was just the last straw.

And then I found out what was the matter. I had agreed to speak at our church on Sunday evening, and the topic I had chosen months ago was anger. The Lord was making me *live* what I was going to teach. He was intending to speak through my experiences to make them real to the people who would hear my message. They could only relate to me if they felt I knew what I was talking about and had lived it. Most people are not into theory—at least I'm not. I believe pastors and teachers should *never* teach anything unless they have filtered it through their life. If they don't do this, then it is strictly book knowledge and doesn't do anyone much good. Christ didn't spend much time behind a pulpit. He was in the street surrounded by the hurting people who could relate to his love and care. We have to be real, and that includes admitting our faults, our anger, and our struggles. And by the way, since we're talking about anger and its causes, be sure not to blame other people and situations for it. People and situations don't cause our anger. They just reveal the anger *in* us. We have the anger inside. People and situations just make it come out.

When I began my study on anger, I first went to Strong's concordance to see how many times anger was mentioned in the Bible. I found three entire columns of single-spaced Scripture references relating to anger. Much of it talked about God's anger. For instance:

> But Moses pleaded, "O Lord, I'm just not a good speaker. I never have been, and I'm not now, even after you have spoken to me, for I have a speech impediment." "Who makes mouths?" Jehovah asked him. "Isn't it I, the Lord? Who makes a man so that he can speak or not speak, see or not see, hear or not hear? Now go ahead and do as I tell you, for I will help you to speak well, and I will tell you what to say." But Moses said, "Lord, please! Send someone else." Then the Lord became angry. (Exodus 4:10–14a)

I can just feel God's anger in this passage. He had given Moses all the gifts and talents he needed to do God's work, but Moses still had no self-confidence and wanted God to send someone else. God got angry with Moses, and I'm afraid he probably gets angry with me, too, as I forget once in a while that *he* is in control, not me.

Jesus expressed anger, too:

> While in Capernaum Jesus went over to the synagogue again, and
> noticed a man there with a deformed hand. Since it was the Sabbath,
> Jesus' enemies watched him closely. Would he heal the man's hand? If
> he did, they planned to arrest him! Jesus asked the man to come and
> stand in front of the congregation. Then turning to his enemies he
> asked, "Is it all right to do kind deeds on Sabbath days? Or is this a
> day for doing harm? Is it a day to save lives or to destroy them?" But
> they wouldn't answer him. Looking around at them angrily, for he
> was deeply disturbed by their indifference to human need, he said to
> the man, "Reach out your hand." He did, and instantly his hand was
> healed! (Mark 3:1–5)

I get the impression from this last Scripture and others that the religious
leaders of his day were the ones who were most often on the receiving end of
Christ's anger. But unlike Christ's anger, mine is not righteous. Mine is self-
centered.

Just what is anger, this frustration, this rage that sometimes tears us apart
and makes us explode, hurting the ones we love? Sometimes it surprises us as
we wonder where in the world *that* came from. Anger is an emotion caused
by the frustration of our goals and desires. It can be brought on by people,
situations, or things.

I guess we were born into the world angry. After spending nine beautiful
months in that warm nest with every one of our needs being met, all of a sudden we experience cold air, a slap on the bottom, and a bunch of strangers
standing around with video cameras. Soon, however, we find comfort at our
mother's breast as we feel her warmth once again. If we stayed dry and were
fed regularly and cuddled a lot, we felt pretty good about life. But try to frus-
trate one of our goals and look out! We got red-in-the-face *angry!*

From reading the book *Facing Anger* by Norman Rohrer and Philip
Sutherland, I learned there are several basic reasons for anger. The first one is
the desire to feel powerful. We feel weak if our behavior is determined by
other people, so we become angry in order to restore our sense of power. The

person who feels powerful doesn't need anger. The person who doesn't worry about tomorrow has power, but the worrier feels weak because he doesn't know what tomorrow will bring. There are all kinds of power struggles: conflicts between husband and wife, parent and child, brothers and sisters, employees and bosses. I can't think of a relationship where there might not be a struggle for power.

Another thing making some of us angry is having too many things to do in too little time. I've already given you some experiences on this from my own life. I have always prided myself in getting a lot done, even though this pressure makes me angry at times when I get into a time squeeze. I even did six things at once recently. I was dubbing a tape, working on a slide presentation, putting a record on a cassette, filling the fountain, flushing the car radiator, and making some audio copies on my tape dubbing machine. After I finished that record-breaking accomplishment, I rushed upstairs to share this triumph with Barb. But guess what? She wasn't the least bit impressed.

I had read the book *Type A Behavior and Your Heart* which seemed to indicate Type A people were always on the go, made impossible deadlines for themselves, hated red lights, had lots of stress, couldn't relax, and were more prone to heart attacks than Type B people. Type B folks relax a little more, don't mind traffic signals, do only what they could do in the time allowed, and usually do only one thing at a time. Barb said I wasn't supposed to glory in my being a Type A. I was supposed to try to be a Type B. Who wants to be a Type B, for goodness sake? We'd still be riding in covered wagons if some Type A in our history hadn't decided to put a motor in the dumb thing because they wanted to go a little faster.

I really get angry when I'm late, which is often caused by trying to do too much at the last minute, or having too many people demanding my time. Remember, anger is not produced by a situation so much as it is by our interpretation of the situation.

I mentioned earlier that Barb thinks red lights are ordained by God to bring order into our lives. From my standpoint, I *know* red lights are a tool of Satan to disrupt my schedule and make me angry. There's a red light on a street by our home that I've asked the city to remove. It is in a lonely part of the neighborhood protecting a street that is seldom used. In fact, only twice in recorded history has anyone come from the other direction. Once on May 14, 1933, Mazie Rathknocker lost her way and came up there, and the other time was August 23, 1962, when Henry Radburner took a wrong turn. Other than those two instances, no one has ever used that red light. And it irritates me to have to stop when no one ever comes the other way.

A loss of power also makes us angry. Many times people feel angry when a person close to them dies. They may even become angry at the dead person. Or we become angry when we lose our house in a flood, or a fire burns it to the ground, or a burglar cleans out the home, or a car accident leaves family members hospitalized. We feel absolutely helpless in such situations. The reason we get angry is that we have no power over the event.

Another cause of anger is a desire to be self-sufficient. The young child wants to tie their own shoes. The teenager wants to fix his own car. The young wife struggles to sew a dress. There's nothing wrong with trying to do these things, but when we fail at our task, we become angry and frustrated. We want to be in control, and sometimes this causes some of us, especially men, not to see doctors, not to seek counsel, not to weep, or not to ask someone for financial help. We want to do it ourselves, and when we lose control, we get angry.

Another cause of anger is wanting to feel important: to be first in line, president of the club, or captain of the team. We want to win at everything we try. Some of this drive for status can stem from childhood when someone in our lives told us we would never amount to anything, so we keep striving all our lives to prove them wrong. I had lunch once with a young man who was a workaholic—a driven man who was ruining his marriage in the process. During the conversation both of us found out he was still trying to prove to his father he was worth something. His father had been dead for ten years.

Another cause of anger is striving for perfection. The straight A student gets all bent out of shape when she gets a B. The concert pianist gets angry when she hits a wrong note. The mechanic swears when he strips a thread, the football player claps his hands in frustration when he fumbles the ball, and the softball player throws her bat when she strikes out. Many people feel they have to be perfect to be accepted. When they don't do a spectacular job, they feel like a failure and get angry. Sometimes we reach for unrealistic goals for which we do not have the ability, time, patience, or resources to reach.

I'm a perfectionist, so I really know all about this drive to be perfect. Earlier in my life when I would get to 80 percent of my goal, my authority, or the world around me would tell me I had done a good job. Sometimes I still felt bad though because I had not reached 100 percent. What I learned to do was give God the remaining 20 percent as long as I did the job that was expected of me and a little extra. The rest of my efforts to be perfect were only to try to make *me* feel worthwhile. I decided that striving for the extra 20 percent was not being a good steward of my time. This is not an excuse to do a poor job, however. It just releases us from unrealistic expectations of ourselves.

One of the big problems with perfectionists like me is we also expect perfection from our kids, our mates, our employees, and the people on the freeway. We get angry when we don't get it. People who see themselves as perfect have a hard time accepting criticism. It makes them angry to learn about their imperfections. It's also hard for perfectionists to ask forgiveness. I sometimes give an assignment to classes I teach. I tell them to go out and destroy an enemy during the next week. I had better quickly explain this does not mean murder. It means asking forgiveness for something we have done. When we do this, most of the time the other person ceases to be an enemy. Therefore, we have destroyed them as an enemy. In fact, many times they become our friends, believe it or not.

After hearing the assignment, one woman in class baked three pies because she was having trouble with three different neighborhood families. She took the pies to the people with whom she was having the difficulties and asked them to forgive her for her unloving attitude. She *healed* that neighborhood with three pies. God does powerful things through our lives when we do things his way.

Anger affects us physically too. When we become angry everything shuts down above the chin. Our blood goes to the muscles and inner organs, and the brain gets less blood than usual. Angry people don't think clearly. They say things they don't mean. You cannot reason with an angry person. Don't even try. Wait until they cool down a bit to begin logical conversations. Try to mirror back the anger if you can, so the other person can get rid of it rather than stuff it.

Well, I hope you can relate to my struggles with anger. If so, then I suggest you make a list of all the things that cause you to become angry, and then present your list to God. Ask him to help you control your anger so other people in your life will see his supernatural strength through you as you learn how to handle your anger. When you and I do this, we can then be of value to others who struggle with this same problem. They will see that a personal relationship with Jesus Christ is the answer to the strength we seem to have in handling our anger better than they can. However, if we don't handle it any better than our non-Christian friends do, why would they need a relationship with Christ? It's an awesome responsibility to be Jesus to the people who come into our life and show them how he can affect our everyday life. Handling anger God's way is one of the best ways to show his supernatural power in our lives.

Barb: Let's see what the Bible says about anger.

"Let all bitterness and wrath and anger and clamor and slander be put away from you, along with all malice" (Ephesians 4:31).

I see in this verse a progression of anger, especially as it relates to conflicts in our marriage relationships. It describes what happens when we don't handle our hurts and our anger properly. Let's take a look at the major words in the verse. Notice the significant progression as we examine these words in the same order Paul lists them:

Bitterness. This is a cutting, pricking sharpness. As a human emotion it's the feeling of hatred, resentment, and cynicism. Hebrews 12:15 says, "See to it that no one comes short of the grace of God; that no root of bitterness springing up causes trouble, and by it many be defiled." This is on the *inside* of us, although others can usually detect it even when we think we're hiding it. You may be sure bitterness affects those around you. A person is not bitter alone. A bitter person causes trouble because they show their bitterness with an angry outburst.

Wrath. This means passion. *Vine's Expository Dictionary of New Testament Words* explains it as hot anger, fierceness, an outburst of wrath, an agitated condition of the feelings. Now the bitterness has shown itself on the *outside*. We have a blowup and may even try to talk about the problem, but there is no resolution. It looks like the problem is over because it has been discussed. But it is not over. Then the next step is anger and it's *inside* the person again.

Anger. This means impulse. *Vine's* says it is a more settled or abiding condition of the mind, frequently with a view to taking revenge. *Webster* defines impulse as excitement to action arising from a state of mind or some stimulus. A sudden inclination to act without conscious thought. A motive or tendency coming from *within*.

First, we have bitterness on the inside, then the wrathful blowup on the outside, then we have anger on the inside again because the problem has never been solved. The other person involved in the conflict may think it was solved with the blowup, but in reality it wasn't.

Clamor. Suddenly, when everything seems to be going well in the relationship, something sets the person off again and the conflict is back on the *outside*. That's because anger has progressed to clamor—that is an outcry, or as *Vine's* describes it, "a tumult of controversy." This is when we say, "But we talked about this. Why are you bringing it up again? We just keep going over and over the same thing." This is because the problem was never solved in the first place. At the first outburst of anger one of the two parties withdrew and hoped the conflict would go away. But there is an outburst or clamor and you know it didn't go away. And because the problem was never talked out with understanding, it progresses and becomes slander.

Slander. This means evil speaking. *Vine's* calls it railing. In Greek it has the root words *blapto,* which means to injure, and *pheme,* which means speech. This is where we just don't care what we say. If it hurts someone else, so much the better. If someone feels injured, who cares. And this attitude leads to malice.

Malice. This means wickedness. *Vine's* says it is badness in quality and vicious in character. *Webster* defines it as active ill-will. It's the actual desire to harm another person. It involves spite and evil intent.

This is where the angry person plans to get back at the other person because they've been so hurt. They just don't care anymore. In fact, they have gone the opposite way from love. Now they not only want to hurt the other person, but they plan to.

And so there's a divorce. Can you see where it all starts? Conflict that's not handled well in marriage leads to bitterness, then wrath, anger, clamor, slander, and malice. And why wasn't the conflict handled well? Probably because of our own selfishness. We want our own way. We want to be served rather than serve each other. We think more highly of ourselves than we ought to think. We are not obedient. Obedient to what? The very next verse after this slippery progression of anger is Ephesians 4:32, which gives us this command: "And be kind to one another, tenderhearted, forgiving each other, just as God in Christ also has forgiven you."

We can cut out the root of bitterness at the very beginning by forgiving each other. We live in a world of people who feel they are victims. Victims of how they were raised or how they have been treated. It's always the other person's fault. People believe they just can't help themselves because after all it isn't their fault. I'd like to suggest that God has given us the solution to feeling victimized. He has told us to forgive.

I ran across this saying once: "Forgiveness is setting a person free and finding out that person was me." I believe so many people feel like victims because they are not willing to forgive. Forgiveness is giving up my right to hurt you because I think you have hurt me. It is not something we have to feel like doing. It's something we do because God commanded us to do it.

Another thing. When I found the Greek word for *anger* in Ephesians 4:31, I wondered if it was the same word Paul used in Ephesians 4:26 which says, "do not let the sun go down on your anger." It was. I believe it is not just the immediate feeling of anger we need to get rid of, but also the ongoing intent to get revenge. Revenge can be the silent treatment, not looking at a person, avoiding them, not showing love, not fixing meals (for the wife), not fixing broken things around the house when asked to do so (for the husband), withholding sex, buying what you know your partner does not want you to, and on and on.

Then I found the Greek word Paul used for anger in Ephesians was the root word for *angry* in Matthew 5:22 where the Lord says, "everyone who is angry with his brother shall be guilty before the court." In this verse the Lord compared anger to committing murder. If we don't stop this type of anger— the anger of wanting revenge and harboring it in our hearts—then the root of bitterness keeps growing and the blowups occur until there is the intent to harm another person. The solution is forgiveness.

Another Scripture about anger is Romans 12:17–21.

Never pay back evil for evil to anyone. Respect what is right in the sight of all men. If possible, so far as it depends on you, be at peace with all men. Never take your own revenge, beloved, but leave room for the wrath of God, for it is written, "VENGEANCE IS MINE, I WILL REPAY," says the Lord. "BUT IF YOUR ENEMY IS HUNGRY, FEED HIM, AND IF HE IS THIRSTY, GIVE HIM A DRINK; FOR IN SO DOING YOU WILL HEAP BURNING COALS UPON HIS HEAD." [emphasis mine]. Do not be overcome by evil, but overcome evil with good.

It's been my experience that when I give up any thought of revenge and decide to forgive (even when I don't want to), the Lord takes over my emotions, and the feelings of anger fade away. Having the emotions fade away may take time, but from experience I know it happens. Sometimes I have to forgive more than once about the same hurt, but it's worth it because I'm set free.

And then the next step is overcoming evil with good. Not only do we forgive, but we act out kindness, goodness, and love. We're told to do good, kind things for the one who hurt us. In Bible times they didn't have matches. Starting fires was not easy. So people tried to keep some of the coals glowing so their fire would not go out completely. If their fire did go out, they had to find someone who still had a fire, get some burning coals, and carry the coals home in a container on their heads. So heaping coals of fire on someone's head was a good thing to do. The people depended on fires to cook and heat their homes. So, even though a person hurts you in some way, the Bible tells you to overcome that evil by doing something good to the guilty person.

In other words, we are to serve one another. We have to deny ourselves with humility and obedience. Sometimes I wish there was another way to overcome anger in our relationships because this is hard. If I find another way before we finish this book, I'll be sure to pass along the information.

Now here's something the Bible is very clear about—divorce.

16

GOD HATES DIVORCE!

Chuck: I want to start with a little disclaimer. Too often evangelical Christians group divorced people in with the lepers, and that's not fair. Some of you have experienced the wrenching that comes with divorce. Some of you have been abandoned. Some of you *did* the abandoning. Whatever the situation, God forgets our sins when we are faithful to ask his forgiveness. No matter what has happened in the past, you can make your present relationship all God would like it to be. Sure there are ongoing consequences of divorce like conflicts between the ex-partners, child visitations, and financial settlements. There are always consequences of sin.

What I would like you to do is start over no matter what happened. When you ask God's forgiveness, he gives you a fresh slate. You are clean and pure and holy in his sight. Now make your present situation pleasing to God without guilt for the past. The Bible says God doesn't remember your past sins. Why should you? I know it's easy to look back at the what-ifs, especially when you read a marriage book about how to do it right. I just didn't want you to beat yourself up as you read about what God asks a husband to do, and what he asks a wife to do.

I was counseling a man whose wife wanted to go out and be a party girl again. She was tired of being a wife and mother. When she left he called me, which is a common phone call for me to get, and told me what happened. He was very upset about his wife leaving. He knew now how much she meant to him. He was very vulnerable, and sometimes God uses this type of thing to get a man's attention.

So I began to ask him questions about how his "awful" wife could possibly leave such a wonderful man like him. I call this my "jerk" scenario, but I don't use that term with the caller at this point. Later I might. I just told him I wanted to go over some of the things a *man* should do to keep a marriage on track just in case he *had* made a couple of tiny mistakes.

I told him a husband who did things right had regular dates with his wife every week so he could keep up on the things that were happening in her life. When she said to him, "Just get out of here," he took her in his arms and *stayed* there to prove she was worth something to him. He helped with the kids, and repaired the broken things in the home quickly. He gave her a woman's night out once in a while and baby-sat the kids himself. He looked into her eyes when they talked and sympathized by saying things like, "What else do you feel?" "That must have hurt, didn't it?" "I'll bet that tore you up." "I don't see how you have survived." He regularly asked about her mom and proactively suggested they visit various members of her family.

He never made a fuss when she wanted to go to a wedding during the NFL playoffs at 1:00 P.M. on a Saturday. He kept his part of the house in order so she didn't have to pick up after him. He loved her unconditionally, so it didn't matter how much she went shopping, or how much time she spent on the phone with her friends, or whether she wanted the blue rug in the rec room, or how much she weighed. He was sensitive to her moods and understood when she had a headache and didn't want to go to bed early. He treated her with tenderness, mercy, forgiveness, kindness, and understanding. He prayed for and with her regularly. He took the leadership in making sure she and the kids were fed spiritually. He spent *quantity* time with the kids, not just quality time.

He insisted they talk over conflicts and tried to be friends again quickly. He was committed to reserve his evenings for her, even if she watched TV and he worked in his shop or listened to music. He was available if she needed him. His work did not interfere regularly with family time. She knew she was his second highest priority behind his relationship with Jesus Christ.

He touched her and held her hand at times when he wasn't thinking about the bedroom. He proactively made a couple of dates so they could do things together without her having the responsibility of the kids all the time.

He didn't complain when she asked him to put on another tie or not to wear black socks with his tennis shoes. He complimented her on how she kept the home and nurtured the kids. He thanked her for providing a soft place to come home to, even if she, too, had a job outside the home. If she did *not* do these things well, he was careful to keep his thoughts to himself and not to let it affect the way he treated her. He made a habit of catching his wife doing things *right,* and he rarely mentioned anything she did wrong.

He made the bed when he was the last one up. He put the dishes in the dishwasher in the proper places. He hung the pictures exactly like she asked. He was patient when she took so long to get out of church or a social event because she needed to catch up on her relationships. He kept the outside of the home shipshape. He spread the yucky fertilizer in the flower beds for her. He was patient with other drivers when she was in the car with him. He was in the Word daily trying to find out what it meant to be a godly husband. He kept the garage clean and made sure she had a spot to park even if it meant keeping his precious Corvette outside under a tarp. When he was waiting in the car to go somewhere with her, he didn't mind when she felt she needed to make the bed before they left for the appointment even though it might make them late.

He was careful of his anger, and he tried to be patient with things he didn't understand, like her standing in front of a huge closet filled with clothes and shoes saying she had "nothing" to wear. He was sensitive to her feelings and didn't try to fix her all the time even though she insisted the moon was a triangle during one of her cycles. He tried his best to put the toilet seat down. He shared the TV clicker with her. In fact, he gave it to her *first* in case she wanted to be chief clicker that evening. When she gave him an emotional message, he didn't try to give her a series of easy steps to solve her problem. He was honest with his feelings and didn't hold grudges. He provided financial support for the family, so she could think about the extras that she would like to have rather than worrying about how they were going to pay the bills.

He complimented her on how she looked. He admired her spiritual gifts and talents. He created an atmosphere for her growth, which meant if she was an artist, he bought her brushes. If she liked to write, he got her a computer. If she liked crafts, he gave her a gift certificate to the hobby shop. If she was a gardener, he got her the right tools. If she liked biking, he got her a Harley and German helmet. If she was a teacher, he found books to support her gift and stretch her. If she was a people person, he was open to having groups of people over to the house for dinner or visiting.

He kept himself looking as good as possible. He kept his weight within reason. He kept his hair cut neatly. He didn't burp or wear his greasy shoes in front of her guests. He was quick to listen and slow to speak. He got right to the things she had on the goal list on her refrigerator door. He quickly agreed to ask for directions when they were lost. He had a male accountability group where he could be weak, cry, laugh, and learn what his wife needed through some of the things the other men had experienced. He didn't resist all the rules she had in the home, like putting the coffee cups on the left side of the dishwasher and the plastic things on top. He didn't resent all the trouble she went to getting the house ready for company. He understood and acted on the fact that the first thing God asks of a husband is for him to serve and give himself up for his wife—meaning he would not always get the things he wanted. He valued the team concept of marriage, and he never made an independent decision she didn't agree with. He gladly went to counseling when she asked and was grateful for the insights he gained into why the two of them were having problems. He took an active and gentle part in the disciplining of the children. He was very patient at the shopping mall and didn't keep looking at his watch while she shopped. He was sparkly at a social event even if he hated being there. He created a list of fun things they could do together, like playing tennis, working out at the club, enjoying film festivals, going to garage sales, sitting on the beach, going for a 10K run, whatever he knew she would enjoy. He was quick to ask forgiveness when he offended her in some way or teased her in public. He was centered on his relationship with God, and his goal was to be obedient in every aspect of his life.

Barb: Wow! And to think I'm married to that man!

Chuck: I'll try not to get a big head. Barb taught me everything I know about marriage and relationships. Now, if my friend the "jerk" is still on the line after all this, it is quite obvious to both of us where the problem lies, and it is *not* with his wife. Now he panics and gets religion and is desperate to get her back. It's hard for him to understand that he is not in control of the situation anymore. He may have even lost contact with her. He wants to send flowers and cards and is amazed when I suggest he not do that. It would be just another control thing to her. What he needs to do now is make God his first priority, and if by some chance his wife ever comes home, at least he will know what to do to please her and meet her needs.

I just got off the phone with a woman whose husband had found a bimbo who would spend time with him in the woods, and he now wants to get a quiet, loving, amiable, quick, no-hassle *divorce*. He knows what he is doing is wrong, but he considers God a forgiving God, so he thinks he'll still be okay for heaven. In fact, he said he was taking his new girlfriend to *church*. Not only is he asking for a divorce, he tells his wife he doesn't want anyone to know about it. This woman made the mistake of asking my opinion, and my advice was to put the news in *bold print* in the church bulletin. Take out ads in the local community newspaper. Buy an ad in the business journal his peers read. Have a plane do some skywriting. Put it on billboards. Tell his family and friends all about it, also his boss and coworkers. Have Larry King interview her on CNN about it. Her husband told her he had found a "Christian" counselor who couldn't imagine he had stayed with his wife for so long and suggested he get a divorce immediately. I asked her to get me the name of the counselor so we could stop this type of blasphemy against God and his Word, but her husband won't tell her. The Bible warns there will be people with itching ears going from teacher to teacher, counselor to counselor, and church to church looking for people who will say what they want to hear, whether it is biblical or not.

Another guy out having his affair told me he was *praying* with his girlfriend. God *vomits* as these so-called Christian men are out doing their own thing while shaking their fists at God and saying by their actions, "Stay out of my affairs."

One man's wife wanted him to leave the house and get an apartment. He made the mistake of asking my opinion. I said, "Don't you move an *inch*. That's your house too, and she only owns half of it. If she wants to leave, fine, but don't you go." Even from a legal sense, a man's leaving is often used in court to prove abandonment. It was safer just to stay put in the house. He complained that she was staying out until the wee hours of the morning, and he was a nervous wreck waiting up for her. I suggested he get some sleep, set his alarm just before he expected her back, and have breakfast waiting for her. He's not supporting irresponsible behavior by doing this. He is proving to a wife, maybe for the first time, that she means something to him. This particular situation had a happy ending. She came home and resumed being a wife and Mom. They now have the delicious joy of sharing how God made diamonds out of the ashes of their lives and are comforting others with what they have learned.

Obviously, it doesn't always work out this way. You women are especially hard to reach when you have been abused and neglected and taken for granted for so long. You give, give, give, give, and then something clicks in your mind. You are now convinced that your husband will *never* change, and you are going to get on with the rest of your life and see if you can find a tiny bit of approval somewhere. In my experience, it is actually easier when it's the man who is the transgressor. It isn't long before his girlfriend gives him an opinion, and he's vulnerable to God bringing someone into his life who can help him do the right thing by going back to his wife and family.

Another so-called Christian told his wife he wanted a divorce, but he would take care of all the details. He wanted a nice, friendly divorce so there wouldn't be a lot of hassles. The wife also made the mistake of asking my opinion. I advised her to get legal counsel to make sure she protected her rights and those of the children. A Christian shouldn't *initiate* divorce proceedings, but I see nothing in Scripture to prevent a Christian from defending themselves using the authorities and governments God has set up for this very purpose. In this case, she found out he planned to take almost all of their savings as well as the house. He wanted to leave her out of any future claims to his salary and wanted to have the kids. Many times the woman will have been mistaught about having to be in submission to her husband even if he wants to cut her throat or leave her destitute. She feels like she has no choice but to give in to his wishes. Or she has some misguided trust that he'll be fair. The *last* thing he will be is fair. He is thinking only of himself. He will pay the consequences for his blatant sin some time, some way. God is not mocked. God feels terrible when people break his marriage covenant.

The natural thing for the woman victim to do is give in, be intimidated, act like a doormat, give more, and serve more. Sometimes the husband will make some stupid statement about the divorce being in the best interests of the children. Besides being blasphemy, that simply is not true. The best interests of the children will be served by the couple *staying together*. Their best interests are served by the husband forgetting his own selfish desires and coming home to nurture, protect, and provide for his family so God can bless him. Even the secular mind can see the advantage that children have with their natural parents.

We humans can make up all sorts of silly ideas to justify what we want to do. I read about a couple of counselors getting a divorce. Their statement was something like, "Who would be better than us to counsel the children going through this and protect them from any harm relating to our divorce." Kids *never* recover from a divorce.

I was reminded of this by something that happened to us with one of our dogs. We always had dogs while the kids were growing up. After the kids had left the home, our dogs Molly Two and Muffit got old and went to be with the Lord. (It would not be God's character not to let us see them again someday.) Barb made it quite plain she never wanted to train another dog as long as she lived. Barb paid most of the price with the spotted rugs.

So I was dogless for a while, but I did the best I could without having furry friends around the house. Then a few years ago we were in Phoenix for a Pro Athlete's conference, and Barb made the mistake of letting me go into a pet shop. Barb says I came out of the shop with tears coming down my cheeks. That is not true. My eyes were moist—but I was in control. I just love animals, that's all.

Then one day I came home to visit with one of our ex-Mariners kids Mike Moore who always came by the house when he was in town for a game. Right there by Mike's chair was a puppy. Barb had been so touched to see my tears (moistness) that she decided anyone who loved animals that much should have a dog, so she had purchased a little lap dog that she could enjoy too. We named her Molly B. I'm sure the people who sold Barb the pup didn't mean to mislead her, but the small lap dog they sold her soon weighed thirty-five pounds and still thought she was a lap dog.

We always had our other dogs sleep in the basement, but now that we had a lap dog, we had her sleep between us crosswise up by our pillows in our king size bed. This is in keeping with Proverbs 12:10 about a good man being concerned for the welfare of his animals that I mentioned to you before, if you would like to have a scriptural basis for this. As she grew, our bed space shrunk because we had this thirty-five pound lap dog laying between us the long way, and Barb always got the good end.

By the way, here are some steely cold rules someone sent to me so I could be more firm with my dogs. I hate to be this harsh, but there is nothing as bad as an out-of-control dog, and we have to take stern measures. I was glad to see someone else was as hard on their animals as I was. Here are the rules:

1. The dog is not allowed in the house.
2. Okay, the dog is allowed in the house, but only in certain rooms.
3. The dog is allowed in all rooms, but has to stay off the furniture.
4. The dog can get on the old furniture only.
5. Fine, the dog is allowed on all the furniture, but is not allowed to sleep with the humans on the bed.
6. Okay, the dog is allowed on the bed, but only by invitation.
7. The dog can sleep on the bed whenever he wants, but not under the covers.
8. The dog can sleep under the covers by invitation only.
9. The dog can sleep under the covers every night.
10. Humans must ask permission to sleep under the covers with the dog.

I'm sorry to make jokes during a serious discussion on divorce, but I do have a point. One night Molly B experienced a tragedy in her life. I caught a cold, so to protect Barb from germs, I slept in another bedroom. Molly B was so upset. First, she went into Barb's bedroom, then came back into mine, then back into Barb's bedroom, and then back into mine. She was in effect being asked to choose between two people she loved very much. This is exactly what kids feel when their parents get divorced. Yes, we try to put a good face on it as we discuss visits and who gets them at Christmas. You don't have to agree, but I believe broken homes have filled our prisons and are the basis for just about every cultural and spiritual problem you can name.

I was helping a couple who had actually filed for divorce and then by God's grace got back together again. During the separation they both had created some friends—he some women friends, she some men friends. After they got back together, the man wanted to continue a friendship with a woman he had dated while he and his wife were contemplating divorce. I tried to explain why he just couldn't do that even though his intentions were pure.

This is one of the byproducts of separation—the introduction of other people into a love relationship. If the couple had not separated, these complications would not have arisen. One of the reasons I am so strongly opposed to separation—except where there is physical abuse that threatens lives—is the fact that a couple can't even practice communication if they are separated. And communication is usually at the heart of the matter unless there is another person involved.

Even physical abuse or emotional abuse, or any other kind of abuse is not grounds for divorce as much as we would like it to be. There is only one grounds for divorce in the Bible. In Matthew 19:9 Jesus said: "And I say to you, whoever divorces his wife, except for immorality, and marries another woman commits adultery" (NASB).

I add the idea of habitual adultery to this. When someone strays, I always advise the abandoned person not to file for divorce, even though they might have technical grounds to do so. This gives God time to change the straying person's heart. I have seen some people get a divorce and remarry too soon, and when the offending person comes back, they are not available to restore the original marriage. This deprives kids of natural parents. If the offending party forces a divorce and gets married, then of course that permanently breaks the marriage bond, and I feel the abandoned one can go ahead and marry again, if they marry a Christian.

I've had some people try to make 1 Corinthians 7:15 grounds for divorce. "But if the unbeliever leaves, let him do so. A believing man or woman is not bound in such circumstances; God has called us to live in peace" (NIV).

I don't read divorce in this. This is just letting a non-Christian depart in peace. It can't mean divorce because Christ said sexual immorality was the only grounds for divorce. This would make two, and the Bible cannot contradict itself. From my study here is what I believe this verse means. If the non-Christian spouse is offended by their mate's Christianity and wants to leave because their husband or wife won't renounce their faith, then the Christian partner should let the other one go. The believing partner is not bound or a slave, as the word implies, to keep the marriage relationship together since the unbelieving partner left. Of course, if the unbelieving partner gets involved sexually with another person, then this would provide the biblical grounds for divorce.

Some Christians are even filing for *legal* separation now so they can't be accused of filing for divorce. Legal separation is just Christianeze for divorce. There is no difference. I've even had a few women file for divorce to save their financial assets. I don't remember that contingency in the wedding vows when they swore before God that they would have a lifetime commitment until death…"For better or for worse."

In Genesis 2:24 we find the concept of why divorce is so wrenching. "This explains why a man leaves his father and mother and is joined to his wife in such a way that the two become one person."

The Hebrew word for joined means to be glued to each other. That's why divorce is so destructive. It's like two pieces of paper that are glued together to become one. If you try to separate them, there is never a clean break. Parts of each remain on the other. There will always be scars whether a person becomes a Christian or not. He or she will still suffer the natural consequences of their actions. God forgives divorce like he does any other sin, as long as we sincerely ask his forgiveness with a broken spirit, agonizing over our sin as King David did in the Old Testament. David became a "man after God's own heart" because his spirit was right. However, he *still* suffered the natural consequences for his sins.

I've already mentioned how many evangelical churches treat people who have been divorced. You would think they had a disease or something. They don't feel welcome in the married couple's class on Sunday morning. They really don't feel comfortable in the singles class either. They don't fit in with the college-career class, especially if they are a little older. They don't belong anywhere, it seems, so they become discouraged and finally come to the conclusion no one wants them. Depression is a common result.

Sin is sin. God put envy right next to murder in the list of sins he gives in

Romans 1:29. Divorce *is* caused by sin by one or both partners—usually both. Sins like selfishness, greed, lust, and apathy abound. However, we need to quickly restore divorced people to the fellowship after they have agonized over their sin, are broken before the Lord, and when they desire to pick up the pieces with God's help and go on with their lives. We need to help them draw a line in the sand, saying to themselves and God, "I will no longer look to the past. From this day on, I will focus on the future and the things God wants to accomplish through me." There *are* natural consequences of divorce. These go on to a certain extent throughout a lifetime whether the people involved are Christians or not, but people don't have to keep dwelling on the negative. God forgives our mistakes. We can forgive others for their mistakes as well and help them go on.

If a divorced person gets into a new relationship they should determine in their hearts that *this* marriage will last the rest of their lives. And that's the key for any marriage—the lifetime commitment. This commitment eliminates any chance of emotional blackmail. How many times do you hear about one partner or the other saying something like, "If you say (or do) that again, I'm out of here." If a person is always threatening to leave, then the other partner can never really say how they feel or bring up a subject on which there will be disagreement for fear the other one will leave. A lifetime commitment allows us to have disagreements and struggles and heated discussions without it destroying the relationship.

Barb: I read in a book called *The Kink and I* that a married couple is to "love each other when they *feel* like it, when they *don't feel* like it, and until they *do feel* like it." Author Margaret Jenson quotes her mother saying, "The Christian life is so simple, it's just not so easy." That about sums it up.

Chuck: It's amazing to me how many people forget the sacred vows they made before God at the wedding. "For better or worse, for richer or poorer, in sickness or in health, forsaking all others, to love and cherish until parted by death." Marriage is a holy covenant between you and God, and between you and your wife or husband. Our culture seems to prefer a marriage contract, but there are worlds of difference between the words *covenant* and *contract*. I don't know who deserves the credit for the following words, but I think they put everything in perspective.

A Covenant is based on mutual trust.

A Contract is based on mutual *distrust.*

A Covenant is based on unlimited responsibility.

A Contract is based on limited liability.

A Covenant cannot be broken if new circumstances occur.

A Contract can be broken by mutual consent.

Barb: In the Bible a covenant is a solemn binding agreement that can only be broken by death. That's the kind of covenant we make when we marry, but we don't realize the meaning of it when we say, "I do."

Here's the reward when we honor our covenant with the Lord and also with our husbands and wives.

"All the paths of the LORD are lovingkindness and truth to those who keep His covenant and His testimonies. The secret of the LORD is for those who fear Him, And He will make them know His covenant" (Psalm 25:10, 14).

The word *lovingkindness* is a word used to show the *Lord* is in covenant with us. When God speaks, he tells the truth. He says when we fear him, meaning we obey him because we reverence his great and awesome power, he will make us know what his covenant is all about. It isn't *until* we obey that we get insights into *why* we had to obey.

In Old Testament times when two people entered into a covenant with each other, they exchanged their weapons. This signified they were taking on one another's enemies. When we entered into covenant with Jesus Christ, 2 Corinthians 5:21 states, "He made Him who knew no sin to be sin on our behalf, that we might become the righteousness of God in Him." In other words, he took our sin and in exchange gave us his righteousness, which means our weapons are not the same as they once were. Once our weapons (our sin) included immorality, enmities, strife, jealousy, outbursts of anger, disputes, dissensions, envyings, and things like these. But now they are love, joy, peace, patience, kindness, goodness, faithfulness, gentleness, and self-control. The apostle Peter tells us to supply godliness to our faith. Godliness is making decisions God would make. It seeks the will of God and the welfare of others. A godly person is one who is right with God and his fellow man. This person makes the right decisions and does not avoid the hard way.

First Timothy 4:7 tells us, "discipline yourself for the purpose of godliness." This discipline involves exchanging our fleshly ways for His ways. I believe many of the people who trust God to save them do not trust Him for their everyday life. They don't use the weapons God has given them to use, but instead they continue using what they have always used, even though their weapons do not bring about peaceful relationships.

Since our marriage is a covenant—between each other and between us and God—Chuck and I want to trust him and be godly. That means using his weapons and not ours.

Chuck: I've heard of husbands abandoning families when a retarded child was born. My heart is torn that anyone could be that callused after they had promised to stay married for better or for worse. I suppose on the wedding day we have an idealized view of married life and only think of the "better" times. We feel we'll never have to go through the "worse" part. But God doesn't get us out of problems. He gives us the tools to go *through* problems so he can build our character and patience and make us valuable to someone else. As I heard Chuck Swindoll say one time, we are much more impressed with men's ideas than God's principles.

Filing for divorce means a person has the wrong concept of God. Personally, I believe God is real. So I want to make sure He won't be holding anything against me when I meet His Son face to face. If He's just a Santa Claus sitting on a cloud somewhere, I guess you can get away with divorce, but I'm not that much of a gambler. I want His blessing, not His cursing caused in part by the tragic toll of little children who have been destroyed by divorce over the ages. He loves little children, and I remember His vivid word picture of tying a millstone around the neck of anyone hurting a little child and throwing them into the deepest ocean. Divorce hurts little people's lives. That makes God cry. Me too.

If you have not verbally made a lifetime commitment to your partner, please close this book and take care of that right now. Everything else we say is pretty meaningless unless both of you have this security.

Now let's look at one of the most mystifying aspects of our relationship with God. Sometimes God allows us to suffer, and some of this suffering takes place in marriage. It is not what we would have planned, but it is inevitable.

17

WHAT TO DO
WHEN IT HURTS

You can tell it's going to be a bad day when:

- You call suicide prevention and they put you on hold.
- You see a 60 Minutes team waiting in your office.
- You turn on the news and they are showing emergency routes out of the city.
- Your car horn goes off accidentally and remains stuck as you follow a group of Hell's Angels on the freeway.
- Your check to the IRS bounces.
- Your income tax refund check bounces.
- Your pet rock snaps at you.
- Your twin sister forgets your birthday.
- Your husband says, "Good morning, Carol," and your name is Linda.
- You wake up and your braces are locked together.
- You put both contacts in the same eye.

Chuck: The author of these wonderful word pictures is unknown, but I think the list of problems would probably cause anyone a little bit of trauma. We are all called to suffer once in a while. For instance, Barb and I have to suffer for the Lord at Pro Athlete Conferences twice a year. They are usually held in Florida or Phoenix or California where we are in danger of getting cancer from the sun, chlorine poisoning from the pool, or burned in the hot tub. Also we are forced to eat high cholesterol meals with the athletes. I'd look like a wimp eating a salad, so I have to eat the steaks along with the rest of them so they can relate to me when I share Christ with them. They wouldn't give me the time of day if I wasn't there at the table with them. Also, because we do group counseling, we have to stay in a large executive suite to get a room big enough for our needs.

You know how dangerous athletics is, so it won't surprise you to learn I hurt my leg at the Mariners spring training this year. We had just finished a moderately high cholesterol meal at the Embassy Suites, and we were going back to our room when I missed a step and strained my metatarsal or something. It was very sore, and I had to sit by the pool and read the rest of the day, so you can see how I sacrifice my body for the sake of God's program. I just wanted you to know this so you could pray for us as we suffer on the mission field for the Lord.

One time when we were still living at our other home, Barb came down to the office. "Are you writing? A fuse blew," she said. It was because of the crummy roof gutters that the fuse blew. We had some workers at the house fixing the gutters, and they needed to plug their drill into the fountain outlet where the circulating motor froze that winter. This was next to the broken stonework someone crushed with his car which was beside the storm drain that was plugged with leaves. Leaves also plugged the gutters which caused the problem in the first place or the workmen wouldn't be here.

It didn't bother me one bit when little trees began to grow out of the gutters. In fact, I liked the effect. It made a nice windbreak around the edge of the house. Barb didn't see it that way. She wanted the gutters cleaned. Barb has a real thing about leaves. We had 9,856 leafing trees around our place, and every autumn they "leafed" all over our driveway and yard. Now my thought, a logical one I'm sure you will agree, is to wait until all the trees have leafed. Then we take our little rake, do the pile of leaves bit, and get rid of them. But Barb has this funny idea about raking several times during the season. In fact, she can hear each leaf or seed pod as it clicks and lets go of the branch and flutters to the ground with a thump. At that point, she wants someone to go out and rake it up, or clean it out of the gutter.

Barb: If it was up to Chuck I don't think he would ever rake the leaves. Then they would be slippery and wet all winter, and we wouldn't have been able to get to the top of the driveway. As I've said, I like everything to be clean and orderly.

Chuck: I have no idea how to start the serious part of this chapter on suffering. Maybe that's why Christians don't do a good job of handling this part of life, because it is so overwhelming. I even know of some churches who preach Christians shouldn't even go *through* suffering. They say if a Christian *does* suffer there is sin in their life, or they don't have enough faith to demand that God change their circumstances. I don't know what Bible they are reading. But one of the main *themes* in my Bible says suffering and trials are inevitable. It's not a matter of *if*, it's *when*. The point is not to get *out* of trials, but to go *through* them. We'll give you lots of Scriptures to prove our point as we go along.

Marriage is God's wonderful idea, and most parts of a marriage relationship are satisfying and meaningful. But for small portions of time, marriage can become hell on earth. And this small portion of time can grow to be a large portion if we don't find out what's going on. One of the hardest forms of suffering, in my opinion, is having marriage problems. They are so immediate and intimate and now. Almost every breath reminds us of the conflicts and misunderstandings we are having as a couple. The tortured silences. The angry voices. The defeat. You just want to run away and start again. Barb and I have been through our share. Even though we still run into each other once in a while, we are more into the laughing stage than the crying stage. Hopefully, some of the things we have learned from our pain can now be of help to you and give you hope. We know many of you reading this are in the crying stage, and we admire you so much for reading a book on marriage. That's probably the last thing you wanted to do, but here you are, and we feel so honored you would trust us as we tell our story of what we learned. It isn't fun. It is pure suffering at times, but after we go *through* the pain, God gives us his comfort and a promise that someday it will all make sense.

Barb: One evening Chuck and I had a particularly devastating argument. We both felt hopeless. He was sitting at his rolltop desk, and I came up behind him, wrapped my arms around his neck, leaned down, kissed his hair, and said, "I don't like you very much right now, but I'm completely committed to you." And that has been our secret. Even though we don't particularly like each other at times, we know our love is so strong and that we are committed to each other. Marriage is falling in and out of like, and that will often happen. But love does not go away. Love is not a feeling as Chuck has said, it is serving. When we do good, kind, loving things for each other, the feeling of like eventually comes back.

Chuck: We don't want to suffer. At least I don't. I want things to go smoothly so I can do all the things I *want* to do, not all the things I *have* to do. I don't like to have things happen that are out of my control, like too much rain, snow, death of a loved one, loss of a job or a large client, an earthquake, or working through marriage problems.

Let's face it. Suffering is part of the Christian life, even though that is not how we would have written the script. Sometimes our natural response to suffering and trials is to assume God doesn't know about them, or that we've done something wrong and he is punishing us. In fact, one of the first things we often ask is, "*Why me?*" There's a better question from God's point of view. Why *not* me? Am I so special God would shelter me from all trouble? In one sense he would be blocking some of the *benefits* the trials would bring me, some of which are mentioned in this Scripture from James 1:2–4: "Dear brothers, is your life full of difficulties and temptations? Then be happy, for when the way is rough, your patience has a chance to grow. So let it grow, and don't try to squirm out of your problems. For when your patience is finally in full bloom, then you will be ready for anything, strong in character, full and complete."

Trials will come no matter how hard we pray, or how many times we go to church. The sooner we accept the fact that trials are inevitable and that they have a purpose, the sooner we'll make an impact on the people around us, especially our non-Christian friends. Divorce is an epidemic in our culture and also in the church, unfortunately. When nonbelievers see Christians handle their struggles and trials of marriage the same way they do, they wonder why they would need God or Christ in their lives. If Christianity doesn't make a difference in the way a Christian acts, who needs it? In order to please God when troubles come, we need to get on top of our circumstances, not let them get on top of us. When we are on top, we can see the big picture as God sees it. But when we are under our load of circumstances, all we can see are the problems, the struggles, and the pain. Barb and I never had a goal to write books. We just hoped we would survive. All we had was a lifetime commitment. We were not always good friends. There were lots of disagreements and silence. Yes, we had some good times, but it was through the hard times that God helped us grow.

Sometimes our trials look like a cross-stitch. Have you ever seen the underside? It's a mess. Colors crisscrossing all over the place. No rhyme nor reason to it. But when viewed from the top, there is a butterfly, or teddy bear, or mountain scene. It's beautiful on top, but underneath it doesn't make sense. That's how our problems appear to God. He sees the peaceful mountain scene, the big picture, the reason, the harmony in what we are going through. All we do is look up from the bottom and see the mess. We need to trust He really is seeing a master plan for our life. It's then up to us to fit into that plan with our obedience and let Him call the shots, especially when it comes to marriage problems. What we need to do is thank God for our trials, assuming He has a purpose in allowing us to experience them.

I have media salespeople calling on me in my advertising business. I have to learn to trust these salespeople as people before I can trust what they tell me about their station or product. The better I get to know them, the more I can trust them when they tell me about their product. I know some of the salespeople so well I would trust them with anything. That's the way our relationship with God needs to be. We have to get to know Him so well we can trust Him to have a purpose even when problems come. And the only way we can know God is by saturating ourselves in His Word. That's been one of the priceless gifts Barb has given me throughout our marriage. She has been a student of the Bible. Every day she spends time in God's Word searching for answers to life's questions. She has been such an inspiration to me in her diligence and has given us a foundation on which to build our marriage, as we reach out to others.

Sometimes God gives us a glimpse of what He has in mind when something goes differently during our day than we had planned. We might put the situation into the category of suffering. At least for a goal-setting, Type A person like me.

One busy day I needed to pick up some audio tapes at an electronics store. I drive a very nice car. It's just another thing I have to do as I suffer on my business mission field for the Lord so my clients and salespeople will relate to me. When I got back to the car from the store, my car wouldn't start. I tried and tried, but no go. Sometimes I fail God at such times by asking, "Didn't you know I was in a hurry?" However, as I've gotten more and more into his Word, I'm able to trust him more and assume fairly quickly he really does have a plan for my situation. I was just grateful the car had not stopped on the freeway, or on a bridge, or when I had a crisis appointment with a client. As it was, the car was in a parking spot on the street. I had an afternoon with no real crises, so I put some money in the meter and walked back to the office, which was only a few blocks away. I thanked God for the situation, assuming that whatever he had planned was okay with me.

Later that afternoon I had the car towed home, and the rest of the week I drove a small pickup truck we had for the business. I'm just a farm boy anyway, so driving the truck was no big deal. In fact, I enjoyed it. Two days after my other car stopped, I noticed I had scheduled a lunch with a brand-new Christian who repaired appliances for a living. I drove to his shop, went inside, and instantly realized why God had stopped my car. The guy had greasy clothes and would have been very uncomfortable riding in a luxury car in his work clothes. He probably would not have been able to relate to me very well because of the car. But he was at home in my truck because he drove one every day too. We had a fantastic lunch, sharing Christ with each other, building each other up, having a great time. I returned him to his shop and drove off in my little truck, with at least a hint of why I had the truck that day rather than my regular car.

When I see Christ face to face, I'm going to ask him, "Did you really make my car stop so I could drive the truck to see my friend?"

He may say, "No, it was just your PCV valve," but I suspect he will say, "Yes, before the foundation of the world, I knew you would be having lunch with your friend, and knowing that he would be threatened by a nice car until he got to know you, I just decided to stop your other car for a while and let you drive the truck."

It's silly, but I have tears in my eyes writing these words about this dumb little story because God is *so* faithful to take care of me. From God's viewpoint, my inconvenience was a thousand times less important than having lunch with my friend. God is just that practical. I thank him so much for Proverbs 16:1 which says, "We can make our plans, but the final outcome is in God's hands." I had definite plans for that day, but God altered them, and it's okay.

Now don't get the idea I do this every time. I'm not some supersaint. In fact, I'm quite the opposite. I *always* seem to struggle to do things God's way rather than having my own way. This time I did it right, and maybe that's why it sticks out in my mind so clearly.

One time we had someone working for us whom we discovered to be dishonest. I had every reason to march into the office, ask the person to leave, and ask him to make restitution for the wrongs done. But I didn't have peace about doing that. So I prayed, "Lord, I know you want this person to leave, and so do I, but I'll leave the timing up to you. Amen."

Several weeks went by, and evidently God was really busy in Africa or South America, because he had not done one thing about my problem. So I took the problem back from him and wrestled with it on my own. I could hardly be around that person, because I was so suspicious and uneasy and worried. Then all of a sudden I realized I had taken the problem back. It was God's problem. So once again I prayed, "Lord, I know you want this person to leave, but it's your problem now. Amen." I went back and forth on this for several months. I went to a cabin to pray and fast and be with the Lord alone. It was there I finally prayed, "Lord, it's a real mystery why you haven't caused this person to leave. Could it be that you want this person to stay? If so, please help me to accept your will in this matter. I really do want to please you, not myself. Amen."

In two weeks the person was gone. A situation came up which caused this person to leave the city. No confrontation, no bad feelings. When I completely turned it over to God, he answered in his own time, which was perfect. I don't think this was my usual desire to avoid conflict. I have been able to be pretty direct in business. It's just with Barb that I tend to run away from conflict. I think it was a simple matter of God wanting me to give the problem to him. I had been holding on to one string—that the person had to go. When I released that last string, then God acted.

There are other reasons for suffering and trials besides maturing us,

building our character, or teaching us patience. Paul wrote about them in
2 Corinthians 1:3–5:

> What a wonderful God we have—he is the Father of our Lord Jesus
> Christ, the source of every mercy, and the one who so wonderfully
> comforts and strengthens us in our hardships and trials. And why
> does he do this? So that when others are troubled, needing our sym-
> pathy and encouragement, we can pass on to them this same help and
> comfort God has given us. You can be sure that the more we undergo
> sufferings for Christ, the more he will shower us with his comfort and
> encouragement.

Time after time, as Barb and I take couples out to dinner and begin sharing some of the problems we've had in our marriage, the other couple will say
something like, "That happened to us last week. What do we do about it?"
Then we are able to share some of the practical lessons we've learned through
trials and from reading Scripture. We can offer them the same comfort God
has given us in those same circumstances.

I have had only a few people come into my life in a teaching or counseling situation who have had cancer. Since I've never had the disease, all I can
say is I will pray for them, show sympathy, visit them in the hospital, and try
to help in any way I can, but I don't *know* how they feel. I have a man in my
Bible study who lost a five-year-old grandchild. I can't imagine I could even
survive such a thing, but he can say to others that he *knows* how they feel and
give them comfort. Another man who is in the study lost a twelve-year-old
daughter to brain cancer a few years ago. I can weep with him, but I can't say,
"I know how you feel" because I couldn't possibly know the pain he experienced.

But when hurting couples come to us with a marriage problem, we can
say, "We *know* how you feel" because Barb and I have usually experienced the
exact kind of problem they are struggling with. There is no doubt about it—
wounds and scars do qualify us to counsel. We must be open and honest as
we share present-day problems, as well as those we have put behind us.

We can even have *joy* through the tears when we run into problems and trials. We might not be happy about the problem, but as our patience develops, our strength grows. As we learn to trust God more each time we go through a struggle, the stronger we become. We learn to stand strong no matter how deep the tragedy or how painful the trial. We know God loves us and will not allow anything to come into our lives that is not in our best interest and his best interest. He goes through the problem with us because His Holy Spirit is right there inside us, filling our hearts with the knowledge of God's love.

As we've mentioned, Barb and I do some counseling with professional athletes here in Seattle and around the country. We see behind the scenes how hard they work before the cheering begins. They punish their bodies, making them do things they don't want to do. They run, lift weights, run, do push-ups, run, work out on the exercise machines, run, sweat, and run some more. Their reward for all the hard work is success in front of an adoring crowd. The world really doesn't expect to see Christians work hard. People have the idea that Christians are pantywaists, sissies, or pushovers. But the apostle Paul wrote in 1 Corinthians 9:26b–27: "I'm not just shadow-boxing or playing around. Like an athlete I punish my body, treating it roughly, training it to do what it should, not what it wants to. Otherwise I fear that after enlisting others for the race, I myself might be declared unfit and ordered to stand aside."

From these verses we can see that a Christian should run his or her race to win, to gain first place and be the best husband, the best wife, the best homemaker, the best business person, the best neighbor, the best church member, the best pastor, the best truck driver, or the best advertising agency person. We as believers are to run with purpose, set goals, eye the mark, and deny ourselves. Time is too short to play games in the Christian life. We either have to get on the ship or get off the ship. We can't have one foot on the dock and one foot on the ship and expect to go anywhere. We can straddle only so long. As Chuck Swindoll pointed out, some of us have too much of the world in us to be comfortable with Christ, and too much of Christ in us to be comfortable in the world. If we continue in that state, it will tear us apart.

I used to work with a man who acted, sounded, and looked like a Christian when he was with a Christian group. But when he was in a social situation with non-Christians, he acted, sounded, and looked just like one of them. Even the non-Christians in his life knew he should not be involved in some of the things he was doing, yet I suppose it gave them some comfort to drag him down a bit.

Which leads me to another reason for suffering. We suffer when we do something wrong. If I go eighty miles an hour on the freeway and get a ticket, I deserve the ticket. I did something wrong. It surely doesn't make much sense for me to grouse around, mumbling against God for bringing this suffering into my life. I simply have to pay the consequences for my sin, then get up and go on. If I divorce my wife, some day I will suffer for destroying a home and children.

I know quite a few people who are suffering for the wrong they have done and are getting impatient with God. It's almost as if they want God to start over, to erase the consequences of their sins. We can start over after we ask God's forgiveness (and that of any people involved), but that does not mean the consequences of adultery, divorce, murder, stealing, or lying will just go away automatically when we get our behavior straightened out. There is a price to pay for sin, and the best thing we can do is be patient and let God work out his will in the situation. Just because the murderer in prison comes to know Christ personally is not a reason he should be released. There is a consequence for murdering someone. But looking at God's big picture, I can't think of a more hurting place than a prison. And to have someone right there in prison with the answer to life is a breathtaking thought. Talk about God making diamonds out of ashes!

Suffering can be one of the consequences of sin. Why do we sin? We sin because we are tempted to sin, and because we didn't resist the temptation. God does not let us be tempted beyond what we are able to stand, but when we invite evil thoughts into our mind to play with them for a while and ignore the escape route God gives us, we can't expect God to intervene. When we toy with temptation, we are saying, "Don't call me, God. I'll call you." God's power to resist the temptation is available at the point of being tempted. If we linger over the temptation, we can't blame God when we give in to the temptation and sin.

Satan knows exactly what makes us tick and where we have weaknesses. If we have a tendency to steal, he will make sure we have lots of opportunities to steal. If our tendency is for lustful thoughts and actions, he will make sure we run into all kinds of TV shows, movies, and magazines that will help feed this weakness so our thoughts will lead to actions. Nobody fishes with a paintbrush tied to a string. The fish would laugh at that. To catch fish we put a wiggly, fat, juicy worm on the end of the hook and pretty soon we've got a fish. That's what Satan does to us. He doesn't waste his time in the areas of our strengths. His favorite fishing ground is with our weaknesses, and he begins his subtle work in our minds. If *Playboy* and Showtime are our daily mind food, then our minds will be sensual. If the Bible is our daily food, then our minds will be spiritual. There may still be an occasional battle, but if we're properly nourished, God can help us win the struggle. Someone said a dusty Bible results in a dirty life.

In a shop class in high school, we made chisels as a project. We put them into the fire to temper and harden them so they would be prepared for the hammer blows later. In the same way, God puts us through the furnace of adversity to make us ready for anything. Someone has said, "God doesn't use us greatly until he has allowed us to be hurt deeply." I don't look forward to that if hurting is part of my future, but my only option will be to assume it will be God's tempering process to make me stronger. God might be saying to me, "I want you to grow through this sickness or hurt. I have another person who will come into your life later who will need the same comfort I am giving you now."

I once visited an aluminum plant. The heated metal is pushed through a specially shaped die and out comes the aluminum shaped as gutters, molding, angles, or rods, according to whatever die was placed in the machine. As Christians, we get heated up a bit with trials and struggles in order to make it easier for God to push us through the die to make us into what He wants us to be. How much pressure and heat is needed to push us through God's machine to make us like Christ? As with the metal, just enough to overcome the natural resistance of the material being molded. What this says to me is that the more we fight or resist, the more pressure and heat God has to exert in order to mold us into the image of Christ.

As we deal with struggles and problems, sometimes we may not know why they happen to us. However, God often shows us the reason for a particular trial *after* we have gone through it. When we face difficulties, our natural tendency is to give up and quit, but God's Word says just the opposite in Hebrews 12:12–13: "So take a new grip with your tired hands, stand firm on your shaky legs, and mark out a straight, smooth path for your feet so that those who follow you, though weak and lame, will not fall and hurt themselves, but become strong."

Even though it seems this passage in Hebrews is talking mostly about getting up after God has had to discipline us, I think we can use the same principle with suffering and trials. For sure, some of my problems are a result of God's trying to get my attention. God does discipline His children as needed—every loving father does. However, God's discipline looks to the future as He helps us back on the path, not back at the past. Paul reminds us in 2 Corinthians 4:17: "These troubles and sufferings of ours are, after all, quite small and won't last very long. Yet this short time of distress will result in God's richest blessing upon us forever and ever!"

Barb and I have shed lots of tears during our forty-some years of marriage. We have had some hard times as God taught us how the World's Most Opposite Couple could learn to live together in harmony. One of the greatest verses in the Bible for me is Psalm 56:8 where it says God saves our tears in a bottle. This implies to me that someday when I have one of my first power lunches with Jesus Christ at the New Jerusalem Denny's, He will bring along God's bottle and say to me, "Remember this tear? This is what I had in mind. Remember this tear? These are the people who were touched by watching your life. Remember this tear? This was the result of the pain you went through." Since we'll have the mind of Christ, His words will make perfect sense. We *will* see His master plan, and what an exciting day that's going to be as He puts purpose behind all the hurts we have gone through in this life.

I think one of the elements of suffering is remembering our past and how we have failed God. It hurts as we remember how we went ahead with the divorce, or left our family, or committed adultery. We suffer as we think back on the days when we were alcoholics, or drug addicts, or addicted to porn on the Internet. Or when we didn't nurture our family, or we didn't live in understanding with our wife, plus a hundred other things we did where we feel we have really failed other people and God and have a hard time accepting his forgiveness.

A man came to our Sunday school class one time and told me about his anger problem. One of the symptoms of his problem was being in his sixth marriage. He said a relationship with Jesus Christ made sense, but he had to get his life straightened out before he could really make a commitment. I explained that he *couldn't* get his life straightened out *until* he made the commitment. Like many others, this man continued to suffer because he had done so many things in his past, and he just never felt like he deserved God's forgiveness.

The thing we need to keep in mind is that we *don't* deserve his forgiveness. We in no way qualify for a pardon. That's why God sent Jesus to earth in the first place. He knew we humans couldn't satisfy God's need for perfection, and there was a death penalty for anyone who was *not* perfect. That was when God stepped into time as the man Jesus, and took on Himself the very penalty He Himself had set up. He created the problem. *Us!* He died to solve the problem. He's now preparing a place of unspeakable glory for us. Not because we deserve it, but because He loves us.

So how do we accept God's forgiveness? The Bible says if we ask God for forgiveness, He forgets our past sins. Sometimes we don't really believe Him. We think that He slightly remembers what we have done. I came up with a word picture that helps me put this in a context I can relate to. Let's say I hurt Barb emotionally with my anger. I ask her forgiveness, and since I have sinned with my anger, I need to ask God's forgiveness, too. So I drop by God's office to ask His forgiveness. I don't have to call ahead for an appointment. If I do call ahead, I never get a menu on His phone service saying, "If this is life-threatening, punch one. If this can wait until tomorrow, punch two. If you would like to speak to an angel representative, punch three." I just drop by because I know He is always there. He doesn't even have a door on the office, and He's never on the phone or too busy working on his web site to talk. He just seems to be waiting for me to stop in.

I come into his office and He gets up and comes to greet me with a big hug and asks me to sit down. Then He gets me a Coke with lots of ice. He puts His feet up on the coffee table, and the first thing He says is that He feels the Seattle Mariners are going to the bullpen much too fast. He feels the starters need to take the team deeper into the game. He's also a little concerned about the series with the Yankees coming up. They have so much left-handed power it will be hard to match up with the pitchers we have available. Eventually He gets around to asking me what's happening in my life. I explain I have hurt Barb emotionally with my anger. I've asked her forgiveness, and now I have come to ask his forgiveness.

He says, "You're forgiven." No big lectures. No Bible verses. No raised eyebrows. No strain in his voice. I'm forgiven. Oh, if I could remember to do that for the people in *my* life, but I fail so often. Then my Lord says, "This is the first time, isn't it?"

I smile and fidget a bit and confess that I have had a problem handling my anger all my life, and I've been to His office more times than I would like to admit. God looks puzzled. He puts on His glasses (so He can relate to me) and goes to look for the folder marked "Chuck" in his filing cabinet. He finds the file, but there is nothing but good stuff among the papers. No sins as far as He can see. He checks His day-timer, and calls up the "Chuck" file on His computer, but the computer says, "Sins not found. Erased by Jesus' blood." He checks His e-mail (His address is God.com in case you want to add Him to your address book). He checks His fax machine, His cell phone, and His answering machine to see if it's something recent, but He can find nothing to indicate I had ever been there before with an anger problem or any other sin. So He comes back, scratches His head, and says, "I can't find anything. Any sins you've committed are washed clean by the blood of Jesus, so of course you are forgiven. You know, I'm also concerned because the Seahawks are going to a 4–3 defense. Now, in my opinion..."

I am free to rest in His forgiveness, and I can stop beating myself up for anything I had done in my past, because He has *forgotten* my sin. If God forgets my sin, who am I to keep bringing it up?

"He has given you all of the present and all of the future" (1 Corinthians 3:22b).
"Forgetting the past and looking forward to what lies ahead" (Philippians 3:13).
"He forgives all my sins. He heals me. He has removed our sins as far away from us as the east is from the west" (Psalm 103:3, 12).

It seems to me that if the past was important to God, He would have said something more about it other than for us to ask forgiveness, get up again on our shaky legs, and mark out a straight path for others to follow. God forgives us and removes our sins from us. He wants us to model His principles of living to all the people around us who are watching to see if this Christianity thing really works. And this is especially important in the area of marriage because broken homes have filled our prisons and shaken the very foundation of our existence here on earth. God's master plan was built on the family as a unit. We have destroyed it, even in the church, and I have no idea if anything can stem the tide of divorce and broken relationships. Each of us can help, however, by making *our* marriage one that reflects God and his master plan.

I was so touched the first time I heard author and Bible study teacher Kay Arthur tell the story about what a silversmith does. He takes the silver ore, puts it in a crucible in a furnace, and turns up the heat a little bit. His goal is to burn the impurities out of the ore. A little bit later he takes the ore out of the furnace and checks to see if there are any specks and impurities still in it. If it is still not completely pure, he puts it back in the furnace and turns up the heat a little more. He is very careful not to let the fire get so hot that it would burn up the ore. He wants it just hot enough to burn off the impurities. He keeps doing this until the time comes when he takes the ore out of the furnace, looks down, and sees his image in the metal. That's a picture of how God works in our lives. When God allows us to go through the fiery trials and struggles of life, it isn't to burn us up or destroy us. He wants to burn the impurities out of our life. When that is done, He will be able to see *His* image in us.

How about you? Are you all bound up with marriage problems, anger, lust, envy, greed, worry, and fear? Are you in bondage to addictions? Are you allowing God to process you into the image of Christ? Or are you fighting your circumstances, questioning God, feeling like quitting or running away. I've felt like this, too, at times, but I've always come back to the realization that God allows these things in my life for a purpose. Many times in hindsight I can see what He had in mind for the trial after the fact. It's natural to want to run away from problems and responsibilities. It's *supernatural* to go through the trials and wait for God's blessing.

Sure it hurts to suffer, but in that suffering we become God's reflection to other people. I love the Sermon on the Mount where Jesus says, "Blessed are those who..." The original word for blessed means having a sense of God's favor and approval. I've never been on a drug high, but I can't imagine anything more fulfilling and wonderful than sensing you are in the middle of God's will for your life. You are working hard to make your marriage relationship everything God wants it to be. You are content and blessed and destined to spend eternity in His presence. It doesn't get any better than that.

Someone has said, and I love this, "God does not make life easy. He just makes it possible!" I alter that to read, "God does not make *marriage* easy. He just makes it possible." Here's a prayer that was written by an unknown confederate soldier.

I asked God for strength that I might achieve;
I was made weak, that I might learn humbly to obey.
I asked for health, that I might do greater things;
I was given infirmity that I might do better things.
I asked for riches, that I might be happy;
I was given poverty, that I might be wise.
I asked for power, that I might have the praise of men;
I was given weakness, that I might feel the need of God.
I asked for all things, that I might enjoy life;
I was given life, that I might enjoy all things.
I got nothing that I asked for, but everything I had hoped for.
Almost despite myself, my unspoken prayers were answered.
I am among all men, most richly blessed.

Now let's look at one of the most powerful ideas God ever invented. It sets the captive free, it gives, it is always others-centered. It's called servanthood.

18

HI, MOM!

Barb: Let me ask you a question: Who do you think has the most authority in the family? Who do the football players say "Hi" to on TV? That's right—Mom. We're aware of that, but we're really not sure why. We know Mom cooks and cleans. She washes the dishes and the clothes. She gets up at night with us when we are sick and takes us to the doctor. She shops for us, acts as our taxi driver, goes to all our sporting events, and helps at school parties. She plans meals for special occasions like birthdays, and pays attention to our special likes and dislikes.

Have you guessed what gives Mom her authority in the family? It's because she *serves*. We were all so touched when we saw that young hockey player looking for his dad after the U.S.A. beat the Soviet Union in hockey during the Olympics a few years ago. It was so unusual to see him looking for Dad rather than Mom. Now it could have been his mom was not living, but even if he had a mom, I'm sure his dad had spent his life serving his son and the rest of his family. Therefore, here is my premise. Headship is not decision making, it is serving. Let's take a look at some Scriptures and see if you agree. The first one is in Matthew 20:25–28: "But Jesus called them to Himself, and said, 'You know that the rulers of the Gentiles lord it over them, and their great men exercise authority over them. It is not so among you, but whoever wishes to become great among you shall be your servant, and whoever wishes to be first among you shall be your slave; just as the Son of Man did not come to be served, but to serve, and to give His life a ransom for many.'"

"And sitting down, He called the twelve and said to them, 'If anyone wants to be first, he shall be last of all, and servant of all'" (Mark 9:35).

"But whoever wishes to become great among you shall be your servant; and whoever wishes to be first among you shall be slave of all. For even the Son of Man did not come to be served, but to serve, and to give His life a ransom for many" (Mark 10:43b–45).

And here is Jesus talking to his disciples as they ate a meal together.

"But let him who is the greatest among you become as the youngest, and the leader as the servant. For who is greater, the one who reclines at the table, or the one who serves? Is it not the one who reclines at the table? But I am among you as the one who serves" (Luke 22:26b–27).

We can see from these verses that God does not want us to lord it over others as the Gentile leaders did, but to serve one another. If our ambition is to be a leader, we are to be servants. Peter told us in 1 Peter 2:21 that Jesus Christ left us an example so we could follow in his steps. The word *example* means an exact tracing. We are to do as he did. He did not come to be served, but to serve, even though he was greater than the ones he served. Both the Old and New Testaments make it plain we are to serve each other. However, when some couples come to the marriage relationship, they think one person is to lord it over the other.

There are some people who believe men are superior to women and they point out Genesis 3:16b which says, "And he [the man] shall rule over you [the woman]." Let me ask you a question. How does the Lord rule? He rules lovingly. He is long suffering. While we were yet sinners He died for us and gave Himself up for us. He serves us. The Hebrew word for rule is also the word used to describe the Messiah ruling over Israel. When a husband thinks of ruling, he thinks it is with a rod of iron like the Lord will use when He rules in judgment over the unbelieving nations when He comes back at the end of the great tribulation. However, the Lord Jesus Christ always rules believers with a scepter of love.

I would like to say it one more time. God tells us in the Bible to serve one another. The commands He gives us as husbands and wives are given so we can serve our mates in the way they need to be served so they can feel loved. I know some people selfishly are afraid to serve because they are sure they will be taken advantage of.

"All of you, clothe yourselves with humility toward one another, FOR GOD IS OPPOSED TO THE PROUD, BUT GIVES GRACE TO THE HUMBLE [emphasis mine]. Humble yourselves, therefore, under the mighty hand of God, that He may exalt you at the proper time, casting all your anxiety upon Him, because He cares for you" (1 Peter 5:5–7).

Here's that word *humble* again. Remember we talked about denying ourselves, becoming a servant, humbling ourselves, and becoming obedient to the point of death? God would not ask you to do anything that is not for your good. He says to cast your cares and anxiety on Him because He cares for you.

There is a quote from G. K. Chesterton that says, "The Christian ideal has not been tried and found wanting. It has been found difficult and left untried." Another quote I've read is, "Obedience belongs to us; results belong to God." Our mindset has to be that God is God. He knows what is best for us, He created us and knows what we need. So I'm not going to presume I know more than He does. I'm going to obey.

There is a story in 1 Kings 12 about Solomon's son Rehoboam who had become king. His rival Jeroboam came to him one day to tell him that if he would take away the heavy yoke Solomon had put on the people, he and his followers would serve him. Rehoboam told him to go away so he could consult the elders who had served his father Solomon and ask for counsel as to how to answer Jeroboam. The elders told him, "If you will be a servant to this people today, will serve them, grant them their petition, and speak good words to them, then they will be your servants forever."

But he didn't listen to the counsel of the elders and consulted instead with the young men with whom he had grown up; they had served him. The young men told Rehoboam to make the people's yoke even heavier than Solomon had done. And because of Rehoboam's decision to be served rather than serve, his rival Jeroboam rebelled and split the country, forming the northern kingdom of Israel and leaving Rehoboam as king of the southern kingdom of Judah.

I believe selfishness and refusal to serve one another is the very reason why so many marriages split and end in divorce. When partners decide to serve themselves instead of their mate, they have set up a situation ripe for conflict. This is not God's way of doing things. Sociologist and author Tony

Campolo points out the difference between power and authority. Power is taken, authority is earned or conferred. Therefore, as a husband serves, the wife looks to him as her authority. He achieves the high position of authority, not by force, or deciding on his own to take it, or by being overbearing. He gets his authority by serving. The Lord tells us when we lose our life for His sake, then we'll find it. Chuck has been my greatest example of how a husband should serve. Whenever he sees a principle in Scripture, he obeys. I'm so grateful for him.

So we've seen that headship is not decision making, it is serving. It is thinking more highly of others than we think of ourselves. It brings us back to the Scripture in Philippians 2:3: "Do nothing from selfishness or empty conceit, but with humility of mind let each of you regard one another as more important than himself."

Chuck: I owe my entire existence to my parents who gave me life. My parents showed God's serving type of love to me. Through the eons of eternity, I will never be able to repay them for their many kindnesses and all of the investments they made in me as a young person. This includes the most important thing that has ever happened to me. My parents introduced me to God and his Son the Lord Jesus Christ. They were so faithful to make God real to me day to day. They helped us so much when Barb and I set up our first household. They made loving contributions to our lives and our kids' lives—physically, emotionally, and spiritually from that day on until the day they died. They are both with the Lord now, and I'm anxious to see them again so I can express my eternal gratitude for the love they expressed in so many ways. I hope Dad has found a place in heaven to practice his clarinet where he won't have to worry about bothering anyone. I also hope the Lord has a large supply of glazed donuts for my mom to have with her coffee as she reads her book in the shade of a heavenly tree.

The person who had the next greatest impact on my life is the one I honored on the dedication page of this book. There are not words enough to tell you about all the contributions Barb has made to my life.

Then I want you to meet my spiritual hall of fame. There have been hundreds of other people who have impacted my life greatly, but these people are the ones who had the most dramatic impact on my life other than God, my parents, and Barb. These were the third parties God brought into my life to teach me God's principles.

Bill Gothard

Ken Taylor

Keith Miller

Gary Smalley

Larry Burkett

Chuck Swindoll

Even though all these people have had a big influence in my life and gave me much advice on how to mature as a Christian, learning to be a servant was something I had to learn by experience. God used a struggle with finances to teach me how to be a servant in my marriage. It happened in the twenty-second year of our marriage. I had turned over my life to Jesus Christ 100 percent following my attending Bill Gothard's Basic Youth Conflicts seminar in 1971. This 100 percent included my time, talents, material things, bank accounts, tennis ball machine, and everything else I owned, plus the business we had purchased that same year. Because God now owned our business, He could trust us with a little surplus. He knew we would be giving a portion of it away to His people and organizations, so He began blessing our business materially.

I have already mentioned, my method of business was to stay small, do personal service for my clients, and perform much of the work myself. That way I could keep my overhead low, do the work at less cost, and, hopefully, do it just as good or better than anyone else in town. Barb's and my business plan was to ask God to bring in more money than we gave away. If He wanted to bring in less, we would give away less. If He took us to zero (which He almost did, but that's another book someday), then we would sell our home and play tennis the rest of our lives. Using this business plan, God could dictate exactly what He wanted us to do through the business income. He was absolutely in control, and I liked that.

During the first years of our marriage, I had not yet given God complete control of my life, so He was not able to bless us as much as He would have liked to. He had promised to meet our needs, and He surely did that. We never missed a meal, and we paid our bills on time, but it seemed like every time we got a few dollars ahead in our savings account, the kids would need new shoes or a tire would blow out. This seemed to reinforce the idea that God would meet our needs, but nothing extra. At that time I really wasn't into the Scriptures much, so I couldn't check this out. But after the Lord and Ken Taylor wrote *The Living Bible,* I could finally read the Scripture in my own language, and it wasn't long before I ran into 2 Corinthians 9:7–8, 11 that said:

> Every one must make up his own mind as to how much he should give. Don't force anyone to give more than he really wants to, for cheerful givers are the ones God prizes. God is able to make it up to you by giving you everything you need and more, so that there will not only be enough for your own needs, but plenty left over to give joyfully to others.…Yes, God will give you much so that you can give away much, and when we take your gifts to those who need them they will break out into thanksgiving and praise to God for your help.

All of a sudden it was very clear that God would not only meet our needs, He would give us a *surplus* if we were really sold out to doing things His way. Not to buy gold dog houses, or a third Mercedes, or pave our driveway in diamonds. This Scripture is *so plain.* The surplus is for us to *give away,* not to use just for our own enjoyment. And the more we give away, the more money He will give us to give away. We won't be able to get ahead of Him. The word *cheerful* in this Scripture means with *hilarity.* It is a rambunctious, pull-out-the-stops, don't-shoot-the-piano-player-Mabel-he's-doing-the-best-he-can type of joy and fun as we give money away in God's name.

Larry Burkett was the one who first introduced us to the concept of a couple not making decisions unless they were both in agreement. Before that, I took God at his word that Barb and I were one. And of course I felt, as Barb told you, that I was the *one!* I'm not sure how I came to that position. I guess we had been mistaught by our churches that if a couple couldn't make a decision, then the man was to make the final decision. As you know from the previous chapter, that's not only selfish on the man's part, it's not biblical.

Early in our marriage, Barb and I had always been pretty much in agreement when it came to helping other people, or spending money on projects, or making investments. We began to tithe during the first year of our marriage. God honored that commitment. Something would come up that involved giving away money. We would discuss it, ask each other what amount the other person had in mind, and most of the time we would independently come up with the same amount. This was one of the ways God confirmed his will to us. This happened way too many times to be just a coincidence, so we were certain God had a hand in our financial giving.

As you'll remember, I'm a dreamer and have hundreds of ideas as to how to change the world. We never had a surplus of money before, but now after twenty-two years of marriage, there was some left over. How exciting! We had too much to give it all away at once, so I began looking around for projects in which to invest. We also wanted some of it to be available for spontaneous people-needs that came up. So I began taking world-changing investment plans to Barb so we could be good stewards of God's money. I would lay this awesome world-changing plan on the table for her approval. Her eyebrows raised a bit and she would say a very strange thing. "I don't *feel* good about the project." I couldn't believe my ears. What did *feel* have to do with anything? Look at these numbers. They fit, don't they? *Feel?* How can we make sound business decisions on feelings? For the life of me, I couldn't find feelings on the business plan I had presented.

Through some tears Barb would release me to go ahead with the investment if I felt it was God's will for our money, but she just didn't feel good about it. Since I had not yet learned that leadership meant serving, not decision making, like an idiot I went ahead with the plan. No, I think that is too harsh as I look back. I wasn't an idiot. I was just grossly mistaught by my spiritual leaders. So I put the world-changing idea into motion, and guess what? I lost the money. The plan blew up in my face. Little did I know at the time I was doing this entirely on my own. I thought God would be pleased with my efforts because all of the projects had spiritual overtones.

In time I would take another world-changing plan to Barb and she would say another strange thing. "I don't trust those people." *Trust?* Wait a minute. I've worked with these people for two years or so, and you just met them at dinner the other night. You don't trust them? I didn't understand, but once again Barb would release me if I thought my idea was what God wanted us to do, and again I lost the money.

There were six or seven different projects I took to her during this time, and I lost money on every one. I was asked by one of the people who worked for a client to cosign a bank note for her so she could buy a car. She was divorced and couldn't get credit and needed the car for work. (I hadn't gotten to Proverbs yet where it says cosigning notes is *stupid!* I think the original Hebrew word is *estoopo* or something like that. I always like to work in some heavy teaching in the stuff I write just in case Barb ever reads it.)

I remember this person's words so well. She said that she would *never* allow me to get hurt, but one day the bank called me to pay for "my" car. She had defaulted, and I have never heard from her again.

I wanted to sponsor a rock band that had a couple of members who professed to be Christians. I won't go into all the details, but I lost a great deal of money on that project. Barb didn't feel good about the project or trust the people involved. I knew this, but I still gave them money, even some behind her back. I didn't do this to hurt her. I loved her. I wasn't a beast. I just thought God had some things for us to do, and Barb never seemed to be on the same page of the program with me. I haven't had one dime of these investments returned, and I don't even know where the people are now.

One of my world-changing projects was to double the Lord's money overnight with a get-rich-quick land deal in Nevada. All I had to do was give this person money, and their contact would resell the land, and I would make a killing for the Lord. (Again, I hadn't gotten to Proverbs yet that says trying to get-rich-quick is *also* estoopo.) Barb suggested a very impractical idea. She said, "Why don't you go look at the land before you give the people the money?" Why should I look at the land? I *trust* the people involved. So I gave them the money and *then* went down to look at the land. I now own a piece of property in the middle of Nevada about seven miles out of Elkheart. It's very quiet out there. There are no roads, phone lines, sewers, or houses. Nothing but sagebrush. How did Barb know it was a con and they were going to cheat me? I haven't heard from those people since either.

Barb: During the time Chuck was making all these financial decisions without me, we would talk and cry and then talk and cry some more. Chuck would often say, "I just don't understand it. I feel I am getting a message from the Lord to do these things. I want to do the Lord's will. Why are we having all this trouble between us? Who am I hearing from?" Neither of us had an answer at the time. I was afraid to resist too much, because I had been taught a wife must be submissive. So I would say, "If you really think this is from the Lord, go ahead and do it." But my heart would be screaming, *"Don't do it!"* I just knew it wasn't right. But I still didn't have a good reason why it wasn't right. I just knew it wasn't.

This was a time in our lives when I used to say that God and Chuck were doing things without me. Always before, we had made financial decisions together, and if one of us did not agree, we didn't do it. I knew we weren't a team anymore. It was a very hard time for both of us.

During this time Chuck was counseling with a couple who said they were Christians but were living together without being married. At one time I thought I saw growth in their lives, so we agreed to help them out financially. Then as time went on they continued to live together. Since I saw no obedience in their lives, I thought we should no longer help them.

We had arranged our finances so we put all income into one account. Then each month we would take an equal amount and put it into two personal accounts. We were not accountable to each other for this money. I could use mine to buy a special blouse, or Chuck could go golfing. But I assumed we would never buy anything we knew the other person was against.

Chuck: I guess I took our arrangement too literally. I thought if we were not accountable to each other, then I should be able to use the money for anything I wanted, including giving it away. This principle doesn't really work if either of the partners can have a say in how it is spent. Barb's point, however, is that I was doing something I *knew* she didn't approve of. Usually the things we use our personal accounts for are a little more innocent.

I was going out of my mind. Here I had dedicated my resources to the Lord. I thought the projects had spiritual overtones, and yet they were blowing up in my face—every one of them. I lost thousands of dollars of the Lord's and Barb's money. What was God trying to teach me? Was he really paying attention? My life's goal was to be in the center of his will. He owned everything I had, and yet things were crumbling around me, including my marriage, since

I was offending Barb at every turn by not including her in these financial decisions and projects. I had not noticed yet that she was 95 percent *right* as to
who to trust, and that her feelings were on target when it came to relationships. I was just mad at God. I wanted to take my dog Muffit (she was the only
one who gave me unconditional love) to Maine and set up a farm and forget
people. The reason I chose Maine was it was the furthermost point away from
Seattle I could think of. I'm sure there are people living in Maine who have felt
like coming to Seattle to farm, too.

After the last disaster, the Lord and I were having one of our board meetings in the car. I was trying to figure out what He was doing to me. I was angry
at Him, questioning His judgment, asking whether He really cared. I said,
"Considering eternity past, and eternity future, would you admit you made
one little mistake—just one—and that's not a bad record." The mistake I had
in mind was him designing Barb so she'd always be against the things I wanted
to do.

God and I have a wonderful relationship. He does not get depressed, or
disappointed, or bothered by the fact that I yell at Him once in a while. He does
not zap me with lightning or reduce me to ashes. He's very sympathetic and
grieves with me, even though this time if I could have seen His face during my
little fuss He probably would have been smiling. Here's His two-year-old throwing a tantrum down in the car. I got the impression He said something like,
"Remember when I opened the Red Sea for the Jewish guys and gals when
Pharaoh was chasing them in the desert?" (Yes.) "Have you noticed the sun
and moon I hung for you to give you warmth and light?" (Yes.) "Have you
noticed my design in nature, the stars, trees, animals, the marvelous way your
body is designed?" (Yes.) "Then what you're really saying to me is that Barb's
heart is much too big for me to change if the project is something I want you
to accomplish as a marriage team."

In other words, God was saying, here I am creator of the universe, and
even though I could hang the moon, and save the Jewish people, I would have
to say, "How are we going to get *this* done, since Barb's against it?"

It quickly dawned on me that the creator of the universe would probably
have more power than that, and He could even change *Barb's* heart if it was
something He wanted us to do. So I said to the Lord, "Okay, I know you can

change her heart, so I'll not do one more thing unless Barb is in agreement." Barb and I were supposed to be a team in our marriage. I knew I had gotten off her team. Now I had great peace of mind and heart but gave up any expectations of ever doing one more project in my life. It seemed Barb had been against just about everything I wanted to do, especially in the area of investments. So I assumed since I had made that vow to the Lord, Barb would now have the last word, and I would just play tennis the rest of my days. I told the Lord, "If something does come up you want us to do, just wait until I'm through with my doubles match, and speak to me through Barb."

Barb: I was looking for our family checkbook one day and accidentally opened Chuck's personal checkbook. I saw entries that indicated he was still giving money to this couple behind my back. I talked to him about this and told him if I knew his heart on something, I would not go ahead if I knew he disapproved. He replied that he couldn't imagine a time when he would not approve of giving money away. (He has the gift of giving, so that is probably true.) I told him I didn't think that was the point of our discussion.

And then it hit me! Would God do anything to break up our team? Would God tell us to do something that would drive us apart? No, He wouldn't. Therefore, I reasoned God would not tell either one of us to do something that the other was against because that would break up the team.

We were having a very heated discussion over the matter when the phone rang. It was a good friend to whom we both enjoyed talking. We talked, of course, like nothing was wrong. I assumed since we had been interrupted in our discussion, we would probably not talk about this again for a long time because Chuck hated conflict so much. Chuck had taken the telephone extension at the opposite end of the house. After we hung up, I walked down the hall toward Chuck, and there he was with his arms open wide saying, "I want to be on your team."

Chuck: I was still a planner and dreamer, and once in a while I brought some more world-changing ideas to Barb, but a funny thing happened. I began saying strange things like, "How do you *feel* about this?" and "Do you trust these people?" I did *not* go ahead with any projects without her feeling good about them. Now she began to be *less* resistant to some of the things I felt God wanted us to do as a marriage team. In fact, she was even *for* some of the things I wanted to do, if you can imagine that. God wasn't trying to teach me about finances just then. He wanted to teach me about serving my wife and to appreciate the gifts Barb had brought to the relationship.

Right about here the men to whom I tell my story get nervous. They say, "What if Barb is wrong? Eve blew it. Sarah got Abraham in trouble. What happens when your wife is against something God *really* wants you to do?" My sincere reply is that's *God's* problem. He hung the moon, so He can surely change Barb's heart if it is something He really wants us to do. If we *do* miss something God wants us to do, He is at fault if He doesn't make it clear through Barb. I'm through making independent decisions and harming our marriage team. Looking back, my "Red Sea" experience, as I called it, might have been the key to restoring our relationship to what it had been before. I had gotten back on her team.

That doesn't mean she's always right, but her track record is about 95 percent right when it involves relationships, and very few things in life *don't* involve people. I went from resenting her ability to feel and trust, to thanking God for her ability to complete me so beautifully.

I've also panicked a lot of dreamers out there in book land because they are married to very conservative, cautious partners who shudder when you bring up a new project. This is not a man-woman thing as much as it is a personality difference. The woman can be the dreamer and the one who rushes off into the unknown. The same principles apply to her, even if for a different reason. If her husband doesn't agree or feel good about the project, *she* should not go ahead of him. My experience is, however, that women tend to be much more practical than men, so I would be wasting God's gift if I was not open to Barb's thoughts.

We dreamers often fail our more conservative mates by thinking about a world-changing plan for two weeks. Then we present it to them at dinner and expect them to get up and run around the table in glee praising our wonderful plan. Instead, their eyes roll back in their heads, they get terribly silent, and sweat more than usual. Then we react to their "lack of confidence" and dump our plans in the trash heap without giving our partner much of a chance to learn why we are so excited about them.

What I've done to help in this area is to write Barb notes when I first start to think of a project or plan. This way she has the same time to think about it as I do, and when we come together at dinner she can talk about it objectively. This also eliminates body language which I tend to read the wrong way.

Now let me repeat, this doesn't mean Barb is in absolute control of the family, and I am just running around doing or not doing what she wants done, while feeling defeated because she is not as much of a dreamer as I am. I just sincerely believe that if it is something *God* wants us to do, He is perfectly capable of changing and softening her heart toward the project. Biblically, I see no other alternative. In practice it works out great.

The only good I can see coming out of all the pain Barb suffered while I was doing my own thing, is that God brought us both to the position where we can share what we have learned with you. It is *great* to make decisions together. At least most of the time it's great. There still are times when I grieve that Barb doesn't see the value of one of my ideas. This teamwork, however, releases so much of the tension. This gives us both security. Now if we lose money by giving a loan to someone who doesn't pay it back, or lose it through an investment where we both were conned, we can *laugh* about it. There is no tension at all. We hate to lose the money, but we *know* we have asked God's guidance in the matter. We *know* we were united in doing what we did, so God must have something to work out in our lives through losing the money. Did you hear that? We can *laugh* about the matter. Prior to my getting back on Barb's team, it would be a time of many gut-wrenching tears and conflict.

One of our best friends just lost a lot of money in the stock market because he didn't heed the warning of his wife who didn't "feel good" about the investment. We recently met a man at one of our seminars who lost a motel chain because he didn't listen to his wife. Another man lost money in a newspaper venture because he didn't take the counsel of his wife. Another man put his family through bankruptcy because he didn't take his wife's feelings and wisdom into his investments. I'm sure there are numerous incidents where a man disregarded the counsel of his wife and has caused his family suffering because of it. Men, you knew you were going to be in big trouble reading this book, but you didn't know *how* big. Now's the time to make a verbal commitment to your wife saying you will not do *one thing* unless she is for it. Get back on her team. Learn to lead by serving. Take her counsel, listen to her feelings, and trust God, and then you can *laugh* with us when God allows you to be conned or lose money. After all, He owns it, right? And your marriage will have less tension as you both learn to serve one another in other areas besides finances.

Our next subject is similar to servanthood. It's called submission, and it causes smoke to come out of the ears of some folks. It's an often mistaught principle, but a correct understanding of submission is one of the keys to having a successful marriage team.

19

GIVING IN OR
GIVING TO

Chuck: Now we want to talk about a very misunderstood biblical concept. It raises the hackles (whatever they are) on the back of some necks, elevates the blood pressure, and makes smoke come out the ears. The word is *submission.* This concept has been abused over the years, especially by men. Ephesians 5 is one of the basic Scriptures that sheds light on this concept. Most men will start at verse 22 where it says, "You wives must submit to your husbands' leadership in the same way you submit to the Lord." To a man, that sounds great. This means I make all the final decisions in the family. I determine all the vacation sites, who takes out the garbage, and what time my wife will have dinner ready.

We men have a problem, however, when we back up one verse and read, "Honor Christ by submitting to each other." That's not quite as clear cut as I thought it was. This sounds more like a *team* relationship rather than one member lording it over the other. We mentioned in the last chapter that men often misunderstand the concept of leadership. Remember, the Bible says being a leader means being a servant. So, rather than making our family conform to our every whim, it appears that it is *we men* who should be conforming to the needs of the family.

Barb: I've thought so much about how to present this. It will not be easy for you to read—nor will it be easy to do. However, what I am going to show you is the key to having a great marriage even though you feel you and your mate are incompatible. We are all so different, and often we can't agree on the things we want. Even this last week, I found myself angry with Chuck because his values were not my values. I had to deny myself to serve him, but I wanted him to deny himself also.

The most important consideration is our heart attitude. Do we want to serve ourselves or serve the Lord? Are we committed to ourselves, or are we committed to Jesus Christ? Are we out to do things our own way, or are we sold out to doing the things God wants us to do?

I often think of 1 Peter 5:7 which tells us to cast all our anxiety on him because he cares for us. Just before that Peter told us to humble ourselves before God so he can exalt us. God knows we'd often rather not do things his way. But God tells us, "Don't worry, I care for you. I won't tell you to do anything that won't turn out for your good." Even the things we consider bad will be for our good. Someone has said the Lord may hurt us, but He will never harm us. Chuck and I have had to hurt for a while in order to find peace with each other. But in the long run, only good has come from the hurt, never harm.

We are told over and over again in the Bible to follow Christ's example.

"You call Me Teacher and Lord; and you are right, for so I am. If I then, the Lord and the Teacher, washed your feet, you also ought to wash one another's feet. For I gave you an example that you also should do as I did to you. Truly, truly, I say to you, a slave is not greater than his master; neither is one who is sent greater than the one who sent him. If you know these things, you are blessed if you do them" (John 13:13–17).

So we see, we are to follow His example, and when we do we will be blessed. He wasn't teaching us to wash feet. He was teaching us how to serve. And serving is not lording it over others. He came to love unconditionally, which means He loves us no matter what we've done in the past, or might do in the future. The question we have to ask ourselves is do I have the same attitude—to love and to serve.

I was once asked, "What message do you think the Lord has given both of you? The one that stands out the most in your minds." At first I talked about serving one another, and of course that is key. But then I thought there was a step that came before serving. It was obeying God's Word. If we have never been obedient to what we read in Scripture and what we know the Lord wants us to do, we won't know anything about serving.

One of the reasons we don't want to obey is we are sure the Lord wants to put us in a prison of some kind. We don't realize that He has set parameters around us to set us free. We think the Ten Commandments were given to bind us up. We have missed the point completely. They were given to set us free—both in our relationship with the Lord and with one another. The Ten Commandments talk about loving the Lord our God with all our mind, with all our soul, and with all our strength, and our neighbor as ourselves.

"But one who looks intently at the perfect law, the law of liberty, and abides by it, not having become a forgetful hearer but an effectual doer, this man shall be blessed in what he does" (James 1:25).

So we must know what the Bible says, remember it, and abide in it. In other words, keep on doing it as a habit of life. Then God will bless us in what we do. And if we obey, we will receive blessing in the form of honor.

"If anyone serves Me, let him follow Me;…if anyone serves Me, the Father will honor him" (John 12:26).

The reason this is so hard is because most people have not decided to make that lifetime commitment to the Lord rather than to themselves.

"If anyone wishes to come after Me, let him deny himself, take up his cross, and follow Me" (Mark 8:34).

The verbs *deny* and *take up* found in this verse are in a Greek verb tense that means to decide to do something at one point in time, and then because of that decision, make it a goal for the rest of your life. The verb *follow me* is in the present tense, which means to keep on following. By the way, *follow* in the Greek here includes the meaning of accompanying or walking side by side. It's the same as being in the same yoke with the Lord. And Jesus says in Matthew 11:30, "My yoke is easy" and *easy* can be translated kind or pleasant. See how the Word fits together? It's a pleasant experience to be honored and exalted because we have decided to be obedient. Then we keep on following and being in the same yoke with him because we've made it a lifetime goal. All of these principles I've shown you relate to what the roles of a husband and wife should be in a marriage. We must make it a lifetime goal to submit to each other because God tells us in Ephesians 5:21 to "be subject to one another in the fear of Christ."

This is a willing personal submission. It is not just the woman submitting to the man, but also the man submitting to the woman. The Greek word for *to one another* is *allelois* and indicates equality of all concerned. It means those of the same kind or of equal value before God. I think this solves one of the problems we wives often face. Somehow, both men and women have come to believe women are in an inferior position. This is just not true, as the Greek word *allelois* shows us. We willingly submit to each other knowing our partner has value in God's eyes. Since God values our partner, we are to value them, too.

The word *fear* in Ephesians 5:21 means a wholesome dread of ever displeasing the Lord. Because you know He is your creator, and He knows the beginning from the end, and He rules over all, you don't want to do anything to displease Him. The controlling motive of your life is to do what He says. Therefore, you submit to each other because you love the Lord.

Picture a triangle with God at the top, a husband at one of the lower corners, and a wife at the other. When you are not submitting to each other, the two of you at the bottom of the triangle draw further apart. The further you get from each other, the further you are from the Lord.

Our granddaughter Kjersten watched *Sesame Street* on TV when she was about three years old. She was in love with Big Bird, so we bought an animated Big Bird for her birthday. It had an audio tape that told a story as its eyes blinked and its beak moved. After she opened her present, she just sat on the carpet in awe of that bird. She would reach out and gently touch Big Bird. Then she would kiss its beak. Then she gently lifted Big Bird into her arms and carried him all over the house while he told her a story. Wouldn't it be wonderful if people cared that much about God and what He says? Wouldn't it be wonderful if we loved Him so much that we would be that much in awe of Him and do what He told us to?

The following verses show us *how* we are to submit. When we walk in the roles the Lord gives us, our partner feels loved because these roles fulfill the other's needs. The roles of men and women are different because we have different needs.

The husband is to be the provider. God said to Adam in Genesis 3:17–19:

> "Because you have listened to the voice of your wife, and have eaten
> from the tree about which I commanded you, saying, 'You shall not

eat from it'; cursed is the ground because of you; in toil you shall eat of it all the days of your life. Both thorns and thistles it shall grow for you; and you shall eat the plants of the field; by the sweat of your face you shall eat bread, till you return to the ground, because from you were taken; for you are dust, and to dust you shall return."

On the other hand, *the wife is to be a worker at home.*

Be sensible, pure, workers at home (Titus 2:5).

With all the talk of equality between the sexes, our thinking has gotten distorted. Our young people do not think a woman can be fulfilled being home with the children. A woman in our culture feels she must have a job outside the home to be fulfilled. Even many young men feel their wives should work to help provide more money for the family. The problem is when young mothers go to work, their husbands and children are left wanting for so many things that only a wife and Mom can do. Scripture does not say a woman cannot work outside the home. In fact, the woman in Proverbs 31 was quite a businesswoman. However, her home was in order and well cared for. She also had lots of help!

The word worker can also be translated keeper or guardian of the home. A woman's primary responsibility is the home. Even when we work in the marketplace, we still feel the need for everything to be in order at home. Are the clothes washed? Do we have the right food in the house? Do we have food in the house at all? Are my husband's shirts ironed? This is a God-given feeling and responsibility. Therefore, it's natural for a woman to be concerned about these things.

On the other hand, when a man has been laid off or retired too soon, and he has nothing to do, his sense of worth suffers. This is because *providing* for his family is *his* God-given feeling and responsibility.

The husband is to be the protector.

For the husband is the head of the wife, as Christ also is the head of the church, He Himself being the Savior of the body (Ephesians 5:25).

Christ is the example of the perfect protector. In Psalm 23 we see He guides us even when we walk in darkness, and He leads us into paths of righteousness. He is always watching out for us and taking care of us.

I love it when Chuck guides me across the street with his hand on my back. Or gives me that feeling of protection in large groups when he keeps touching me to let me know he is there. He shows his protection in so many ways. He takes care to see my car is in good shape. He keeps the walks free of snow in the winter. He always checks to see if I've left the iron on before we go to bed. He brings in the bags of groceries when I buy food because he knows they are heavy for me. When he does these and many other things, I feel protected and valued.

From the same Scripture we see that *the husband is to be head of the wife as Christ also is the head of the church.*

We've already talked about what true headship is when we talked about servant leadership. Again, Christ is our example. He served rather than lording it over other people. Husbands need to do the same thing.

Most men think they are going to be served when they get married. Maybe we all want to be served, for that matter. But remember, "God's ways are not our ways." When we serve, we are served in return. To be served in return should not be our motivation for serving. Husbands should lead by serving just because God said to. However, the Lord has wonderful surprises for us when we obey.

Next we see that *the wife is to be in submission to the godly headship of her husband.*

Wives, be subject to your own husbands, as to the Lord (Ephesians 5:22).

Be sure to note that we are to be subject to our *own* husband. We would get in lots of trouble trying to listen to someone else's husband and our own too. According to the Greek scholar Spiros Zodhiates, Th.D., the Greek word for *be subject* or *submit* is *hupotassomai* which means to place oneself in one's own category under one's husband. The Greek language makes it clear a husband cannot make his wife do this. She must decide to do it. We wives are to subject ourselves to our husbands to accomplish a common goal. As Dr. Zodhiates says, it is the wife placing herself in the proper, divinely-fitted position under her husband. This is a decision a wife makes. Again, it is not something a husband can command or make his wife do. It is her decision alone. If she recognizes she is doing this the same way she submits to the Lord, it is easier for her to place herself in the proper position under her husband. Dr. Zodhiates points out this submission is a response to a husband's love.

Here are some examples of how Jesus Christ responded and submitted to God's love.

"And He who sent Me is with Me; He has not left Me alone, for I always do the things that are pleasing to Him" (John 8:29).

True submission is doing what pleases your mate. When I know how Chuck feels about something, I can make a decision without consulting him. However, if I don't know his heart, then I wait until we have talked. He does the same thing for me. He did not show true submission when he used to make investments on his own against my counsel.

If I go out and spend money I know Chuck doesn't want me to spend, that would not be true submission either. True submission is doing what you know pleases your mate. Again, it is serving.

"For I have come down from heaven, not to do My own will, but the will of Him who sent Me" (John 6:38).
"I can do nothing on My own initiative As I hear, I judge; and My judgment is just, because I do not seek My own will, but the will of Him who sent Me" (John 5:30).

If we seek the will of God the Father, He will give us wisdom and good judgment. True submission is not doing your own thing, but doing the will of your God-centered husband. Another word that can be used for submission is adapting—adapting to the one God has given to you, so you become knit together into one piece of fabric.

The question often comes up, "If I am in submission, will I never again be independent? Can I ever make independent decisions again?" The answer is no. That's what marriage is all about. Two people becoming one, never again able to make independent decisions. When we get married, we enter into covenant with each other. This means we are responsible to each other and for each other. We are to care for one another and put the other one before ourselves. But do I lose all my authority when I am in submission?

> "And He gave Him authority to execute judgment, because He is the Son of Man" (John 5:27).

Because I am Chuck's wife, I have his authority also, but I'm not going to abuse that authority. Hopefully, I am only going to do those things that please him.

Some people worry about being inferior if they are submissive. Jesus Christ submitted to God the Father, but he was not inferior to God.

> "I and the Father are one" (John 10:30).

When two people marry, they become one flesh. Neither one is superior to the other.

> There is neither Jew nor Greek, there is neither slave nor free man, there is neither male nor female; for you are all one in Christ Jesus (Galatians 3:28).

This Scripture says essentially the same thing as Ephesians 5:21. Remember the verse about submitting to one another? The *one another* means those of the same kind or equal value before God. We are all of equal value, but we do have different responsibilities and functions to perform. In all of Scripture the Lord never tells us one person is superior to another in any circumstance.

When a husband is in headship over the wife, he shows his submission to the Lord by being a servant-leader. And when a wife is in submission to her husband, it is loving submission, the kind of submission that serves. God is the husband's example of loving rulership. He does not rule with a rod of iron as when He judges the nations, but with a scepter of love. Therefore, a husband is not to be the judge of his wife. And Christ is the wife's example of loving submission, doing only those things that please the Father. Can't you see how wonderful it will work if we will obey the things we have learned so far?

The wife was created to complete her husband.

> Then the Lord God said, "It is not good for the man to be alone; I will make him a helper suitable for him" (Genesis 2:18).

The words *helper suitable* have also been misunderstood. It means one who corresponds to him. One who completes him. God created woman to complete her husband. Sometimes I think of how God gave this gift to man, and he's been trying to refuse it ever since.

As we've been discussing, men and women are not the same. We *do* have different views and opinions, and that is precisely the point. We bring strengths to the relationship that our partners do not have.

If I was the only one writing this book, you probably would not get to laugh very often because I do not have the sense of humor Chuck has. Also, because I have a teaching gift, I don't see as many practical things as Chuck does. But together we are both stronger. Together we present a more balanced picture. However, the key has been for us to learn to accept each other's differences.

The wife is in the supportive role.

> For indeed man was not created for the woman's sake, but woman for the man's sake (1 Corinthians 11:9).

I know this is a shock to many of you women, and you men are excited. But it's true. We wives are the support to our husbands.

Whenever I talk with wives and explain this, I get lots of nods and smiles of affirmation. Just think about your own relationship with your husband. How many times have you been his support? How many times have you had

to be strong when he felt weak? What happens when our husbands have inse-
curity on their jobs? Aren't we women the ones who have to be strong so we
can support our husbands?

The trouble comes when we as women do not realize we're called to support our husbands. Instead, we go out and get a job or get so busy on committees or whatever that we don't have any energy left over to be the kind of
support our husbands need. You know that just being there to cook his
favorite meal, or to do something special that only you know your husband
needs, makes such a difference to him.

I believe having clean clothes ready is one of the most supportive things
we do for our husbands. It takes time and energy to be supportive. The question is, have we as wives figured this priority into how the Lord wants us to
be submissive?

I find great joy in supporting Chuck. When he is content, I am content.
When I push my way with him, and I know he is not happy, but going along
anyway just for me, I'm not happy. It's just not worth it. Our culture tells
women to do their own thing. Scripture tells us just the opposite. Even though
this might seem like a hard message, women, just stick with me a little longer,
and I think you'll see the big picture and like what you see.

The husband is to love in an unconditional, initiating way.

> Husbands, love your wives, just as Christ also loved the church and
> gave Himself up for her (Ephesians 5:25).

Husbands are told to love their wives with an *agape* love. This is a Greek
word for loving unconditionally; the kind of love with which Christ loved us
when He died for us while we were yet sinners. We did not have to perform
for Him in order to deserve His love. He initiated it. Romans 5:6–8 tells us
Jesus died for us while we were helpless, ungodly, sinners, and while we were
His enemy. First John 4:19 tells us we love God because He *first* loved us. In
other words, He loved us with His heart before He loved us by giving up His
life for us. This is how a man submits to his wife—*by giving up his life for her!*

Recently I said something Chuck didn't agree with. I could tell he was upset. He left the room, but before long he came back and filled my coffee cup and asked if there was anything else he could do for me. That's unconditional love. I did not have to perform for Chuck to show me that he loved me.

When we were younger, however, when I wanted to discuss something, he would walk away and stay away from me if my voice got too tight or too high pitched. He would say, "You should just hear yourself." He was not giving me unconditional love. I would have to shape up before we could talk any further. I agree I needed shaping up once in a while, but I did it out of fear, not respect. I just knew I had to perform to get his approval, because if I didn't, then he would withdraw his love. In defense of Chuck, he did not know his love was supposed to be unconditional, but when he found out what God commanded, he changed and no longer had me on a performance basis. (Most of the time!)

Here's how God asks men to love in that self-sacrificial way.

So husbands ought also to love their own wives as their own bodies. He who loves his own wife loves himself; for no one ever hated his own flesh, but nourishes and cherishes it, just as Christ also does the church (Ephesians 5:28–29).

Our bodies are very important to us, and we make sure they are taken care of. We clothe them, keep them warm, feed them, and treat them in a special way. A wife is supposed to be just as important to her husband as his own body. In fact, she is to be so important to him that he would give up his life for his wife.

Chuck has given up his life for me so many times. Take for instance the tennis court cover he wanted so badly. He wasn't angry because I didn't want to put a warehouse on our property. He doesn't always agree with me, but he still treats me nice and doesn't make my life miserable just because we don't see eye to eye. He gave up something important in his life in order to make me happy. I knew I was more important to him than a cover for the tennis court.

Another way he gave up his life for me was not setting three alarm clocks to go off fifteen minutes apart in the morning. As Chuck already told you, he likes to wake up gradually. He enjoys knowing the first two alarms mean he still has a little more time to sleep. Earlier in our marriage I would hear the alarms, but just go back to sleep until the next one went off.

Then something happened to me. Chuck would go back to sleep each time, but I would stay awake. When I finally told him about the problem, he didn't fuss and fume around. He just started to get up after the first one. It's called adjusting or even giving up one's life for another. It's also called serving.

Wives also have to show unconditional love because the Lord tells all of us in Ephesians 5:1–2 to "be imitators of God…and walk in love, just as Christ also loved you, and gave Himself up for us, an offering and a sacrifice to God."

This kind of love is not one-sided. I show Chuck unconditional love when I continue to cook meals *he* likes rather than what I like. I do make spaghetti once in a while, but I make sure I cook him a steak to go along with it. I go to events with him to which I would rather not go, and I do it with a good attitude.

Have you noticed women seem to be able to adapt better than men? Over the years Chuck would go to weddings with me. However, before we arrived I would have to hear a barrage of comments. "Why don't they just seat the parents before we get there?" "They could have the candles lit beforehand and hurry this thing up." "I've got so much to do. Let's just see the ceremony and get out of here." The comments continued endlessly through the whole ceremony. Finally, after forty years of marriage I told him, "You don't have to go to one more wedding. I would like to go alone so I won't have to listen to how miserable you are." I invited him to go if he wanted to but from this point on I made it clear he did not have to go.

Something interesting happened when I took the pressure off. With a good attitude I will tell him that I am going to such and so's wedding. No comment from Chuck. Then on the morning *of* Chuck says, "I really think I should go. Those kids mean a lot to us."

I'm telling you, it's like night and day. He goes with a wonderful attitude and I'm thrilled to have him with me.

I just found another Scripture that backs up both of us having a good attitude. It's 1 Corinthians 7:3: "Let the husband fulfill his duty to his wife, and likewise also the wife to her husband." I have always assumed this Scripture only talked about sex. Now I've learned the words *fulfill his duty*, as it's translated in the New American Standard Bible, and render due benevolence, as it says in the King James Version, can also mean it is our duty or debt to one another to be kind—to have a good attitude.

Also, when it says in Ephesians 5:28: "So husbands ought also to love their own wives as their own bodies," the word *ought* is the same word as *duty* or *due* in 1 Corinthians 7:3. It means the husband is indebted or under obligation to be kind, to have a good attitude, and to love his wife as his own body. First Corinthians 7:3 makes it plain it is the wife's obligation to do the same.

Once a friend told me what her husband had observed. He told her he had been watching how Chuck treated me. Then he told her, "I don't have to be mean to you. Chuck isn't mean to Barb."

Showing kindness and having a good attitude is another way to show unconditional love. But though women are also to show unconditional love, the Lord never gives specific instructions for a wife to love her husband in this way. He knows husbands need a different kind of love.

A wife is to love in a friendly, responding way.

> Older women likewise are to be reverent in their behavior, not malicious gossips, nor enslaved to much wine, teaching what is good, that they may encourage the young women to love their husbands, to love their children, to be sensible, pure, workers at home, kind, being subject to their own husbands, that the word of God may not be dishonored (Titus 2:3–5).

Actually the type of love we wives are to show our husbands is an affectionate love; a responding love. It is seeing something in another person you admire and enjoy. It is letting your husband know by word and action that if you were ever picking another husband you would pick him. This is not an unconditional love. It is more fragile.

As I've said, all Christians are asked to love each other with an *agape* or unconditional love, so wives have this obligation, too. But we wives are asked to have more of a responding love to our husbands. Chuck *initiates* and I *respond*. Once the good circle of love gets going, it's hard to tell who is doing which kind of love.

In this passage from Titus a wife is told to love her husband with what in Greek is called a *phileo* type of love. It is friendship love. As I've mentioned, it is seeing in another person something you especially like and enjoy. It is to have a fondness for and an attraction for someone. When you have this kind of love you make fun for and with that person. You flirt with them, laugh with them, look into their eyes, admire them, value them, prize them, and pay attention to them.

What man couldn't love a wife unconditionally who treated him like that? Both *agape* and *phileo* love involve putting the other person before yourself.

Personally, I think we women do too many things outside the home. I know when I get too busy I have no energy left over to be all I want to be for Chuck. I think this is particularly true of young mothers who have to work or choose to work.

The Scripture from Titus which started this section gives us a list of things God wants women to be and do. We wives are to:

> love our husbands,
> love our children,
> be sensible,
> be pure,
> be workers at home,
> be kind,
> subject to our own husbands.

Why? So the Word of God won't be dishonored. God tells us in 2 Timothy 3:17 that God's Word has "equipped us for every good work." God means, "You can do it because I will help you!" When we get too busy it takes all our energy just to survive. We have no energy or time to get all the things done that are expected of us. We become self-centered and not self-controlled. We say things like, "I'm so tired and no one cares. I don't get any help around here. No one cares about *me*. My husband can just forget it. The kids can too!" This is when the Word of God is dishonored, or as it says in another translation, it is blasphemed. Women start thinking and then expressing out loud, "Marriage doesn't work." "How much can God put me through anyway?" "Our culture is right! I'm going out and do my own thing and my family can just take care of themselves!"

But God never told us wives to get so busy. He said to love our husband and love our children with this love that is full of affection and fun. It's our *own* fault we get so burned out. Then we blame God and His name is dishonored.

God has told wives to be *sensible*. In Greek this word means to have a sound mind and voluntarily limit our freedoms to benefit ourselves. Wives aren't the only ones told to do this. In the book of Titus Paul tells the same thing to young men, overseers, older men, all men, older women, and younger women. It is this quality in our lives that allows us to serve others in the way they need to be served, and not to be selfish.

We've been talking about how to love our mates. Did you know you can substitute the word *serve* for *love* and come up with the same meaning? Both serving and love are shown by doing something kind for another person. If we would walk in the parameters and guidelines God has given us it would be much easier.

I feel confused when I have too much to do, when I feel time pressures, and when I am overcommitted outside the home. Chuck and I find ourselves doing this too often. However, I really think I feel the pressure more than Chuck. Chuck thrives on pressure—I wilt. I know Chuck has lots of pressure at his work too, but he can come home and take a nap or go out to his work-shop and not even see the things that have to be done around the house. In fact, he doesn't even know what to look for. This is not meant to be a put-down to him. It is just the way things are. When I don't have enough time to do everything, I feel edgy and resentful and don't have the energy to be fun and flirty for Chuck.

I can just hear some husband saying, "So don't do so much! Let some of the things go at home." And I will reply that it's just not in most of us to let things go at home. First Timothy 5:14 tells us: "Therefore, I want younger widows to get married, bear children, keep house, and give the enemy no occasion for reproach." The term *keep house* means to be an absolute ruler in your home; to govern or manage a household or the domestic affairs of a fam-ily. This Greek word for *keep house* is the word from which we get our English word *despot*.

I think this is why we just can't let things go at home. God has put this into our beings, and we have this need to keep up with our homemaking tasks. So, when we add working outside the home to these already existing needs of the family, it's too much.

I wish every husband could understand what he is missing when he insists his wife go out to work. Even more, I wish mothers would understand this too. God asks mothers to love their children in the same way they are to love their husbands—to be there for them, to make them feel special, to play with them, and to be everything they need. I think sometimes all that's needed when things aren't going well is a good laugh. Our families know we like them when we have fun with them. It's our job as wives and mothers to create those times.

A husband is told to nourish and cherish his wife.

Let's look again at Ephesians 5:28–29: "So husbands ought also to love their own wives as their own bodies. He who loves his own wife loves himself; for no one ever hated his own flesh, but nourishes and cherishes it, just as Christ also does the church."

A husband is to treat his wife as he does his own body. We all take special care to create an atmosphere that makes us most comfortable. The word *nourish* in this verse means to bring to full maturity. *Cherish* means to create a warm atmosphere in which the wife can be brought to full maturity. When young people get married today, our culture seems to be asking the *wife* to bring her husband to full maturity by paying *his* way through school and working until *he* can get established in his career. We feel this is the opposite of what the Bible teaches. I don't want to imply that when young people marry, the husband can't finish his education and the wife help him do it. What I'm talking about here is an *attitude of the heart.* Is this what she wants to do? Have they talked it over, or has he just assumed this is what she *will* do?

Those of you who wear soft contacts know they have to be kept in the right atmosphere to be usable. If they are not, they dry up and get brittle like a corn flake. Then they can't do the job for which they were created. It's the same way with a wife. If the husband is not creating the right atmosphere for *her* growth, she will become sad, or angry, or unhappy, or resentful, and she will not be the wife the man thought he had married.

We once heard author and speaker Howard Hendricks of Dallas Theological Seminary tell about a man who told him how terrible his wife was. Hendricks asked him if she was like that when they got married?

"Oh no," he said, "she was beautiful, wonderful, kind, loving, and just perfect for me."

Hendricks said, "Do you mean you created her this way?"

His wife had not been living in the right atmosphere for growth. In fact, he tore her down instead of building her up. This is a perfect illustration to show what happens when a husband does not nourish and cherish his wife as he would his own body.

When you see everything a man is commanded to do as the head of his wife, it adds up to a big responsibility. The Lord says that in order for the man to be in headship, he needs to provide for his wife, to protect her, to be a servant-leader, to love unconditionally, and to nourish and cherish. That's a big job!

A wife is to reverence her husband.

Let the wife see to it that she respect her husband. (Ephesians 5:33b).

On the other hand, the woman is told to respect or reverence her husband. This word *reverence* means to have a wholesome fear of ever displeasing him. This is *not* codependency. This is pleasing your husband because you love the Lord and want to reverence him also. This same word is used when the Bible tells us to reverence the Lord. *The Amplified Bible* indicates this word means she is to notice him, regard him, honor him, prefer him, defer to him, appreciate him, venerate and esteem him. She is to praise, prize, adore, enjoy, love, and admire him exceedingly.

When you reverence someone, Scripture says it is to be a controlling motive of your life. All you do and all you are is tied up in that person. I want to be all Chuck wants me to be. He often asks me what my five- and ten-year goals are. I wrote them down once and they never change because my goals have to do with my relationship to God, my husband, children, grandchildren, family, and friends. We always laugh when he asks me that question because our goals are so different. Most of the time he's just teasing, but there is definitely a difference in our goals. His are usually *doing* and mine are *being*. My goal is to have as a controlling motive of my life to reverence the Lord and to reverence Chuck. I haven't arrived yet, but I'm working on it every day. When we submit to one another in the roles God has given us, we build each other up.

Another way for a husband to serve his wife is not to embitter her.

> Husbands, love your wives, and do not be embittered against them (Colossians 3:19).

This *being embittered* mentioned here is an active, deliberate approach on the part of the husband. It's refusing to pick up your things that are lying around the house. It's not being willing to go on a date—just the two of you— even though your wife hasn't been out of the house for two months without the kids. It's not fixing that leaky faucet or broken chair she's been asking about for six months, yet you've fixed things for the neighbors. It is ignoring her and her wishes. Every couple will have a different list.

You could embitter your wife by not wearing the clothes she thinks are right for the occasion. Our son and daughter-in-law, Tim and Tammie, came to one of our seminars where we explained that a wife's self-esteem is involved in the way her husband looks. Tim had been wearing a greasy old pair of deck shoes, but that afternoon he went out and bought a brand-new pair of white tennis shoes just so Tammie would feel good. He called them his "love" shoes. That's an example of not embittering your wife. Even his mother thought he looked better!

Or you can embitter your wife by coming home from work and watching TV or reading the paper while your wife gets dinner, bathes the kids, gets them ready for bed, and does the dishes. Then later when she is exhausted and barely sits down, you make little hints about going to bed early. *Bed?* She feels she is just too tired, and then you feel rejected and have no idea that you have embittered your wife all during the evening.

The word for *embittering* in the Greek means pricking, or putting a knife in and twisting it. It hurts terribly, and it's anything but unconditional love, dying to yourself, or nourishing and cherishing. It is being selfish and living for yourself only.

To avoid embittering his wife, *a husband is told to live in understanding with her.*

> You husbands likewise, live with your wives in an understanding way, as with a weaker vessel, since she is a woman; and grant her honor as a fellow heir of the grace of life, so that your prayers may not be hindered (1 Peter 3:7).

Living in understanding also means *according to knowledge.* Each husband has a unique wife with her own personality and ways of doing things. What are those ways? What are her needs? How does she like things? Did you ever suspect that if you don't live in understanding, your prayers would be hindered and go unanswered? It makes sense because disregarding God's commands is sin. Why would He honor someone who is not obeying?

The wife needs a true leader—one who does not put himself first but leads by serving. She needs to be loved unconditionally just as the husband loves his own body. She needs to be provided for and protected. She needs to be nourished and cherished. She needs her husband not to be embittered against her.

She also needs him to wash her with the Word.

> That He might sanctify her, having cleansed her by the washing of water with the word (Ephesians 5:26).

The wife needs her husband to be in the Word so they can talk about the Lord together. When Chuck and I were young, we could never talk about the Lord without getting into an argument. I didn't understand what was happening, but I think I do now. At the time I was just beginning to study the Bible. I was learning faster than Chuck was, and I think it threatened him. In his heart he knew he should be learning too but just didn't have the motivation. When he did commit himself 100 percent to the Lord, he started growing and learning. The arguments stopped. We began sharing the Lord, rather than making him a battleground. I love to talk about Scripture with Chuck. We probably will never agree on everything, but we are able to give our viewpoints to each other without the conflict.

When Chuck is in the Word, I have the confidence that he is going to do the right thing. I know I can trust him because he is getting his guidance straight from the Lord. It is so much easier to submit to someone who is following the Lord, rather than his own impulses.

I really think a lot of resistance that husbands feel from wives is because the wife is not sure her husband is hearing from the Lord. She never sees him in the Scriptures. I know Chuck is in the Scriptures. He has a Bible in every bathroom. He has a Bible with him in the car. When he goes to a counseling breakfast early in the morning, he takes his Bible so if they don't show up, he has time to read. When he gets home, he talks about what he has been reading and then we are both washed in the Word.

The wife is to be chaste in behavior, with a meek and quiet spirit, with her hope in God, not her husband.

> In the same way, you wives, be submissive to your own husbands so that even if any of them are disobedient to the word, they may be won without a word by the behavior of their wives, as they observe your chaste and respectful behavior. And let not your adornment be merely external—braiding the hair, and wearing gold jewelry, or putting on dresses; but let it be the hidden person of the heart, with the imperishable quality of a gentle and quiet spirit, which is precious in the sight of God. For in this way in former times the holy women also, who hoped in God, used to adorn themselves, being submissive to their own husbands. Thus Sarah obeyed Abraham, calling him lord, and you have become her children if you do what is right without being frightened by any fear (1 Peter 3:1–6).

Once again we see that wives are to be submissive to their *own* husbands. And, since some husbands are not going to be in the Word to find out what it says, wives are told to be submissive even if their husbands are disobedient to the Word. And a wife is to be submissive *without a word*. Isn't that awful? But, the verse goes on to say that disobedient husbands can be won by respectful and chaste behavior. Again, *respectful* is having a wholesome dread of ever displeasing him. Therefore, you build him up, you admire him, you defer to him, you praise him, you appreciate him, you prize him, you adore him, and you enjoy him. All this even for husbands who do not obey the Lord. You see, it doesn't matter if your husband is a Christian or not. He is yours and God's directions to you are clear. The rules don't change even though at times your husband may not be listening to God.

Our behavior is not to depend on how another person is behaving. We must be obedient no matter what's going on. I think a problem we all have is expectations. We *expect* others to change toward us when we're being nice to them. And more than that, we *expect* to have change when we do what is right. The reality is that things may *not* change. Our motivation for doing what is right has to be for the Lord, not to get someone to change. We must obey simply because God says to. So get rid of those expectations, and you will save yourself a lot of heartache.

Chaste means to be physically pure and morally righteous. No matter what our husbands do, we remain physically true to them. The reason we can keep our mouths closed and be respectful and morally righteous is because we are developing the qualities of a *meek and quiet spirit* that are so becoming to a wife. The word *meek* can also be translated as *gentle*. Meekness is strength under control. It is having a serenity of spirit because we know God rules over all, and we know nothing can come into our lives unless God allows it. This quality recognizes the sovereignty of God—that He rules in the lives of people just as much as He rules in the universe.

The Greek word translated *quiet* means *to keep your seat*. It means to be tranquil and undisturbed by outside circumstances. You know us women. We get excited and jump up and start talking rapidly. Well, this tells us to do just the opposite.

We can be calm and *seated* because our hope is in God. We don't have to depend on outward circumstances to control our inward state. We can be peaceful and serene no matter what *because* our hope is in God. When someone has a quiet spirit, they cause no disturbance to anyone around them. We know this is an inward quality because the Lord says, "Let it be the hidden person of the heart."

I believe we need to put our trust in the Lord more instead of always trying to work out our own problems. If we would just keep quiet and know that God is God and let Him take over, we would walk in that meek and quiet spirit.

Men are to walk in meekness too. I say this because meekness is a fruit of the Spirit. Also Jesus says in Matthew 5:5, "Blessed are the meek" (NIV). All Christians need to be developing this fruit of the Spirit. We need to remember that all things work together for good because God is in control.

We all say hurtful things to each other at times. And probably the reason we're hurt is because there is some truth in what has been said about us. But when we walk in meekness, it doesn't matter what someone says to us. Our response should acknowledge that God has allowed this. We should ask our-selves, "Is there any truth to it? Is there anything God wants me to learn from this? Does He want me to change? Do I have a blind spot He is trying to point out?"

We can walk in meekness because we know God loves us and wants only our good. Sometimes it hurts and it's uncomfortable, but we become more usable for the Lord when we persevere through a trial in a God-honoring way.

The Greek word for *meekness* is also used in describing a stallion under control and trained for his master's use. A horse has great power, but when it is not under control, the horse is not usable. That is why the Lord spends so much time on us. He wants to mold us into His image and make us usable.

Scripture goes on to remind us that *both the husband and wife are coheirs of the grace of life.*

> You husbands likewise, live with your wives in an understanding way, as with a weaker vessel, since she is a woman; and grant her honor as a fellow heir of the grace of life, so that your prayers may not be hin-dered (1 Peter 3:7).

In the body of Christ, no one is above another. We are all equal. It is the same in a marriage. We do not have a hierarchy. We are in this together. We *do* have different roles, but one is not inferior to the other. They are just different.

There is another Scripture that has caused some controversy on this subject because it seems to be teaching a hierarchy.

"Let a woman quietly receive instruction with entire submissiveness. But I do not allow a woman to teach or exercise authority over a man, but to remain quiet" (1 Timothy 2:11–12).

We believe this Scripture speaks to the husband-wife relationship and not to men and women in general. We need to look to see what the Greek means in this passage. It's vital that our interpretation does not contradict another Scripture. The words *woman* and *man* can also be translated wife and husband. In fact, these same Greek words are translated "husband" and "wife" in 1 Timothy 3:2. So we believe these verses about teaching and receiving instruction refer to the husband-wife relationship in marriage.

The Greek word translated *quiet* comes from the same word we discussed in 1 Peter 3:4 with the meaning of *keeping your seat*. It is an attitude of the heart. It does not mean a wife cannot speak. She is just to speak with the gentleness and quietness of spirit that is so becoming to a woman.

The verbs *teach* and *exercise authority* are in the Greek present tense, which means a continuous habit of life—something that is done over and over again. This would be illustrated by a wife who habitually takes the teaching or headship role in the marriage or a wife who usurps her husband's position.

The Greek word for *exercise authority* means a self-starting authority or when a wife acts on her own authority. It does not mean a wife never has authority, just not self-starting authority. For example, I would never go ahead and make a decision that Chuck is against. However, I can make any decision that I know Chuck would approve. In the same way, Chuck would not make a decision he knows I am against if he is loving me with *agape* love and giving up his life for me. When we are both serving and submitting to one another, neither of us will do what the other is against.

The next point is the most important in our discussion, and that is wives are supposed to be submissive to their *own* husbands. A Greek scholar has shown me that the genitive singular is used when this verse says, "I do not allow a woman to teach or exercise authority *over a man.*" This then should read, *"over her man."* If this passage is interpreted to mean that a woman is to be in submission to every man, then we're making the Scripture contradict itself, and this cannot be.

Therefore, Chuck and I believe this Scripture teaches what every other Scripture on the marriage roles teaches. It fits with Ephesians 5, 1 Peter 3, and Colossians 3 as they talk about the husband-wife relationship. If it is interpreted to mean a woman is in subjection to all men, no other Scripture backs it up—it just hangs there alone. One of the principles of interpretation is that the Bible cannot and does not contradict itself. If we have an interpretation that contradicts another Scripture, then our interpretation is wrong. So you see, husbands and wives really *are* fellow heirs of the grace of life.

Man is the glory of God, and woman is the glory of man.

> But I want you to understand that Christ is the head of every man, and the man is the head of a woman, and God is the head of Christ. He [the man] is the image and glory of God; but the woman is the glory of man (1 Corinthians 11:3, 7b).

We have talked about how Christ is our example. God was Christ's example. Remember the Lord said he only did those things he saw his Father doing. That's where we get the principle of the husband following Christ's example. Christ follows God because God is the head of Christ. Men follow Christ because Christ is the head of men, and a woman follows a man because a man is her head. In the Greek, *the* is singular. It is not men over women, but *a* man is the head of *a* woman.

One day I was listening to a portion of the Bible on tape and heard these words from Ephesians 5:25–27:

> Husbands, love your wives, just as Christ also loved the church and gave Himself up for her; that He might sanctify her, having cleansed her by the washing of water with the word, that He might present to Himself the church all her glory, having no spot or wrinkle or any such thing; but that she should be holy and blameless.

The word *glory* caught my attention. Christ was presenting the church to himself in all her glory, as (implied) a husband should present his wife to himself in all her glory. What could this mean? I thought immediately of 1 Corinthians 11:7 where it says a woman is the glory of man.

I decided to look up what *glory* meant. It means an opinion (always a *good* opinion in the New Testament). It is to have a correct estimate of a person or thing, or to praise and honor someone. Then I went to *Webster's Dictionary*. It defines glory as:

1. A great honor and admiration won by doing something important or valuable. Anything that brings fame and honor.
2. Worshipful adoration or praise.
3. The condition of highest achievement, splendor, and prosperity.

Then I thought of the Proverbs 31 woman and all her achievements: how well her house was run, how well her children were cared for, and how all her businesses were prospering. And then it says in Proverbs 31:23: "Her husband is known in the gates, when he sits among the elders of the land."

This man had let his wife be all she was meant to be. He let her do all she did. Not only did *she* receive honor for her accomplishments, but *he* did as well. He would not have received that honor unless he had created the atmosphere in which she could grow. She reflected glory back to him.

Then I thought of the description of Christ in Hebrews 1:3: "And He is the radiance of His glory and the exact representation of His nature."

Christ reflects back to God exactly who God is. Man is supposed to reflect back to Christ exactly who He is. A woman is supposed to reflect back to her husband exactly who he is. When I treat others in a Christlike way, I receive a reflection back of what I am to them. So a man presents to himself his wife, just as Christ presents to himself the church in all her glory.

Some men present to themselves a happy, contented wife. Some men present to themselves a sad, discontented wife. I have even heard of a husband who said to his wife, whom he had been neglecting, "If you'll just get happy, we'll do something this weekend!" When a husband does something that deserves honor and praise, I believe the wife will reflect that back to him.

Are we presenting to ourselves the type of relationships that bring glory to God? Or do our relationships dishonor God? Do we present to ourselves relationships that honor ourselves, or dishonor us?

To honor each other, the husband and wife cannot be independent from each other.

> However, in the Lord, neither is woman independent of man, nor is man independent of woman (1 Corinthians 11:11).

This fits so well with servant-leadership and servant-submission. It fits the example given to us by the relationship of God and Christ. Neither God nor Christ make independent decisions. It also fits the principle of being fellow heirs together of the grace of life. If we are going to honor each other, we cannot and must not make independent decisions. When anyone enters a covenant relationship, he or she watches out for the interests of the other person.

In marriage we are in a covenant. In the body of Christ we are in a covenant. We should always be putting the interests of others before our own. We are not independent in any relationship, especially not in marriage. Since marriage is a picture of our relationship with Christ, we should never do anything unless we first ask ourselves, "Is this what the Lord wants me to do?"

The question is, how do we know we are being submissive to the Lord as well as to one another? How do we know how the Lord wants us to respond? Two passages of Scripture give us special help on this.

> For you have been called for this purpose, since Christ also suffered for you, leaving you an example for you to follow in His steps, WHO COMMITTED NO SIN, NOR WAS ANY DECEIT FOUND IN HIS MOUTH; and while being reviled, He did not revile in return; while suffering, He uttered no threats, but kept entrusting Himself to Him who judges righteously; and He Himself bore our sins in His body on the cross, that we might die to sin and live to righteousness; for by His wounds you were healed. For you were continually straying like sheep, but now you have returned to the Shepherd and Guardian of your souls (1 Peter 2:21–25).

Therefore, since Christ has suffered in the flesh, arm yourselves also with the same purpose, because he who has suffered in the flesh has ceased from sin, so as to live the rest of the time in the flesh no longer for the lusts of men, but for the will of God (1 Peter 4:1–2).

Our purpose in life should be to please God by following the example Christ left for us, as Scripture tells us to do. In 1 Peter 3:1, it says, "In the same way, you wives…" In 1 Peter 3:7, it says, "You husbands likewise…" These two phrases tell husbands and wives to act as Jesus did when he submitted himself to God when He suffered unjustly. This is what Jesus did:

He committed no sin.
No deceit was found in His mouth.
While being reviled, He did not revile in return.
While suffering, He did not threaten.
He kept entrusting Himself to God because He knew God judges righteously.
He bore our sins in His own body.
Because He was willing to bear our sins, He healed our wounds.

When it says there was no deceit in His mouth, it means He didn't say one thing and mean another. He didn't do anything underhandedly, secretly, or insidiously.

It would be like going out and buying a blouse you know you can't afford and keeping it under wraps for two or three weeks. Then when your husband asks if it's new, you say, "I've had it for weeks." Or for a husband to say he is just too tired to finish painting the bedroom as he has promised to do for weeks, when in reality he just doesn't want to get it done.

One of my friends told me when she was young and had a disagreement with her husband, she would always fix him tuna fish casserole for dinner and then tell him that was all they could afford. But she really prepared it because she knew he did not like tuna fish casserole.

Or it may be telling your partner everything is okay, when all you really want to do is avoid a conflict. If you do things like this, *you are not being submissive* to each other.

The word *revile* means *to openly abuse*. When the Lord was openly abused, He did not openly abuse in return. He didn't return evil for evil, nor did He threaten. He didn't say, "You'll be sorry some day. Just wait until you see what I'm going to do to you!"

Open abuse is when a marriage partner says, "I'm going to divorce you if you ever do that again." That is openly abusing and threatening. If you find yourself saying things like this, *you are not being submissive*.

The Lord prayed about the situation in which He found himself. It says He kept entrusting Himself to God, who judges righteously. He could do this because He knew He had done no wrong. He knew He was doing the will of the Father, and God is pleased when we obey Him even when we're falsely accused. Psalm 50:15 says, "And call upon Me in the day of trouble; I shall rescue you, and you will honor Me." Jesus knew God would be true to His Word.

Another thing the Lord did was to bear our sins in His body, and because of that we were spiritually healed. Are we willing just to forget all the bad things our mates have done to us even though they don't recognize what they've done? Can we give them kindness and healing? If a wife keeps her mouth shut and doesn't even say a word, it's a form of bearing another person's sin. Or when a husband lives in understanding with his wife, even though he doesn't like it, he is bearing her sins in his own body. He can do this because he knows God judges righteously.

Make sure, though, to follow Christ's example with the right motivation. Don't do it to get a desired response from your mate although this may happen. But do it because your foremost desire is to walk pleasing to the Lord. Do it because you want to obey.

And further, we can be submissive in spite of ill treatment because we have armed ourselves with the same purpose with which Christ armed Himself as it says in 1 Peter 4:1–2. It is because we have decided not to live the rest of our life in the flesh following the lusts of the world. Instead, we've committed ourselves to do the will of God.

So, following Jesus' example, this is how to know if you are being submissive:

You do no wrong.
You don't deceive or openly abuse.

You don't return evil for evil.

You don't threaten.

You keep praying.

You trust God to judge righteously.

You keep your mouth shut.

You live in understanding.

You decide not to live for yourself.

You live for the will of God.

You arm yourself with the same purpose the Lord had.

This decision has to be made before the conflicts come. We need to realize again that it isn't God's harshness that wins us, it is His kindness. It isn't our harshness that will win others either. It will be our kindness and our obedience to God.

Chuck: I guess the bottom line for me was learning from the Bible how God expected me to treat Barb and then trying to do it right. If you're fighting our view that submission is mutual, or headship doesn't mean decision making, or loving is dying for and serving your wife, then check out the Scriptures for yourself and see if you don't come to the same conclusion.

This is a hard message, especially for men, because so many of our churches are doing a poor job presenting the balance in the relationship between a husband and wife. If you are a true Christian and have asked Jesus Christ to come into your life and take control and asked Him to help make you be the person He wants you to be, then you have the power to change.

If you and your partner are not Christians, you may be able to change for a few weeks, but usually the relationship deteriorates back to where it was because neither partner has the supernatural power to do the right thing regardless of how they feel. Love is action not feelings. We are to be ministers to each other. We are to focus on each other's needs. The good feelings will come *after* the obedience of doing the right thing and not before.

Barb has already mentioned that a man is to nourish and cherish his wife. Here are some practical guidelines on how we can nourish and cherish each other.

20

KNOW YOUR FLOCKS AND HERDS

Chuck: Ann Landers once published the definition of a devoted husband. "A devoted husband is one who stands by his wife in troubles she would never have had if she had not married him."

I'm not sure whether to laugh or cry, but it was certainly true in my case with Barb. One of the best lessons Gary Smalley taught me was how to value and pay a price for Barb. That was a significant breakthrough because I was not valuing her like I should have been. I was not nourishing and cherishing her like God wanted me to. I learned that my example was Jesus Christ who thought I was special enough to die for. I found out that as a husband I should be ready to do the same for my wife. And God's joke—something He does not tell us about ahead of time—is that when we nourish and cherish and value our wives, they can't keep themselves from beginning to meet our needs, too. And the marriage grows stronger.

Barb: We talked a bit ago about husbands nourishing and cherishing their wives. Remember nourish means to bring to full maturity. Cherish means to create a warm atmosphere. This again is where we get the principle of the husband being in charge of the atmosphere of the home. It is the idea of a hen brooding over her chicks, keeping them at just the right temperature so they will be healthy and brought to full maturity.

We keep our homes at the right temperature so we can be comfortable and productive. During the day when we are working full speed ahead we keep the thermometer at 69 or 70 degrees. But in the evening when we sit and read or watch television we raise the thermostat a couple of degrees. The thermostat controls the temperature so we remain comfortable.

So it is with the husband nourishing and cherishing his wife. He is the thermostat controlling the temperature or atmosphere in the home. If he comes home from work irritable and grumpy and wants his wife to be a bright and shining light for him despite how he's acting, he's got another *think* coming. But when he comes home and is kind and thoughtful and shows value to her, she is more likely to reflect back to him the glory we talked about earlier.

Through the years we have heard over and over again, "The wife is in charge of the atmosphere of the home." That may be true, but Chuck and I believe the husband is in charge of the atmosphere for his wife, so she can create a soothing and peaceful atmosphere in the home.

Chuck: Wives are a little bit like a rhododendron bud. If we nourish and cherish our wives like the Bible tells us to, then they can grow and blossom and bloom and get perfume all over us. They radiate back to us exactly what we are giving them. If you see a happy wife, you can assume the husband is doing a good job nourishing and cherishing. If you see a sad wife, you can bet the husband is failing in the nourishing and cherishing department.

I went to a Christian management seminar once, and the man up front was talking about how he and his wife were teammates in the ministry together and how much they thought alike and had similar priorities. However, his wife was sitting over in the corner as far away from him as she could—all shriveled up like a prune. She had a pinched face and folded arms, and she didn't laugh at his jokes. She was probably screaming on the inside. I think she radiated back to him exactly what he gave her.

This is not to say a woman doesn't have a responsibility to grow on her own, too. Just as the husband is responsible to God to learn how to be a godly husband and father, the wife is responsible to be a godly wife and mother. The man just has an extra role, and that is creating the atmosphere for his wife's growth.

I remember on the farm a hen would go out into the weeds and lay eggs. Pretty soon she would appear with this cute little line of baby chicks following along behind. When the dogs would bother them, she would squat and ruffle her feathers to make space underneath her wings, and the baby chicks would hightail it into this refuge. If the dog came too close, the mom would peck him on the nose, and pretty soon he decided there were other things to bother that didn't hurt so much. After the dog would leave, mother hen would get up, and the chicks would come out. What a beautiful picture of protection. I know my feminist friends cringe at the idea of a man being a woman's protector, but God gave us that picture to portray what a husband is to do for his wife and family. I have no idea why that is so bad. It doesn't denote weakness. I feel it pictures the man protecting priceless jewels—an irreplaceable wife and children. God has given men the physical ability to protect, and during wars and other times they give their *lives* for their family.

The problem is we men haven't been taught what it means to nourish and cherish our wives. We need a third party, another man—usually older—who can come into our life and teach us what our wife needs from us. We don't know these things naturally, and we usually don't have good role models, so an older trusted friend is essential. Gary Smalley and Larry Burkett each had a major part in teaching me about teamwork with Barb. Chuck Swindoll, through his tapes, added a practical foundation to my marriage.

I now have the privilege of being a third party to other men as God brings them into my life. I've mentioned before that I teach a small men's Bible study at 6:30 A.M. on Thursday mornings. We go through the Bible to see if we can apply the principles to our everyday lives—and our conversation almost always reverts to some aspect of relationships with wives. We laugh and cry together when we discuss our failures, and then the men give a happy report the next week about how their wife responded to what we had learned. A woman cannot teach her husband what she needs. Most churches are not equipped to teach men how to value, nourish, cherish, and die for wives. Parents are too close to the situation to be of much help. It takes a third party to get the job done.

One of the problems I find is that most men don't *have* any friends with whom they can be honest and share their lives. Men have been taught not to share weaknesses because it reveals our failures. We are independent and therefore want to do everything by ourselves. We don't need help. Most of the men I run into are ignorant of the ways of a woman and don't have one person they can turn to in times of trouble. If that is your case, maybe Barb and

I can be *your* third party though this book. I have given our address at the close so you can get in touch with us if you have specific questions.

Here's one of the things about Barb that mystified me when we were going through our hard times. When we had a conflict, she would not only talk about the present crisis, she brought up everything I had ever done in the past. I would say, "I thought we talked about that. Why are you bringing that up again?" She never had a good answer, but Bill Gothard and Gary Smalley taught me what was going on. She didn't feel I really knew how badly I had hurt her in the situations she kept bringing up. They suggested I make a list of all the times I could remember in the past where I had hurt her.

The idea is to get by yourself somewhere. An early morning breakfast in a restaurant is perfect so there will be a minimum of distractions. Think back to your dating days with your wife, and then make a note of every instance you can remember where you have done something to hurt your wife. Then take her out on a date and ask her forgiveness for each thing on your list. Get a booth in the corner so you can cry. And be sure *not* to use the words *I'm sorry*. I'm sorry means "I'm sorry I hurt you, *but* it really wasn't that big of a deal." "I'm sorry I hurt you, *but* it's your fault too." "I'm sorry I hurt you, *but* I don't think anyone noticed." The operative words for this assignment are "Would you *forgive me* for…" There's something special about the words *forgive me*, rather than *I'm sorry*.

One guy's list was so long he refused to carry through. It was just overwhelming what he had done to his wife over the years. I've lost track of him, but I hope he finally got around to it because it is a life-changing process. I know it was for us. I look at that evening when I asked Barb's forgiveness as one of the major events that taught me how to live in understanding with my wife. I asked her forgiveness for making all of those investments I told you about earlier without taking her counsel and losing so much of her money. I asked her forgiveness for putting so much pressure on her about entertaining while we were living in our big house, for playing golf sometimes when I really should have been home with the family, and a number of other things.

Go back to your dating days. Maybe you were sexually intimate before marriage. Ninety-nine percent of the time it's the man's idea, so ask forgiveness for taking advantage of her that way. Maybe you tried to control your wife and make her just like you. Maybe you physically or emotionally abused her. Maybe you used a budget to put her in chains. Maybe you chose the furniture and paint colors and other things in the home without any regard to the fact that *she* is the manager of the home, not you. You will probably list some events where your anger got out of control. You're the one to decide what your list will contain. All of our lists will be different.

After you have gone through all of the items on your list, then ask, "Can you think of any other times I have hurt you?" Since our wives remember if we put catsup on our hamburgers on our first date, she might just remember some things you left out. Don't be defensive. The whole point of the exercise is to open up her spirit, as Gary Smalley calls this process. It doesn't sound sincere to our male brain if we have to be reminded to do something. Just take my word for it, your wife does not care why you are doing this. She will just be overwhelmed that you had the courage to ask forgiveness and that you cared enough to be real and vulnerable. She knows how hard this is for you. That makes it all the more special for her.

After you have done this, you are back to square one. Your spirits will feel so free—if not instantly, at least within a fairly short time. You will be best friends again. Now, the idea is to keep short accounts. When you make a mistake, ask her forgiveness quickly, and try not to let things build up. That way you can nourish and cherish her without a lot of past events clouding the atmosphere.

Now you're on a roll. Take your daytimer and mark down all the important family dates. Everyone's birthday, your anniversary, Christmas, her mom's birthday, the anniversary of your first date, pending vacation times, some women's night outs where you pay the bill for the dinner or movie and babysit the kids. Make a goal list of the things that would please your wife—fix the kitchen door, give her breakfast in bed, surprise her with a vacation, take a trip to her mom's, put the backyard fence back up, clean the garage, put the front door back on its hinges—whatever you have been putting off.

One Thursday morning after we had discussed some things we could do for our wives, one of the men in the study, who had been married for only a few months, decided to stop by the florist and take some flowers home to his new wife. He told me later that he came in the door and found her reading my

Assembly book where I ask the husband whether he was still doing the things he did when he was dating. I was so proud of him. What a narrow escape.

Another time we discussed some of the things the men had done to win their wives in the first place. One man told us his girlfriend was being courted by a number of guys, so he wrote her a note every day telling her of his love. Our discussion took place some thirty-five or so years after they had gotten married. Old meddler me—I asked him if he was still doing that. We laughed and kidded about the fact that since he *got* her, why would he still be sending *notes!* I think he went home and wrote a note to her that day.

There are some traps we have to accept with the territory, men. One husband bought a davenport for his wife's birthday. Dangerous, of course, since the man may or may not have the same furniture taste as his wife, and she is in charge of decorating the home. She was upset that he spent that much money when a simpler present would have been just as good. One man scored high on the *in*sensitivity scale when he went to Europe on a trip—and brought his wife back a German frying pan. He disregarded that ancient proverb that says: "Wise husband never gets present for wife that plugs in."

I've already mentioned that a husband can also help his wife develop some of her gifts. I like to try new things all the time, and some years ago I took some art lessons at our local YWCA. I had a great time, but I made the mistake of leaving my paints and brushes out one night. Barb tried them the next day, and while my pictures resemble Grandma Moses, her work resembles Rembrandt and Norman Rockwell. So I retired and encouraged her to carry on with this new talent. Many of the pictures in our home are those she has painted.

Barb and I have different spiritual gifts. Her main gift is that of a teacher, and she loves to spend hours at a time getting into the Bible, doing word studies, examining the Greek tenses and the sentence structure of Scripture. My principal gift is one of exhortation. That means I like to come alongside someone and encourage them when they hurt and help them put Scripture into shoe leather.

The key to nourishing our wives is to make them our highest priority—a number ten on our list before sports, TV, hunting, camping, working, and even ministry. I see some pastors and teachers violate this principle all the time by saying, in effect, "Lord, you take care of the family, I'll take care of the sheep."

Here is what we believe the Bible says a man's priorities should be:

1. His relationship with Jesus Christ
2. His wife
3. His kids and grandchildren
4. Making a living
5. Ministry

I've met people in full-time Christian service whose families were on welfare because the husband and father wouldn't provide for them adequately. Often what God is telling a person like that to do is, "Go get a job," but somehow they are deaf to that.

After you have provided for your family and have a little time left over, then you can be a youth leader, or camp counselor, or pastor, or sing in the choir, or teach Sunday school, or run the Awana group, or minister with Campus Crusade, or something.

We were on the same speaking program with a man who had a worldwide ministry. He was gone over three hundred days a year traveling for the Lord. We were eating at the same table, and he was called to the phone. He came back and told us his teenage son was having all sorts of problems and how excited he was to have the opportunity to *pray with him on the phone*. God vomited, and I felt like it, too. This guy should be *home* with his thirteen-year-old boy and make sure he survives his teenage years. I don't care if he flips burgers, works as a security guard, or runs a jitney in a warehouse. His son is hurting, and, according to the Bible I'm reading, he isn't supposed to be ministering until his home is in order. "He must have a well-behaved family, with children who obey quickly and quietly. For if a man can't make his own little family behave, how can he help the whole church?" (1 Timothy 3:4–5).

As I said earlier, I paraphrase this to mean, don't even ask a man to *sweep out* the church until his family is well managed, or served. I can't tell you how much it grieves me to see men running around "serving the Lord" while their family is dying at home.

I heard of an army chaplain one time who had a very successful ministry overseas where we was not able to take his family. He had completed a two-year tour, and because of his successful ministry, he was being urged by his superiors to serve for another two years. His family *begged* him to come home. He took another tour. I think that man will have to answer to God someday about the blasphemy of doing ministry while his family was hurting. If you want to serve on some mission field where you can't take your family, don't have a family in the first place. Remember, I'm just an old farm boy and like things simple. God gave us priorities, and it is the height of spiritual arrogance to ignore them.

Honoring, valuing, and serving our wife and family does not come naturally. *Selfishness* comes naturally. We have to make the *decision* to look after our family's needs first, after our relationship with Christ. This means we won't always get our own way. Christ didn't always get His own way, and He is our example in this. We might not go hunting or fishing or golfing as often as we would like. We might not watch TV as much as we want. We might have to go to more funerals, anniversaries, and weddings than we feel our systems can tolerate.

Barb: At one of our conferences a woman raised her hand and said it sounded like Chuck had done all the changing in our relationship. I knew I had changed a lot too, but it was hard to think on my feet, so I didn't give a very good answer. Later a friend came up to me and asked, "Don't you know how you've changed, Barb?" She then reminded me of all the projects where Chuck had involved me, like speaking engagements, cooking for and entertaining the groups he invited to our home, and ministries like being chaplains for the University of Washington football team, coteaching the Mariners baseball couple's Bible study and the Seahawks football team's couple's Bible study, traveling and teaching at retreats, serving on the national staff of Pro Athlete's Outreach, and more. I came to see through her that I had changed in the *goal* area, and Chuck had changed in the *relationship* area.

I've also changed by trying to honor Chuck and cook the things he likes. If I had my way, there would be some all-vegetable dinners and not so much meat. He also loves the same thing over and over again and doesn't like many of the foods I do. I'll compromise by adding some things to the meal for me, but also I have what he likes, too. Once in a while I'll remind him how much he hates to do the same thing over and over again, and that's how I feel about cooking the same meals over and over.

I'm a perfectionist when it comes to keeping the house clean. However, I have compromised for a couple of his areas. He can keep them like he wants (messy), but before company comes he picks them up and makes them presentable. We don't even talk about it anymore. He just cleans his areas automatically when we have people coming over.

In one of our homes we had a dining-room table that Chuck called the Bermuda Triangle. It was one of the first things you saw when you entered the front door, and the family kept putting things on it when they came home from school or work.

Chuck: Hold it! Now what's the use of having a dining-room table if you can't put things on it? Somehow Barb didn't share this thought, so the things the family put on the table would disappear. We used to have four kids, now we have just three because one of the kids sat on her table. Poof, the child hasn't been seen since. I set my briefcase on it one time. It went poof, too. I panicked because all of my "brains" were in there, but Barb somehow summoned its return after some anxious moments.

Barb: Well, it just wasn't "me" to have the dining-room table messy. I have, however, given in as far as Chuck's home office is concerned. He loves having it look like the Smithsonian museum. He has cameras and recorders and film and papers all over the place. I used to give him a bad time, but I've changed and now just ask him to straighten things and clear the floor when we have company. I don't dare look into the closet. When we don't have guests, I just let him be who he wants to be in his office. He is comfortable with his things in a mess.

Part of this has to do with his personality style. Chuck was born with high energy. He likes to keep doing things, not just sit or stand around. However, when Chuck realized people were eternal and things and projects were temporary, his whole priority system changed.

I was his secretary at the time he learned this. He had an appointment to counsel someone. They went into his office and talked and talked. I got very nervous thinking he would be upset because he had so many deadlines that day. After the person left, I noticed Chuck was as relaxed as he had been when the person arrived. I asked him about it, and he said that counseling was much more important than getting his commercials written. He could always write at night, but he could not always be there when someone was hurting. He has operated on that principle ever since.

Chuck: We recommend married couples have a weekly date, especially if they are having lots of conflicts. The whole purpose of the date is to talk about your relationship, and whether you have hurt each other during the past week. The discussion takes place when emotions are even, and both can talk about the situations without much anger. It's really up to the man to initiate this procedure. He's not going to be real excited about doing this because he is usually mostly at fault, and it's painful to have his failures pointed out. However, he must do this because it is all part of nourishing and cherishing a wife and loving her as Christ loved the church and died for her. The feelings follow after the action is taken.

And by the way, don't let one person (usually the man) unilaterally determine everything is going well, so you won't have to have your date this week. Chances are the other person is screaming inside, and they are not being heard. So make a covenant with each other to have your weekly date without fail. Put it on your calendar, and don't let anything short of World War Three keep you from that appointed time. Your discussion won't always be heavy and emotional. In fact, when you keep short accounts with each other, your blowups will become less and less frequent. This is because you are forcing yourselves to talk about them at your weekly date and then becoming friends again quickly. What's going to happen is that most of the time when you sit down to talk, you will both agree that everything's fine, and you can have a fun evening together.

Men, one of the most important nourishing and cherishing days is Valentine's Day. That's a big day in most women's lives. Most men go to bed on the night before Valentine's Day. Suddenly, he remembers what the next day is. So he very quietly gets up again at 11:00 P.M., puts on his clothes, and runs out to the drug store. He's sure his wife is not aware he is gone, so it's not a big deal.

There are some men who do it a bit differently, however. There is one guy in Sioux Falls, and one in Fargo, I think. Those are the only two I know of who do it right. What they do is put a note on their daytimer on January 28th say-ing: Valentine's Day shopping. Then on February 3rd they have another reminder and actually hit the street to compare fourteen different gift ideas the friendly stores have as suggestions. After selecting the one of their choice, they safely hide it in a drawer in the garage. (This is hard goods by the way, not flow-ers. Flowers don't last too well in a drawer.) Then they put another reminder on their calendar for February 9th at which time they line up a baby-sitter and make a restaurant reservation for the evening of February 14th to make sure they can get a window seat at her favorite eating establishment. By the way, they don't choose Tony's Bar, Grill, and Card Room. They make it Helen's Rose Palace for Elegant Eating or something like that. So take out a loan.

Then February 13th after work on their way home, they get some flowers that will barely last that evening, rather than the ten-year cactus plant *you* usu-ally choose the few times you remember to get something. Then they excuse themselves from the dinner table for a moment that night and put a love note on her pillow telling her how much they have been thinking about her and how much they appreciate all the things she does for them. Then on Valentine's Day morning, they bring out the flowers, a card, and the hard goods, and confirm the time for dinner, and there's *no way* their wife will have a headache the next time they want to go to bed early.

Because women are into relationships, Valentine's Day is one of the most important days of the year. We forget it because we still have to go to work if it falls on a weekday. We also forget Christmas and Thanksgiving and for sure her birthday and our anniversary. I don't want to lay a big guilt trip on you men, but this is a *horrible* way to treat God's gift to us. It's an insult to her, and I think also to God because we don't value her more than a last-minute shop-ping trip and a little spit and a promise. I know you didn't mean to forget. That's my whole point. Be *proactive* in remembering these things. That's why God made daytimers.

If you blew it this year, you can gain back a little momentum by stopping by a variety store on your way home tomorrow night and getting her six or seven women's magazines—on gardening, fashions, cooking, computers, dec-orating, or motorcycles—whatever she's into. Wrap them up in some heart-type paper and present them to her with some red tulips and the mushiest generic card you can find since it won't be a holiday of any kind. Look for cards that say, "I was just thinking of how wonderful you…" "You will always be number one in my heart because…" "How do I love you? Let me figure out the ways." The words "let me count the ways" would even be better if you can find a card that has them in it. *You* usually get the kind of card that says "Knock, knock" (Who's there?) "Olive" (Olive who?) "Olive you very much." Har, har. Guys, do the mushy bit—it really pays off.

Barb: Noted author and speaker Steve Brown has written an article about everyone needing soft places in their lives. Even our Lord Jesus Christ had a soft place in the home of Mary, Martha, and Lazarus. It was this home where he stopped to rest before his ordeal on the cross.

Steve writes about visiting in someone's home and being comfortable enough to take his shoes off. Even if he falls asleep in a comfortable chair while the others visit, it's okay. That's a soft place.

Or when we have given our all and been rejected and left alone, and then a friend calls and says, "I know what that cost you to take that stand, and I know that not a lot of people understand. But I want you to know that *I* understand, and I'm praying for you." That's a soft place.

Then he tells of his daughter Robin calling from college quite often and after talking with him for a few minutes asks, "Is Mom there?" He would give the phone to his wife Anna and she and Robin would laugh and talk and cry for two or three hours and have a wonderful time. "And as I watched," he says, "I realized Anna was the soft place in our home. And she's very valuable because she's the soft place."

I've read Steve's article many times in our seminars and Bible studies because we all need to create soft places for each other and for our mates. That's what Chuck and I have been trying to show you throughout this whole book—*how* to create those soft places. As Chuck says, "It really pays off."

Chuck: Now let's talk about what to do when all else fails.

21

WHAT TO DO
WHEN ALL ELSE FAILS

Chuck: It's been said if you let something go that is yours, it will come back to you. If it doesn't come back, it probably wasn't yours in the first place. This principle of releasing is one of the most powerful tools in helping solve marriage conflicts.

I had lunch with a young man one time, and when I am with men, I always try to get the subject around to marriage because most men don't have many opportunities to learn much about it. I asked him how everything was going at home. He said everything was great except that his wife wanted to go on vacation to Phoenix in August. He had put his foot down. It would be way too hot, and besides they couldn't afford it. He and his wife were having some heated discussions over this.

He asked my advice, so I suggested if he was to die for his wife, and if she was his highest priority, he should make arrangements to go to Phoenix in August. I suggested he tell her she was the most important thing in his life, and if she wanted to go to Phoenix in August he would be glad to go with her. I added, however, that he probably would not have to go. He didn't quite understand that but decided to take my advice. He sent a note a few days later to report that they were not going to Phoenix in August. His wife thought it would be too hot, and they really couldn't afford it.

They had a power struggle going. He was insisting they were not going to go to Phoenix in August. She was resisting him and was determined that they *were* going to go. When he released her, she did the right thing.

We had a couple come to us for advice as to what to do with a rebellious teenager. She wasn't awful, but her spirit was resisting the family. She was almost eighteen so we suggested they release her and let God put the pressure on her to be less resistant to the family. Somehow parents think if they say something just one more time (even though they have said the same thing 1,198 times) the teenager will hear it. But all it does is drive them further away. We suggested they tell their teenager that because she was almost an adult, they would no longer tell her what to do. They were turning her over to God. They would be her support, however, if she needed them. It wasn't long before she was back in the family unit with a positive attitude.

If we release our children, we of course worry about them getting pregnant, becoming an alcoholic, starting to do hard drugs, and ending up in prison. Some of these things might happen. But they are breaking the rules anyway, so maybe if you stop being their Holy Spirit and become their friend ready to step in if needed, they will come back to what they know are your standards.

I feel like apologizing to our son Tim because I am going to tell his story again. He's made every book we've written so far. I guess that's because he is such a good example of how kids do grow up when their parents get out of the way. He has encouraged us to share his story so other young people will be helped. I probably should begin giving him some royalties, but I'm sure he's not into material things, so he wouldn't want money. I don't have time to ask him about this because I'm writing this book with Barb, but I'm sure he wouldn't want this world's goods. I'm pretty sure, anyway. I won't bother him about it, and then he won't have to compromise his position.

Tim was a right-brained, creative child. He had two problems. First, his parents didn't know anything about personality styles and brain wiring. Second, most schools are for structured kids and left-brain subjects like science, reading, arithmetic, biology, chemistry, and so on. Right-brain subjects like art and music are shuffled into the if-you-can't-do-anything-else category.

Tim was a dreamer like most creative people are. He would sit in class and all of a sudden wake up to the fact that the teacher had been talking for fifteen minutes, and he hadn't the foggiest notion what she was saying. His grades reflected this, too.

By the way, as long as I'm going to the trouble of writing part of this book, let me take a shot at our school systems. They spend 70 percent of the time on reading, writing, spelling, and math. These are good subjects, but 70 percent of our *lives* are spent listening, speaking clearly, and trying to figure out how to be a good husband or wife, how to handle our finances including balancing a checkbook, how to look for a job and please a boss, how to serve others, how to raise kids, and how to forgive an enemy. Things are a little out of balance in my opinion.

Typing was by far the most important course I ever took in my entire sixteen years of schooling. It's even more important these days so kids can handle computers and get a job. Doctors spend seventeen to twenty years preparing for their profession. Lawyers, scientists, and schoolteachers all spend many years in formal training, but how much time do we spend on preparing our kids for marriage? None, or at least not very much. It seems like we spend way too much time on nonessentials in school and miss the heartbeat of what life is all about. But that's just an old guy speaking who has clear hindsight now but didn't know how to be a good parent to Tim then.

Tim always seemed to be a half step out of phase with the rest of the family. If we wanted to go to the zoo, he wanted to go to the beach. If we wanted to look at slides, he wanted to look at movies. If I wanted him to mow the lawn, he decided to clean out the garage. I only wish I had known what made him tick. He was creative. Even as a small child he spent hours underneath his toy car "fixing" it. He took apart every piece of machinery, clock, toaster, recorder, and toy he could find, including some things I wished he had not taken apart. If only I would have had the maturity not to have cared so much about the things he took apart and had been more understanding about how Tim was put together.

He got into what we perceived as the wrong crowd. It was just one of his gifts we didn't recognize. He loved to help people in trouble, and when he did, they accepted him for who he was, and this helped cement their relationships. Through all of this Tim was a fortress as far as not bending to peer pressure. He was a wonderful kid, but just a little out of step with the family, and we didn't know why. He knocked over a gas pump one time with his car, and for his discipline he was to go through the book of Proverbs and write out in longhand every verse that had the word "son" in it. Then he was to explain to me what the verses meant. He worked and worked and even took his Bible to school.

Finally, one morning he woke me up and wanted to go over the Scriptures he had found. We had only gone over a few verses before I noticed he had missed some of the key ones. I pointed this out and he said, "Even the ones that don't apply?" The ones he missed were of course some of the zingers that *really* applied. He went back to work, and later we went over the verses, both of us in tears, as we realized just what God had in mind for a son.

As he approached eighteen years of age, we decided to release him to God. If He wanted to put the pressure on Tim to change some of his attitudes toward us, that was fine. We had done all we could. Saying it one more time would not make any difference. So we told him he was now responsible to God, not us. We would always be his parents. Our home would always be his home. We would help whenever he wanted, but he was free to have any companions he wanted, come in anytime day or night, or have any lifestyle he wanted. All of a sudden he was calling us at 3:00 A.M. and saying, "Don't worry, I'm just over here at my friend's house." We weren't worrying. We were asleep. We knew God was watching out for him. Tim was now *God's* responsibility, not ours. It wasn't long before Tim was home at midnight, then he was in bed by 10:30 P.M., then he was in school.

He escaped high school with a 1.9 GPA and looked at his diploma as a pardon. Since he could take the motor out of his car every afternoon, dust it off, and make it run again, we decided to encourage him to go to diesel mechanic's school. He signed up and began to get straight A's. He hated math in school, but now he was bringing home fractions and decimal problems. I mentioned to him that his homework looked a lot like math. He said no, it wasn't math. It was piston ratios, spark plug gaps, and valve clearances. Someone had finally hit his hot button, and we were so grateful. He now has given us a beautiful family and has his own diesel shop in Seattle. Even though she is perfect in every way, his firstborn daughter Kjersten reminds us of him once in a while. Barb says it serves him right.

Barb: I guess every parent says this, "If we had only known then what we know now!" I can remember when Tim was born my dad said, "Good thing he's a boy. He'll be strong while you experiment." I didn't understand what he meant then, but I do now. So despite us, Tim was strong and survived his parents to be a godly son, husband, father, and man. We are proud parents.

Chuck: I'm reminded of the phrase, what goes around, comes around. I finally was able to afford my first really nice car. I was so proud. I brought it home, and Tim wanted to take it to the gas station and fill it up with gas for me. I said, "Sure," but a small problem arose. He put a big scratch in the side by getting too close to the gas pump. He was mortified and worried about what my reaction would be. My life had been changed a few weeks earlier at Bill Gothard's seminar, and I had given up my rights to everything I had, including my nice car. So I told Tim, "If God wants to scratch up his car, it's none of my concern. It's just a car, a piece of metal, so don't worry. How's breakfast?"

Years go by. Ten-year-old Kjersten goes on a white water raft trip with a school group. She comes home. She asks her dad, "Do you want the good news or the bad news." He opted for the good news first. Kjersten said, "I'm alive." Well that *was* good news. What's the bad news? "I lost my glasses." Tim and Tammie had just a few weeks earlier purchased some very expensive glasses for her. Tim was able to say to her because of the nice car incident, "Kjersten, you are much more important to us than those dumb glasses. They are just bits of glass and metal, so we'll get you some more. No problem. How's breakfast?"

Releasing is such a powerful tool in the hands of spiritual men and women, especially in the case of kids and marriages. There are so many odds against a marriage making it with all the cultural, parenting, personality, men-women, and environmental differences that we bring to the relationship. It takes supernatural help and self-sacrificing work on our part to make it work. Two people can be taught how to have a satisfying marriage, but it doesn't come naturally. We simply cannot easily break those chains of self that so tightly bind themselves around every part of our being. The man can feel magnanimous when he mows the lawn without being asked, cleans up the basement, or takes his wife on a date for dinner to talk. The woman can feel magnanimous when she makes his favorite meal or suggests going to bed early and puts on her frilly, frothy, nothing outfit for him. Doing good, thoughtful things like this on a regular basis takes work, commitment, preprogramming, and self-reminders because it is so much against our natural way of doing things. Our feelings so often get in the way of our obedience.

One of the big problems in being so different is that we expect our partner to think and have the same needs that we do. It is not even logical to think otherwise unless you have been told about God's plan for a man and woman completing each other. Not only are men and women different, they are *completely* different. Dwell on that thought for a minute—COMPLETELY different. And God designed us to be different. Other than a few physical items like hair and toenails (maybe these are different, too; I haven't checked), we are as different as God could make us. The problem comes when we try to change the other person into another one just like us. It just doesn't work.

Men probably have the hardest job and make the most mistakes in a marriage because God made women to be more naturally into nurturing relationships. Men are more naturally into goals and work and sports and things and doing. Unfortunately, a man can go twenty-five years and not even *know* he has a wife who needs a relationship with him.

We expect so much from a wife, mother, friend, and lover. What we don't know is that she has killed herself working all day at home or has come home from the office dead tired. She still fixes dinner, probably loads the dishwasher without help, picks up clothes and toys, and puts the kids into bed. She has battled PMS all week, is dealing with a cranky neighbor, has deadlines at church or school, and he wonders why she doesn't have time to go to bed with him every time he sees the boat ad in *Popular Mechanics*. He has not approved of her or acknowledged all the yucky things she has had to do all day, and then he wants more. I know this can be so discouraging to you women. I'm sure sometimes you get to the point where you just want to give up.

On the other hand, if your husband was quick to help you around the house, gave you a hug once in a while, grieved with you over your busy schedule, made all the repairs around the house quickly, made time to visit and share your life, proactively made couple time and farmed out the kids so you could have a little romance once in a while without pressure, what a difference it would make. If he helped you with the children, kept your side of the garage clean, gave you a woman's night out once in a while, put his arm around you and held your hand when his goal was not the bedroom, and all the other things I have already mentioned a godly husband would do, there would be nothing you wouldn't do for him in return.

Barb and I just had an interesting discussion. It is Saturday around noon and I have been working hard on this book. It is filling all the cracks I usually have in my schedule of making a living, doing ministry-related projects, counseling, and keeping the home shipshape. Therefore, I have not been as available to her as I would like to be. I had just finished the rough draft of a couple of chapters and wanted to make a connection with Barb. I finally found her in the sewing room. She was ironing and listening to one of the prophecy tapes I gave her for our anniversary. She is teaching Kay Arthur's Precept course on the book of Revelation, and she is very much into learning about the last days. I said, "If you would like to do something, go to a movie or go looking for antiques, or go for a walk, I'm available."

She said "I only have a few more things to take care of and I'm available. What would you like to do?"

I said, "I don't necessarily want to *do* anything, but I want to meet *your* needs in case you want to take a break or do something later this afternoon."

She said, "Do *you* want to go?"

I said, "I want to go if *you* want to do something."

She said, "I'm available if you would like to do something."

I said, "I don't necessarily have to do something unless *you* want to do something." (Some more he-said she-said conversation.) I finally asked her whether she had a *need* to do something. "No," she answered. "I don't have any need to do anything." She asked if I needed to do something.

I said, "I'm here to meet *your* needs. I don't have any needs right now."

She said, "Neither do I."

So I went back to my writing, and she started the audio tape again. My focus was meeting her needs. Her focus was meeting my needs. *That's* the way both our needs can be met—by focusing on the other person. This is one of the best kept secrets about how to succeed in marriage—spend full time focusing on, being creative about, and thinking how you can fulfill your husband's or wife's needs. When you take them on as a project, it gets your eyes off yourself, and that's *exactly* what God wants, and He will bless your relationship because of your giving attitude.

I love how Barb's and my friendship has grown over the years. We are very comfortable together. I want to make sure it stays that way, so I'm always look-ing for tears from Barb or a tense countenance just in case I'm involved in some way. We have even developed a type of shorthand communication that tells me how she is. Not too long ago I came into the living room, and Barb looked like she had been crying. I asked her if anything was wrong. She nod-ded toward the TV. She was watching a movie. I asked her, "Cancer, dying, or someone run over?"

She answered, "Dying," and I went out to fix myself a sandwich.

Now, before you start to think I'm wonderful, let me confess that *most* of the time I miss those signals. In fact, a few years ago Barb got up feeling bad about a situation that didn't involve me and came to the breakfast table with red eyes and tears on her cheeks. I was reading the paper. She just wondered if I would notice. Since I'm not into the details of life, I was glad to have her at the table, but I surely didn't notice that anything was out of the ordinary.

I want to repeat something I said in an earlier chapter because it is so *vital* to handling marriage conflict. The two of you must have a lifetime commit-ment to your marriage. I know I hit that pretty hard earlier, but it is vital that you verbally say to each other that no matter what happens, you will not leave the other person or seek a divorce. You *will* work things out even though there may be times when you feel like walking away. When your marriage has the foundation of "till death do us part," then you can have conflict and resolve it in a healthy way.

I had a woman tell me she had prayed and God said it was okay to divorce her husband. I thought, How interesting. God had just contradicted Himself, and I didn't think He could do that. He said very plainly in the Bible that He *hates* divorce. It makes Him nauseated. He vomits. She just couldn't imagine God wanting her to stay with a husband who was not meeting any of her needs. You can be pretty sure when someone says divorce is okay, they don't know the Word very well. There is a way that seems right to a man or woman, and so often it is *our* way that feels so right. The "God wants me to be happy" philosophy has reached epidemic proportions in the Christian church these days. But it's wrong. God wants us to be *obedient,* which may or may not lead to happiness. One thing you can be sure of; God wants to bless us and He *looks* for ways to honor and encourage us when we are obedient to His way of doing things.

Sometimes the problem in a marriage relationship is a matter of control. I have contact with lots of men who have their wives all bound up in *their* rules and desires, without any regard for what she needs. It's often so subtle the man doesn't recognize he is controlling his wife until he makes the mistake of asking my opinion.

I had a man tell me about his wife who was going out on him. He had no idea where she went, with whom she was with, or what she was doing. His track record was one of control. I suggested he have *un*conditional love with no expectations, especially during this time he was trying to court her back. He was even doing the courting wrong. He was leaving her little love notes and expressing his desire to go to counseling with her and wishing her happy birthday. He hadn't done that before, so this seemed false to her, especially the counseling thing. She had asked him to go many times before, but of course he wouldn't go. Now his note said, "I know God wants us to get back together, so please let me know when you would be available to see the counselor." You can recognize what's wrong, can't you? Control. He was still trying to run her life.

He disappeared from my life for about five years. I didn't give their marriage any chance to survive. She finally filed for divorce. But what a nice surprise when I ran into him recently and he told me the story of how he had stood for the marriage and finally she came back and they were remarried. Control is such a subtle thing, and I see it in many of the hurting marriages that come into my life.

Having expectations is a form of control. A husband cannot expect his wife to pick up his dirty clothes, be available for sex every time he is in the mood, pick him up on time from work, love going to see his mother, have the dishes done, or dinner on the table when he gets home. He can't expect her to be understanding when she has scrimped for a year saving money for some curtains, and he buys a new hunting rifle for three times the amount the curtains would have cost.

On the other hand, a woman cannot expect her husband always to be home on time from work, always to pick up after himself, or always to be available to talk. She can't expect him to keep his shop clean, buy the right kind of clothes, eat the right kind of food, go to the doctor enough, quit smoking, or even stop having his affair. The principle here is that the other person is out of our control and many times even out of *God's* control. We are not robots. We can tell God to get lost. He will let us go. He is not going to force anyone to be obedient. He *could* have done that when He first got the idea of creating men and women. He could have programmed us to love Him at all times and be obedient. He could have made us so we'd never sin and only produce the fruits of His Spirit.

Maybe this is making God too human, but I wonder if He even had second thoughts about making men and women independent. I guess He decided He would rather have us love Him because we *wanted* to, not because we *had* to. Of course God, who knows all, had already read the next chapter of human history and He knew He would lose His gamble, but I still think He feels He did the right thing. It's a wonderful feeling to know our awesome love for God is because He first loved us with no strings attached.

As far as our mates our concerned, we can't force them to change, or come back, or love us, or serve us, or like us, or anything. We can't have a *goal* that they will ever change. We can have a *desire* they will change, but not a goal. A desire is something we can have on our own. A goal depends on the cooperation of the other person.

Releasing someone is a wonderful example of *unconditional* love. This means the wife can't weigh too much, talk on the phone too much, work too much at the office, delay doing the dishes too long, or bring her briefcase home with work too many times in the evening. This means the husband can't weigh too much, spend too much time in his shop or at work, watch TV too much, spend too much money, or go out with his men friends too much. If any of these things (and hundreds of others I could name) affect our *doing* love, then the love we have for them is *our* love, not God's. His love is unconditional.

I know this is not what you want to hear. But have you ever had success *forcing* your wife or husband to do something and have it turn out positive? Yes, the more submissive, nonexpressive pleasers of the world can be used as doormats and will do what the more dominant, controlling, expressive mate

WHAT TO DO WHEN ALL ELSE FAILS

says. But I can't believe this is very pleasing to either one to have a dictator relationship rather than a team relationship.

Here's what you do. Work hard at being the man or woman God wants *you* to be in the marriage with no expectations that your wife or husband will *ever* change or ever meet *your* needs. Do you know of a Bible verse that says people are to meet *our* needs? The ones I read tell us to serve others with an *unconditional* love. Forgive others, think of others first, honor others, defer to them, help them, and die to ourselves. The alternative to this is being miserable because your marriage partner is not meeting *your* needs. You can keep the pressure on him or her and make them bleed. You can control and demand and manipulate and connive and create a hellish life for both of you. Or you can serve your mate with an *unconditional* love. Will it be easy? No. It might not even be possible, but it's worth the pain and effort, and many times you can restore your marriage unilaterally. I've seen it done.

Now I want to say a few more words to you women before we close. I shock some people when I say that I believe 90 percent of all marriage problems are caused by men. When people have a chance to think about it, even men, I haven't had anyone disagree yet. This isn't a perfect survey, and I'm sure I'll run into some guys who will object to this. But I think deep down, when a man is really honest and looks at his marriage objectively, it is hard to escape knowing who causes most of the problems. This is not man-bashing. This is acknowledging a fact that men are not into relationships like women are. It is not as easy for us to give ourselves to others like women do. It's not as easy for us to serve. We are into *winning*, not connection. We have to be *taught* how to serve. Serving doesn't come easy for us. We are fighters, not lovers. This means there are probably millions of women around the world who are starving for love and attention. They have to live with someone who doesn't know how to meet their needs and doesn't seem very interested in learning. You have worked so hard at trying to understand your husband, but for some of you discouragement is your reward for all your hard work and effort trying to keep the relationship together.

By the way, ladies, I don't share the 90 percent idea to give you leverage. I share it so you will be more understanding when your husband blows it. He is usually untaught. He does not know how to love and serve naturally and will probably admit he is mostly at fault for problems in the marriage. Hopefully, this will help you look for things he does *right*. When you see him doing the right things, praise him out of his mind since you know it is not his nature.

There is one small thing you can work on, however. You women have a tendency to fill vacuums. I had lunch with a young woman who was struggling with how different she and her husband were, and she gave me some examples.

First of all, he was more of a dreamer and entrepreneur than she was. He was trying to run his own business, but it wasn't going real well. She wanted him to go get a "real" job but couldn't bring herself to tell him directly. Her salary was paying most of the bills, and he seemed down most of the time because his work wasn't going as well as he wanted. I explained to her how a man's self-esteem comes from what he does. Also, a man tends to look down the road further than most women, especially the dreamer type. He says, "In two years this thing is really going to click, and we're going to be successful."

His wife says, "How are we going to eat tomorrow?"

He says, "Well, I don't know about that, but I know in two years this thing is really going to work out well."

He is looking into the future. She is looking at tomorrow afternoon. The advice I give husbands at this point is to go out and get any kind of job, whether it meets his career goals or not. The purpose is to stabilize the family finances. When that is going well, he can work on his dreams.

One of the problems in this case was that the woman's husband didn't feel as much financial pressure as she did because she had assumed the responsibility for the finances. It was an out-of-sight-out-of-mind type of thing for him. He didn't feel much pressure because *she* handled the bills. She got all stressed out because their outgo was more than their income, and they were dipping into savings. This fits the way a man thinks. It's called no-news-is-good-news. If his wife isn't crying or creating a crisis like saying, "Let's talk," then he thinks his marriage is one of the best in the world and his wife is happy and contented. It's the wife who must always say, "Can we talk?" when things need to be resolved. The man is either oblivious to any conflicts or hates disagreements. He won't bring up anything that might lead to one.

If you as a wife are in this sort of situation with finances, I would suggest you say something like this. "Sweetheart (honey, precious, dear, whatever your term), I think I have taken way too much of the responsibility for the finances. Would you forgive me? God has asked *you* to be the provider for the family, and I've been getting all uptight about paying the bills when the money is in short supply. You had no way to know what our situation is. Therefore, I am going to resign my job since the kids are so small, and I am turning over all the finances to you. I'm sorry I took over. I still want to be your teammate in the financial area, and I know neither one of us will make independent financial decisions, but from now on you are in charge of the day-to-day finances. If you want my opinion on something regarding our finances just ask. I'm sorry I have been usurping your role as the family provider."

Some of you just fainted! "You mean turn over the finances to that spendthrift, irresponsible, husband of mine?" I acknowledge the risk. I'm sure there *are* husbands who might take advantage of this, but my experience has been that when the wife steps back from paying the bills, *God* puts the pressure on the husband to go out and get a job that meets the family's needs. It appears to me the only alternative to this is to become bitter, uptight, resentful, and worried about whether the family is going to make it financially. So put the responsibility in God's hands, and ask Him to work in your husband's life to motivate him to do the right thing. Then when the bill collectors come to the home or call on the phone you can say, "Oh, just a minute, you want my husband. I'll get him for you."

You then have a free spirit because you have given the situation to your husband and God. Now you can sleep nights and have a cheerful loving attitude, free in the knowledge that the problem is God's, not yours. God has committed himself to meeting your needs, and you can count on Him. Now you can meet your husband's needs with a fun, loving, free spirit—just like God would want you to.

Yes, there are a few uncaring men out there who would let the family suffer because of their irresponsibility. And if this is your case, go back to the chapter on suffering and review God's promises when you hurt. But let me say again, of all the thousands of men I have met, none come immediately to mind as people who would purposely harm their family in any way. Most of the time no one has ever taught them what they need to do to be responsible providers.

This is easy for me to say and might be impossible for you to do. This is going to sound harsh, but I think we excuse needing double incomes because the cost of living is so high in our culture these days. And it is. So you might have to rent instead of buying a home. Take the bus or car pool rather than your own car. You might not be able to afford going out to eat. You might have to do your own lawn. You might have to take the laundry to the laundromat. You might have to wash *out* the diapers instead of buying disposables. You might have to shop garage sales, thrift shops, and rummage sales for clothes and kids' toys. You might not be able to have a big screen TV or the latest computer. You might not be able to afford vacations.

For the first years of our marriage, Barb and I lived out of envelopes. We had a food envelope, a clothing envelope, an entertainment envelope, and a miscellaneous envelope. When the money in the envelopes was gone, we waited until the next paycheck to refill them. We rented our home. Our kids had secondhand toys. Our vacation was putting up a tent in the backyard. I bought a complete set of golf clubs at the Goodwill for a dollar a club. I was making $350 a month, and we were even putting a little bit into savings and giving the Lord his 10 percent. I know that times have changed. I'm just asking that you at least look at what would happen if you had to live on your husband's salary alone. I look at our days when we were "poor" with a little bit of envy sometimes because we had it so good in other ways than money. Barb would trade permanents with other young mothers. We traded baby-sitting with other couples. We had pie socials in our home for our entertainment. It was a rich, memorable, precious time of life, and the memories make me cry.

Back to the example from the woman I was counseling. Her second problem was trying to be her husband's Holy Spirit with regard to his not being the spiritual leader of the home. In her mind this meant praying with her and the family, doing family devotions of some kind, and taking an active part in a local church. Not all of you will agree with me, but my feeling is that being the spiritual head of the home does not necessarily mean doing any of these things. The man might have the gift of service or mercy and not feel comfortable praying out loud, or teaching the family, or anyone else. A spiritual leader creates the atmosphere so his wife can do the teaching for the family if she is the one with a teaching gift or enjoys reading Bible stories. We've already learned that being the spiritual leader or head of the home means being a servant, not necessarily the one who is up front.

As far as praying together, some couples can do this, some can't. Barb and I don't pray together except at the dinner table. I tear up much too easily, and I can't talk when I get moved, and I feel very uncomfortable. There is no Bible verse that says a man and wife have to pray together. That is the invention of somebody who was gifted in that, and they then put the guilt trip on everyone else who is not "spiritual" like they are. If you and your husband can pray together, great. If not, don't worry about it. Pray at the table together and include some of the same things you might pray for if you were praying before bedtime or in the morning. God believes in diversity. We see it in nature. We see it in the way he designed men and women. We see in it the way he structured the different personalities and learning styles. Our tendency is to try to make the other person into someone just like us. God wants us to *release* them to be who *they* are, not who we would *like* them to be. Here's the problem with men. The more a woman presses, criticizes, and expects from her husband, the more he feels pushed away. He knows he will fail in your eyes. So why try? When you release him to be who he is in the spiritual area with no expectations, everyone is free to be who *they* are.

If you have a husband who is not open to change, then I suggest you give him to God. Then find or create a support group of some kind for yourself. I've mentioned that Barb teaches this marvelous Bible study material written by Kay Arthur called *Precept upon Precept*. Barb has 120 women from all kinds of different churches gather to study the Bible and support each other on Tuesdays at a local church. It is life changing. Within the group there are many women whose husbands are not supporting them at home. Just to find someone else who is going through the same situation is therapeutic and helpful. If you can't find a group, start one. If you're not working outside the home, find three or four other women in the same situation and meet in each other's homes for fellowship, prayer, and Bible study while the kids are in school. Or if the kids are small, chip in and hire a baby-sitter or trade baby-sitting with other young mothers. You don't have to have the gift of teaching to do this. Just read through a book of the Bible picking out practical helps for everyday living. Or get a book on marriage or child rearing or depression or anger or stress and have everyone read a chapter. Have them be prepared to report on the things that touched them the most.

If you're working in the marketplace, then find a restaurant with a back room and develop your relationship group during the lunch hour. There's a danger in this, of course. You could begin enjoying the small group fellowship so much you wished you didn't have to go back to work. So have a mobile phone handy in case you get carried away and are late getting back. The only skills you need are the ability to call a restaurant and reserve a table in the back room and drive a car to the restaurant. The rest is automatic as God works through you to the group. It's life changing. I know from firsthand experience. Barb has helped change *my* life through the things she is learning as she teaches the study.

If you have a fairly harmonious marriage, this would be a great way to reach out to help others who might be going through struggles in their own relationships. If you have a horrible marriage, it will be a way for God to give you comfort as you learn the principles of being a godly wife in *spite* of what your husband is doing.

Barb: We mentioned earlier how the woman reflects back to the man how he treats her. I think it's interesting to note that a woman gets most of her self-esteem from her relationship with her husband, but a man usually gets his self-esteem from his work. Even if a woman works in the marketplace, most of her good feelings come when her home and family are in order.

Men tend to be a little more objective in their approach to life. Women tend to relate things to themselves. If a woman's husband said something at dinner like, "Where did you get this meat?" the woman would probably reply, "What's wrong with it?" All the husband wanted to know is whether it was from the big market on the corner or the small meat shop down the street. Usually he is impressed with how good it is, rather than how bad.

The same thing would probably happen if the man looked at the woman on the way to church and said, "Where did you get that dress?" Again the reply would probably be, "What's wrong with it?"

Even the fears of a man and woman tend to be different. These fears are felt when we do not treat our mates like the Lord told us to.

When a wife is not submitting to the Lord and her husband by respecting and loving her husband with friendship and admiration, he realizes his two greatest fears. The first is the *fear of failure*. The second is the *fear of being dominated by a woman*. These are God-given fears. God made men to be providers and protectors and to be in headship. When we as women don't give our husbands trust and respect, they feel like failures. You know how it is. The first time our husbands make a mistake, we decide to take over. We tell them what they should or should not have done. If they do as we say, they feel like they have failed and have been dominated by a woman.

When a husband does not submit to the Lord by loving unconditionally and giving himself up for his wife, then she feels her great fear which is *being taken for granted*. He wants her to cook his meals, take care of the kids, make sure he has clean clothes in his dresser drawer, and keep his house clean. In addition, he expects her to go to all his business parties and meetings but never includes her in his thoughts or talks to her as a friend. He spends money for things *he* wants, but tells his wife she is spending too much on food or clothes for the family.

He makes decisions that involve her future as well as his but never talks those decisions over with her. He teases her about how much she weighs and about getting older and then wonders why she does not want to go to bed with him. She has been treated like a thing, rather than the lovely person she thought he saw in her before they were married. *She has been taken for granted.*

I read a wonderful book called *You Just Don't Understand* by Deborah Tannen, Ph.D. She is a linguist who has studied boys and girls into adulthood in order to know how they talk to one another. What she has seen fits with some of the things I have seen in the Bible about husbands and wives. She says it so well in her book I would like to show you some excerpts:

> The male is seen as normative, the female as departing from the norm. And it is only a short step—maybe an inevitable one—from "different" to "worse" or "wrong."
>
> Furthermore, if women's and men's styles are shown to be different it is usually women who are told to change. Talk between men and women is cross-cultural communication. The effect of dominance is

not always the result of an intention to dominate. That is the news
this book brings.

Dr. Tannen tell us women speak with the motivation for connection and intimacy and to avoid isolation. Men, on the other hand, speak from an adversarial
position. They speak from a position of opposition, independence, and status—
they feel they are either one up or one down. They speak to avoid failure.

Do you see? God made women relational. We are concerned with connection and intimacy and do not want to be isolated from our relationships.
God also made men competitive because he has given them the job of going
out in the world to earn a living and provide for their families. That is why the
Lord has told wives to honor them, defer to them, and appreciate, love, and
admire them exceedingly. When we don't, our husbands feel like failures.
Every man has to feel special to *someone* and God knew it must be their wives.

In the same way, husbands are told to honor their wives by nourishing
and cherishing them so the wives feel your relationship with them is so intimate you would give up your life for them.

Dr. Tannen has outlined in her studies the exact reason why God gives
specific ways we are to love our mates. He gives one set of instructions to husbands and a different set of instructions to wives. God does this so we will love
our mates in the way *they need* to make them feel loved.

The women's movement has been operating on the principle that women
are equal with men. God has said that we *are* equal, but we are different. Most
women have figured out that talking to a man as another man would does not
work. Some of us have learned to build them up and defer to them whether
we realized that is what we were doing or not. I don't think that is wrong or
bad. It just *is!* In fact, I believe most women know this instinctively. And sometimes it makes us angry.

A repairman came one day to fix our dishwasher. He found a wet soggy
toothpick holding open the little black rubber ball that closed off the drain.
He said it would cost a certain amount to replace the ball.

I told him, "Let's just leave it the way it is since it doesn't seem to be dam-
aged."

He said, "That's not the way we do it!"

I told him, "I'd like to try leaving it and see if it works." Let me tell you he checked everything there was to check on that dishwasher, taking a long time to do it, and the bill came to more than if I'd just let him replace the little black ball in the first place.

After that episode, I decided I wouldn't tell a repairman what to do again. I should have known because some time before that I told a stove repairman what I thought was wrong, and that was the last thing he checked. No woman was going to tell *him* what to check! At least that's what I imagine he was thinking.

There you have it. I think if we would obey what the Lord tells us to do for our husbands and wives, we would not have to deal with our great fears. The Lord gave us the golden rule in Matthew 7:12 when he said, "However you want people to treat you, so treat them." I know I want to be loved in a way that makes *me* feel loved. So I'm learning how to love Chuck in the way that makes *him* feel loved too. That's what the golden rule is all about.

What is true for Chuck and me is also true in many marriages. It's our different perspectives on the "little things" that cause us trouble.

Most men tend to be stable when it comes to handling disasters like earthquakes, storm damage, or wars—but can go out of their mind if their nail clippers are missing. Chuck has been known to go out and buy ten flashlights or five pair of scissors or six sets of nail clippers just because the one he usually uses is missing.

Also, while most men tend to have their eyes set on the end result down the road and don't want to be bothered by disruptions and details, women seem to be able to handle the little details and interruptions of life. It's a good thing because there are so many of them.

We can let our mates be who they are rather than who we want them to be because God has given us the fruit of the Spirit, *meekness.* Remember, this is the quality in us that is strength under control. That strength is the Holy Spirit in us. I've already told you that meekness is a serenity of spirit that accepts everything that comes into our lives as coming from the hand of God, whether we think it is good or bad. The reason we can look at trials this way is because we know God rules over all. He is in absolute control of every situation. He could have prevented the trial we are going through if he had wanted to. He allows circumstances in our lives to mold us and make us into his image. Trials come to us to mature us and to make us complete and lacking in nothing as the book of James tells us. God never tempts us, and yet He does design trials for us once in a while. Not to trip us up, but to approve us. "In this you greatly rejoice, even though now for a little while, if necessary, you have been distressed by various trials, that the proof of your faith, being more precious than gold which is perishable, even though tested by fire, may be found to result in praise and glory and honor at the revelation of Jesus Christ" (1 Peter 1:6–7).

Chuck and I have already told you how different we are. I am just amazed sometimes at how different we still are after over forty-three years of marriage. Because of these differences, we have had a number of disagreements and conflicts.

My dream for marriage was never to have arguments and to live in peace with each other all the time. Chuck's dream for marriage was the same. But after we got married we discovered we even handled disagreements differently. Remember, I want to talk, he wants to withdraw! Chuck thinks if we don't talk about it, it will go away. I think if we don't talk about it, it will become bigger.

"Blessed are the peacemakers, for they shall be called sons of God" (Matthew 5:9).

He didn't say peace*keepers*, He said peace*makers*. On the surface the peacekeeper appears calm. But inside there is a boiling caldron of unspoken thoughts which can turn into a root of bitterness. We are told: "Pursue peace with all men, and the sanctification [that means being set apart for God's use only] without which no one will see the Lord. See to it that no one comes short of the grace of God; that no root of bitterness springing up causes trouble, and by it many be defiled" (Hebrews 12:14–15).

To be a peacemaker, one must pursue after peace. The problem is when someone pursues peace, it can look like they are causing war. The fact remains, one way or another there is going to be an explosion. For the peacemaker it's now. For the peacekeeper who avoids the conflict to keep the peace, you never know when the explosion might happen.

By the way, when a wife gives her opinion or feelings to her husband, his reaction is sometimes so harsh she becomes afraid. After she experiences this a few times, she tends to quit giving her true opinions.

There have been times in our relationship where I have not been completely honest with Chuck because I just couldn't bear his disapproval again. It's not easy to always have a different opinion than your husband. Most wives don't plan to disagree on purpose with their husbands—it's just that we do think about things differently than they do.

When Chuck and I had a disagreement, the usual pattern would be for him to withdraw. I would often ask him, "Can we talk?" He took this as a sign of trouble. To me, it meant I was trying to make peace. We didn't know it at the time, but I was being a peacemaker, and Chuck was being a peacekeeper.

As we've said before, the nonexpressive finds peacekeeping much more comfortable. The expressive finds pursuing the nonexpressive to talk is not necessarily comfortable, but it is vital for the relationship. Maybe this is why the Lord puts these two different types together so often. He knows bitterness might be the result if two nonexpressives were married to each other.

When a person is meek and knows that whatever comes into their lives is ordained by God, then they can live through the harsh replies or the disapproval, and be a peacemaker. Sometimes peacemakers have to go through a lot of guff before peace is made. Often they are attacked personally. Peacemakers may even be accused of disrupting the peace. It's not easy to be a peacemaker, but it is the best way because that's what the Lord commands.

Chuck and I know there are times we fail to be all God wants us to be for him and for each other. Yet the word that keeps coming back over and over to my mind is obedience. The way we have described to you is a narrow way, but the way of the Lord *is* narrow. It's our own ways that are broad. The Lord said just a few would be willing to walk on the narrow way while many would choose the broad way.

Chapter 2 of the book of Romans tells about the religious people of that day, describing them as teaching others not to break the Law, while they themselves were breaking it. They did some of the right things, but in their hearts they were going their own way. The root meaning for the Greek word *breaking* in Romans 2:23 means that which is not on the true line, either by falling short or going beyond it. Because we haven't known what the true line is—because we haven't put all the principles together in our minds—we have not walked on the true line. We may have been close, but still our relationships have not worked out right because we haven't been on the narrow way.

Besides, some of the things the Lord tells us to do just don't seem right. They don't seem to make sense in our circumstances. And so we settle for short-term joy and get long-term misery because we have not been willing to be obedient. We want happiness for ourselves *right now*. We just don't see the big picture. We don't see reality.

Chuck and I have quoted 1 Peter 5 several times already, but it fits here, too. God tells us to cast all our anxiety on Him because He cares for us. He tells us to humble ourselves before Him so He can exalt us. If we choose to obey what He says, we may have short-term pain, but we will have long-term joy. Doing things His way always turns out right.

I believe the big picture must include knowing the final result of disobedience. "But to those who are selfishly ambitious and do not obey the truth, but obey unrighteousness, wrath and indignation. There will be tribulation and distress for every soul of man who does evil, of the Jew first and also of the Greek, but glory and honor and peace to every man who does good, to the Jew first and also to the Greek. For there is no partiality with God" (Romans 2:8–11).

It's interesting to note the Greek meaning for the words *tribulation* and *distress*. Tribulation means a pressing together, crushing, squeezing, and pressure. Distress means a narrowness of place, forcing through that narrow place and the distress and anguish that results. It has the dominant idea of constraint.

When we think about the mansions the Lord is preparing for those of us who obey Him or the green pastures where He restores our souls talked about in Psalm 23, we think of a broad way. In *this* life, however, if we stay on the broad way and do our own thing, we end up in a narrow and constricted place. Our disobedience puts us in prison. On the other hand, if we stay on the narrow way in this life, we end up in a broad, spacious place. Our obedience gives us a freedom.

In the book of James we are told the Scriptures or the Law are the perfect law of liberty. Some people think if we do things the Lord's way, we will be put into prison, but the exact opposite is true.

Our good works do not get us into heaven. What makes us a Christian is our trusting in the risen Lord Jesus Christ, acknowledging His death for our own sins, asking for forgiveness of our sins in His name (and receiving and believing in that forgiveness), and then following Him and accepting His authority over our lives. After trusting in Him, obeying Him keeps us on the narrow way. God asks us to enter through a small door onto the narrow path. When we do that, we experience the peace that comes from doing what the Lord says is right. We *stay* on the narrow way—a staying that equals obedience to doing things God's way in our marriages and in all our relationships.

Chuck: I'm often asked by hurting couples if I would do "extended" marriage counseling for them. As softly as I can, I say that I don't believe in extended counseling unless there are other factors involved like abuse, addictions, mental problems and the like. If it is just good old-fashioned garden variety marriage problems, all a couple has to do is read this book or listen to our audio tapes and take the Taylor Johnson temperament test, and they will know everything I know about marriage.

Now the operative word is OBEDIENCE. Our wish and prayer for all who read this book is that you will be obedient to God's ways so you can experience not only eternal life, but also a wonderful marriage. You can have fun again with your mate, just like you did when you were dating. You will know a love for one another that you never thought possible.

Obedience—that's the key. And with the Lord's help, you'll discover that incompatibility can *still* be grounds for a *great* marriage!

With God's Love and Blessings,

Chuck and Barb Snyder
PO Box 819
Edmonds, WA 98020–0819
www.chucksnyder.org

Printed in the United States
by Baker & Taylor Publisher Services